Amir Pirani

Trauma, Addiction, and Trauma

Portraying the Cycle of Suffering in Addiction

Senior Editors & Producers: Contento
Translator: Mor Shavit
Book and Cover Design: Liliya Lev Ari

ISBN: 978-965-550-351-7

International sole distributor: Contento
22 Isserles Street, 6701457, Tel Aviv, Israel
www.ContentoNow.com
Netanel@contento-publishing.com

Trauma, Addiction, and Trauma

Portraying the Cycle of Suffering in Addiction

Amir Pirani, MSW

Rothschild 2 Therapeutic Center

CONTENTO**NOW**

Table of Contents

Foreword 7

Preface 9

Structure of the Book 11

CHAPTER ONE: *Rothschild 2.* 15

CHAPTER TWO: *Trauma and Addiction Epidemiology* . . . 21

CHAPTER THREE: *Addiction-Induced Trauma* 59

CHAPTER FOUR: *Addiction-Induced Post-Traumatic Syndrome* . 101

CHAPTER FIVE: *Addiction* 137

CHAPTER SIX: *Addiction-Induced Suffering and Delinquency* . . 169

CHAPTER SEVEN: *Treating Substance-Addicted Trauma Victims* . 207

CHAPTER EIGHT: *Animal Assisted Therapy for SUD.* . . . 273

CHAPTER NINE: *Prolonged Exposure Treatment for SUD* . . 303

CHAPTER TEN: *The Cycle of Suffering* 329

CHAPTER ELEVEN: *Epilogue* 363

References 373

Appendices 379

Foreword

In 1992, Amir Pirani founded, and today continues to manage, the Rothschild 2 Treatment Center for Substance Abuse in Neve Tzedek. The center runs in association with the social services administration in Tel Aviv-Jaffa. I have guided and witnessed the work of Amir and his highly devoted staff for many years.

Substance addiction has been a strategic problem for many years now. Most violent crimes in society, including moderate vandalism, stem from problems resulting from substance and alcohol addiction. This book addresses the sources of these problems.

Approximately 40 percent of all heavy substance addicts who approach the Rothschild 2 Center manage to rehabilitate themselves, successfully completing a detoxification program, therefore minimizing work on a myriad of police and court cases, the addicts' suffering, as well as their relatives', and the public's as a whole. The key to such therapeutic success lies within implementing innovative models for coping within the framework of treating individuals with a history of substance abuse and their rehabilitation while relying on identifying the cycle of suffering in which they have been captive for many years.

The author illustrates how personal trauma in the addict's early years correlates with his drug addiction later in life.

The book opens by epidemiologically examining the substance addiction issue. The following chapters review the professional literature addressing trauma and sexual abuse due to addiction, thereby triggering further causes for addiction, such as environmental and parental neglect, as well as physical and verbal abuse. The author then progresses to discuss the development of post-traumatic anxiety, which often constitutes a predisposing factor to addiction. The book's conclusion offers a portrayal of unique therapeutic methods developed at the Rothschild 2 Treatment Center, some of which involve working on revealing trauma and animal assisted therapy.

The author calls for establishing a multi-professional work setting, where the parties involved offer guidelines for research, planning, and treatment of substance addiction issues that stem from trauma.

There is no doubt in my mind that this book is an innovative one. It includes a sound theoretical foundation, successfully implemented professional interventions with substance abuse victims. *Trauma, Addiction, and Trauma* is mandatory for those who engage in preventing substance abuse and treating the addicted, as well as those engaging in law enforcement and social work.

Professor Shlomo Giora Shoham

Preface

———————————————————————

A wound full of worms festered on a black rabbit's back. For fear of its near death, we released it from its cage. A rooster with a handicapped leg wandered around, rejected by its flock. The rooster pecked out all the worms from the rabbit's wound. They are both alive, at Rothschild 2.

Structure of the Book

The book portrays an issue, a place, and people.

- Issue: Mental stress and trauma related occurrences

- Place: Rothschild 2

- Active Participants: Substance addicts, who experienced the damages resulting from stress, trauma, and abuse

The book portrays the four components that comprise the theoretical model I developed:

1. Stressful and traumatic experiences

2. The resulting mental condition, namely, post-trauma

3. Substance abuse and delinquency

4. The fact that crime yields further mental suffering, namely, trauma-prompting addiction, which, in turn, results in further trauma.

The book comprises 11 chapters:

The preface, which is the conceptual description of the processes unfolding at Rothschild 2 as described in this book, introduces the reductive connection formed by treating thousands of individuals addicted to substances, who seek treatment at public welfare services.

This connection implies that most of my patients are characterized by a traumatic past preceding their substance addiction, thereby inspiring me to provide justification and to portray the cycle of suffering's theoretical structure.

Chapter Two presents epidemiological research findings, thereby being of particular interest to professionals engaging in psychological therapy. In addition to several studies lacking in Israeli professional literature, I present numerous important studies, conducted worldwide, measuring the relationship between the repression of severe psychological trauma and substance abuse.

Chapter Three addresses theoretical and evidence-based knowledge in literature, relating to psychological stress and trauma events. The stress events experienced by patients is similar in character to the stress and trauma damaging combat field soldiers, citizens who experienced terror attacks, stressful situations, and abusing others. In their interventions, professionals witness these conditions with sexually abused individuals, those who experienced environmental and parental neglect, or those who experienced physical and verbal abuse. Trauma is trauma, no matter the source.

Chapter Four discusses the anxiety disorder Post-Traumatic Stress Syndrome (PTSD), a psychological syndrome common among a high percentage of Israelis, many of whom have experienced domestic abuse, or trauma from the wars throughout Israeli history, or have experienced terror attacks. My patients have suffered wounds and stress induced by sexual trauma, physical assault, violence, and civilian acts of horror. Their trauma and post-trauma victimization preceded their substance abuse.

Chapter Five presents various research approaches to the drug addiction issue. The chapter presents some of the existing professional knowledge regarding the factors affecting an individual's addiction to drugs, and the circumstances that induce it. Investigating the prolonged addiction to drugs is supported by the viewpoint implied throughout the book; accordingly, addicts bear the burden of past stress and trauma events that went untreated.

Chapter Six portrays situations associating delinquency and further so-called "psychological suffering." I address delinquency situations where an individual acts to obtain money, which often covers the purchase of the substance. Delinquent acts often yield further psychological suffering, accumulated layers one on top of the other result in a downward spiral of mental suffering, namely, obtaining money in order to use substances, and using in order to obtain money.

Chapter Seven discusses treating substance addicted trauma victims (SUD). This chapter identifies the similarities between treating stress or trauma victims and treating substance addicts, emphasizing the professional uniqueness compelled by treating substance abusers who have suffered stress and trauma.

Chapter Eight addresses various treatment techniques developed by the professional staff at Rothschild 2 Treatment Center. Animal Assisted Therapy (AAT) and animal assisted group intervention take place with emphasis on the important rules dictated by AAT and the role of responsibility and compassion present in the treatment process. Additionally, Rothschild 2 highlights the importance of a safe environment in a therapeutic setting.

Chapter Nine presents another therapeutic tool for treating trauma victims, Prolong Exposure (PE), developed by Professor Edna Foa.

This tool was tested at Rothschild 2 as an experiential intervention among SUD.

Chapter Ten presents the Cycle of Suffering theoretical model I developed, extensively addressing its four components, briefly addressed in the preface: trauma, post-trauma, delinquency, and further psychological suffering.

Chapter Eleven offers insights I have acquired as an individual, author, and therapy professional.

The book presents various cases that are merely a drop in the ocean of the human suffering I have encountered throughout my career. All the characters appearing in this book remain transformed and mixed by my imagination, to maintain anonymity. In writing, I seek to draw the reader closer, even to the slightest extent, to understanding the enormity of human suffering, the source of the damage caused to my patients prior to their substance addiction.

The following chapter addresses research findings that imply the strong relationship of stress and trauma and using drugs.

CHAPTER ONE

Rothschild 2

I decided to write this book following many years of working with stress and trauma victims, who became addicted to substances. The thousands of clients whom I have treated since 1992, at the Rothschild 2 Treatment Center, inspired me to relate their story.

An abundant body of literature related to stress and trauma resulting from wars, terror events, and abuse is available in Israel. It is sufficient merely to refer to several books: *Mental Health in Terror's Shadow* (Eli Zomer & Avi Bleich, 2005); *The Shattered Secret* (Eds. Zvia Seligman & Zahava Solomon, 2004), as well as books by Lahad, Eilon, Shalev, Noy, Klein, Berger, Arnon, Omer, among others, that address trauma victim treatment in Israel. However, professional literature discussing stress and trauma among substance addicts is scarcely available. The professional literature I found in Israel addresses the relationship of trauma and addiction to a rather limited extent.

In my writing, I place focus on this relationship, which acts as a guideline throughout the book. I am well aware that focusing on the relationship of trauma and addiction is not to be taken for granted, because as thoroughly as it may be explored and investigated, it will not be sufficient for the readers to illuminate the areas where suppression, denial, and shame still dominate.

Approximately twenty years ago, a few years after leaving my kibbutz, I established a substance abuse treatment center at the request of the Tel Aviv-Jaffa municipality social services. In its initial planning stages, Rothschild 2 stood to service a population of prolonged substance abuse victims, living in the center of Tel Aviv. I have lived in Tel Aviv since 1987, coming to the big city from Kibbutz Nir David, located in the Beit She'an Valley. In Tel Aviv, I was in for an entirely new, and strange, world—the other side of humanity, as a matter of fact. In urban Tel Aviv, I came across four core insights, which also inspired this book.

I. Conversations with many of my clients indicated that they did not choose substance abuse. Rather the substance abuse was a consequence of prior psychological suffering. Those who came to therapy were individuals hurt by others: a stranger, relative, acquaintance, sibling, mother, or father. For their benefit, I established *Kibbutz Acher* (Alternative Kibbutz), a therapeutic structure integrating love for nature, animals, and humans—a place in nature, a world where humans and animals are equally treated. I did not embark on this work with any pre-meditated, structured theory. My existence until then came to life inside me and channeled itself to manifest in my new position. Family, adulthood friends, kibbutz childhood friends, the impression of nature by which I was surrounded while growing up, including the Asi Stream crossing the kibbutz, a tributary of the Sachne Spring, the huge lawns, the eucalyptus and ficus trees, the singing of the birds, the kibbutz dogs, all join together in my mission. My longing for my childhood's natural scenery inspired me to reconstruct memory images of visual, emotional, and sound experiences in the very heart of tumultuous Tel Aviv. There, the professional psychology and social work studies and the many years of engaging in psychotherapy as well went into fulfilling a significant role. My first few years in Tel Aviv channeled a life of supposedly flowing routes that would not normally intersect, into a point where they would meet. In the one course of my life, my professional practice, I had heard horrific stories of individuals hurt by others. They are ordinary people that we meet every day. Meanwhile, in the other course of life, I attempt to offer a humble contribution to those victims. I realized there were very few intersection points where I would be able to assist, and only to a handful of people.

2. My clients lost their natural ability to feel because of the severe abuse they had undergone, but it's possible to restore and revive this loss through contact with pets. I thank my devoted employees: Alex, who shared my dream of "rabbits rubbing against our feet," Effye, Zehave, Ilan, Moshe, and Eli, mature, experienced facilitators who have worked with me for many years. I include the social workers Marganit, Rama, Niva, Tal, Maya, Michal, Carmit, Dr. Marina, Liat, Daphna, Inbar, and many others. Thanks to the assistance of my clients who know what true love is and the assistance of my daughters, who came with me to feed the pets and clean the petting zoo every weekend. The natural therapeutic jewel, Rothschild 2, developed, expanded, and flourished, thanks to all of you. From a dilapidated shelter on south Rothschild Street, bordering with the Neve Tzedek neighborhood, the place became a flourishing garden full of trees, vegetation, and pets, immersed in a pleasant therapeutic atmosphere. Rothschild 2 is a professional structure with a sound foundation, having established behavioral rules, appearance, and policy. It is not only a structure of therapy and employment, but also a second home to those who enter its gates: the clients, who come at moments

of sadness and joy, their relatives, the professional staff working collaboratively, mutually consulting and updating, and its many guests. I always get a grasp on any professional doubts in the narrow hallway connecting the therapy rooms, colleagues sharing while the aroma of espresso wafts in from the small kitchen to the corridor and the therapy rooms.

The book *Trauma and Recovery* by Judith Herman (1992), to which I was introduced in 2003, played a dominant role in my writing. This book allowed me to draw the following conclusions:

3. Most clients were troubled by intense stress experiences, sexual traumas, extreme physical or psychological abuse, and other human cruelties. They resorted to substance abuse and long term addiction not only because they remained silent about the abuse they experienced but also due to the limitations associated with the budget allocated for assisting substance abuse victims, their treatment, and rehabilitation. My clients resorted to substance abuse due to a prior shock they had to endure. Thanks to my clients, I realized that using substances served as some sort of self-medication, a relief from their painful, open wound in their soul. For a while, the substance relieved, if only superficially, the pain of stress and trauma they had experienced. Even I did not know, nor did I realize, how dearly this self-medication cost. What consequences Israeli human society had faced, and would face, for choosing to turn a blind eye.

4. Those clients who found temporary relief and a source of relaxation were those who did not receive any professional treatment for their abuse, resorting to theft, harming others, engaging in substance trafficking, and selling their bodies in order to obtain money for the next dose, for relieving the pain of traumatic memories. The

trauma resulted in addiction, which, in turn, resulted in another psychological trauma. The complete cycle of suffering revolves continuously. This suffering cycle needs breaking.

I believe that with the assistance of the clients' strength, my family, my wife Atalia and my daughters Yuli, Ziv, and Aviv, the emotional support of my female dogs, Kamma and Choco, who became my friends, and my colleagues, I was able to muster the strength to slow down the cycle of suffering and even break it in some cases. I present the therapeutic process in this book.

Chapter Two

Trauma and Addiction Epidemiology

───────────────────────────────

Since 1999, Kamma, a speckled shepherd's dog, lives with us in the therapeutic center. Kamma once barked at two types of people: those wearing hats and those wearing glasses.

Reviewing the epidemiological studies that investigate the relationship between substance use disorder (SUD) and post-traumatic stress disorder (PTSD) is complex. This chapter addresses the professional literature that explores the relationship of substance addiction and PTSD, namely trauma and substance abuse, as titled by various researchers.

On a daily basis, I hear rough life stories from individuals addicted to drugs and who have additionally suffered violent experiences, namely, verbal and physical assault, sexual assault, abuse, and abusive situations.

Each day, for 20 years, I discover the close connection between the violent experiences in clients' pasts and their substance addiction to date. Every Sunday at 11:00 a.m, I facilitate the "Life Stories" therapy group, where in due course one of the group members relates his or her life story for ninety minutes. The group members are Yitzhak, Marilyn, Yoni, Menny, Nitzan, Yair, Alex, Shoshi, Sivan, Sima, Ami, Tityana, Ofer, and others. This morning, we heard Yitzhak's life story.

Yitzhak, born in Acre, is a handsome 45-year-old man, married to a woman who is a substance addict herself. He is the father of three children aged 25, 22, and 20. While Yitzhak relates his story, his green eyes incessantly shed tears.

"My paternal uncle abused me, even as a small child. I had no childhood whatsoever." Thus, Yitzhak begins his life story, clean from heroin for three months. According to group regulation, the members must listen to the story from beginning to end, without interrupting the story-teller. When the story is complete, the group members provide feedback to the story-teller, which illuminates other aspects of his personality, behavior, and nature, hopefully to assist him later in the course of his recovery.

For a long time, that uncle lived at my parents' home, where he turned me into his personal servant, an outlet for his sadistic and sexual needs. When the uncle came home wearing a police uniform, I felt pride and awe on the one hand, perhaps even admiration for him while being paralyzed with fear of him on the other hand. The uncle would ask me to take off his shoes, stroke him, massage his back, soothe and calm him down after the rough day he had gone through. I would massage his shoulders and back for hours at a time. As an eight-year-old child, I did not understand a thing and was very scared of him; always scared. If I stopped the back massage for even one moment, the seemingly quiet, calm uncle would immediately turn into a raging monster. He would mercilessly beat me in every body part, forcing me to keep massaging him, through intimidation and threats. Now I understand the bond of silence we maintained. The uncle warned me not to tell anyone our secret, not even my parents, who would not be home until the late evening hours.

Yitzhak draws in a few deep breaths. Apparently, they do not reach his lungs, but remain stuck in his throat.

I once tried to rebel against that monster. I tried to run away from home before he returned. Unfortunately, he found me at the playground and dragged me home, where I underwent a series of physical and mental tortures. To this day, I have not been able to realize the extent of his cruelty. That uncle was not satisfied with just the beatings. He dragged me to an ancient sheikh's grave in the town's Muslim graveyard, lowered me into the grave's depths and threatened to kill me. I trembled with fear; my body broke out into a cold sweat… I recall a huge snake approaching me, standing erect, and hissing, my terrified look locks into his frozen one. I was paralyzed with indescribable fear. I fainted. I do not remember at what point I was taken out of the pit. I was wet with urine, shaking from the cold and fear.

The group sits, fascinated, alert.

And so began the sexual contact, too. The monster uncle would come to me from behind, hurting me tremendously, raping me. His smell was revolting. I remember his moans were like the screams of a black raven. This episode was not a one-time thing.
At 14, a friend from the neighborhood offered me a toke of marijuana. I was finally able to get some sleep at night. Later, the heroin came on the scene. At last, I was spared the queasiness. I couldn't stand myself, the disgust, nor could I fall asleep, as I was afraid of the dark. Never in my entire life had I enjoyed an undisturbed night's sleep.

I had burdened myself with delinquency, crime, and suffering for thirty years, as well as the burden of the nightmarish uncle secret. Thank you for listening to me, thank you for giving me the strength to relate the story of my life. I hope that with your help I will be able to begin a new life, free of drugs.

Yitzhak's story is sorrowful and touching, inspiring compassion and empathy, as well as a feeling of terror. Following similar tales I've heard from my patients, not once did I wonder whether the next would bring another heartbreaking life story. How cruel humans can be. Through the years, I have learned from hundreds of stories that, apparently, stress, trauma, and abuse could relate to future drug addiction.

Every Sunday at 8:00 a.m., I begin my workweek at Rothschild 2 Treatment Center. While taking a brief walk through the site, I see the clients first to arrive, greeting them good morning. I hear guinea pig shrieks, they may associate human movement with the food they are about to receive. I whistle to Kamma, who comes enthusiastically wagging her tail and barks, as though saying "Where have you been for two days? I have missed you!" My day begins with an espresso, sitting with my colleagues, recalling the previous week's events, consulting with them, considering the therapeutic interventions needed for this day and the week ahead. Each day, we gently touch the wounds of souls, some indeed covered with bandages, but most of them have never formed a scab, nor healed. I know I am in for an eventful, complex workday. Engulfed in the coffee's steaming, sweet scent, I plan my day.

The professional literature review published in Israel for 20 years until 2008 reveals very few articles discussing trauma and addiction issues, save for a few studies investigating the connection between both phenomena. I cannot help but wonder why.

Examining circumstantial connections and searching for justifications to account for the intensity of both phenomena's connections between PTSD and SUD is the first step toward clarifying the findings for which I search in this review. The epidemiological research attempts to address the research of two phenomena or more, as such a study addressing patterns of events, and/or phenomena within the population, as well as causes affecting those patterns (Ouimette & Brown, 2003). This research yields findings based on studies of the connection between PTSD and substance abuse in the following modes:

1. Studies investigating the presence of PTSD within the population, facilitating the search for the presence of substance abuse issues within the same population

2. Studies investigating the substance abuse rate within the population, facilitating the search for PTSD symptoms among substance abusers

3. Other research examines PTSD victims (such as soldiers who fought in wars or terror victims) and the prevalence of substance abuse prior to traumatic experiences and afterward (Kulka, Schlenger, & Fairbank, 1990)

First, we must state that the data cited from such diverse research worldwide indicates the connection between previous stress events of sexual assault or traumatic experience and substance use in a later course. Below, I address trauma and addiction studies conducted in the past decades in Israel first.

A handbook issued by the Israel Anti-Drug Authority summarizes a decade of research in the field of substance addiction in Israel (Bar-Hamburger & Tal, 1999). Of the approximately one hundred and thirty studies, none explored the connection between mental stress or other trauma and the subsequent addiction to drugs in a later course.

Content analysis of the research presented in the handbook called into question the following issues, which, as an addiction-induced trauma specialist, have occupied me for many years:

1. What research parameters and content analysis served the studies investigating substance abuse and addiction in Israel at that time?

2. What is the scientific process that results in the approval of research by the Israel Anti-Substance Authority, and what were the parameters for receiving the research budget?

3. Were Israel Anti-Substance Authority research trends specifically targeted through 1988-1998?

4. Do the targets of the studies that explore stress, trauma, and abuse modes as they relate to later substance addiction not occupy the boards of experts who approved that research field at that time?

5. If those studies had indeed been published, how would the substance abuse victim treatment have been established in those years?

What significance do the above questions and their presentation hold for me?

I possess a somewhat simplistic professional view, maintaining that the subject of research is of interest to the researchers. It is easy to understand, but raises the question of whether or not the researchers' interests are of importance to the field of practice and therapy. If not, something must be falling through. I, therefore, question the direction of knowledge and which therapeutic and rehabilitation-related implications were not studied throughout that period in relation to addictions in Israel, and what are the implications related to human suffering in that context?

The following procedures regard the approval of research by the Anti-Substance Authority, as portrayed by Bar Hamburger & Tal (1999):

> Research grants have been awarded once the head researcher submitted a research proposal for thorough review and contemplation by three to five expert-judges (usually scholars). The judges' opinion is presented to the research committee of the Anti-Substance Authority, which discusses each and every research proposal.

Apparently, no research proposal addressing the mode in which stress, trauma, and abuse connect to substance addiction was ever submitted to the committee. There is no fair statement expressing the reason why such studies in those years did not appear at all in the handbook summarizing substance and addiction research in Israel. The fact that scholars worldwide have extensively investigated these issues—thereby proving their degree of relevance—has rendered this lack of Israeli literature even more remarkable. At this stage, those issues and questions remain unaddressed.

In his book, *Living in Another World* (1989), Israeli addiction expert Professor Meir Teichman refers to addiction as a condition where one responds to severe emotional problems and coping difficulties. The writing of those assumptions was sufficient to call for an examination of how modes of stress, trauma, and abuse relate to addiction, since it no coincidence they are dominant within the circle of severe emotional problems. As I demonstrate in Chapter Six, stress, trauma, and abuse constitute some of the landmarks to clarifying the phenomenon of delinquency and crime among individuals who struggle with addiction. Teichman's book does not explore this field further.

The book *Substance*, edited by David Green (1995), is an anthology of articles discussing the facts known at that time as causes for substance abuse: "The book integrates some of the knowledge and experience accumulated in recent years while coping with the substance phenomenon in Israel." The book also presents theoretical models, addressing the circumstances and causes for prolonged substance abuse. The most prominent researchers in the drug use field in Israel rely on it.

In a perspective yielded after the twenty years since the publishing of this book, I seek to explore and address the following additional questions:

- Why are there no literary works, even small ones, by professionals who daily encounter for many years victims of addiction to drugs?
- If there were any such works, might they have been classified?
- Why was the subject of stress and trauma as it is connected to substance use not investigated during these years?

As a student of many of the researchers in Israel at that time, I learned a great deal from their work and I am unworthy to criticize or assess it. However, having been exposed to the vast knowledge accumulated by the admission questionnaires (handed to every client) to thousands of therapeutic sessions, and to the vast information yielded by guiding hundreds of therapeutic groups for substance abuse victims at the Rothschild 2 Center, I hear other opinions and approaches. Underneath the protective shield, keeping the client from being exposed to psychological pain, voices are heard that may be of interest to the professionals treating addicts. In my opinion, the client questionnaires, the scientific research, and the various statistical analyses all stand as insufficient. It is clear to me that another research approach did not exist in those years.

It is difficult to obtain authentic information in a sensitive, troublesome field, addressing memories related to trauma and stress. That purpose naturally demands a greater extent of involvement and cooperation from therapists and other professionals who encounter clients coping with addiction for many years. Studies might be biased. They might direct their search into the clarity zone while the information they seek remains concealed. While encountering the clients' competent defense mechanisms, studies may miss important, sensitive information that is within their grasp, but hides in the darkness of human suffering and shame. There are research instruments for investigating stress, trauma, and abuse, yet studies addressing substance abuse victims in Israel have not sufficiently exhausted them.

As for the therapeutic practice, I state deductively that traumatic experiences, including sexual assault and abuse, among substance addicts are significantly more common than known even to the current research in Israel. As a therapist, I state that confidently. First, I maintain that most of those seeking treatment in public institutions for treating and rehabilitating substance abuse victims have experienced abuse, trauma, and psychological suffering preceding their addiction to drugs. From a clinical, therapeutic point of view, those cases have not been sufficiently expressed in terms of research to this day. Thus, the present research in Israel should direct its efforts toward further channels, or alter its course. Further courses may be identified in later studies in Israel such as the study of Zomer, Leventhal, & Tzoref (2005), which I address later in this review.

Since the beginning of the millennium, we notice the significant worldwide expansion of PTSD research. Such progress may be attributed to civilians coping with the Twin Towers bombing in the United States (Foa, Doron, & Yadin; 2004; Adams & Boscarino, 2005; Schulman et al., 1999). Thus, apparently, though indirectly, the civil trauma issue is raised within a wider public discourse, even among researchers in Israel.

In his book *From the Gods Nectar to the Poison Cup* (Teichman, 2001), the author discusses alcohol abuse issues – causes and reasons, prevention, and the way in which trauma, violent assault, and sexual assault relate to substance abuse. Teichman writes:

Many professionals – psychologists, social workers, psychiatrists, and counselors refer to alcoholics as individuals who attempt to treat themselves, so to speak, seeking psychological welfare by means of alcohol.

He also states that this field, one of the most fascinating research fields at present, attempts to explore the relationship of alcohol consumption and past traumatic experiences (childhood experiences such as neglect, abuse, sexual abuse, and rape).

The book also refers to "the expanded public and scientific awareness in the past decade of the consequences of traumatic experiences, and the prevalence of chronic post-traumatic disorders, and of prolonged use of alcohol, medications, and other substances." Unfortunately, this issue is addressed only partially in this book, leaving the reader with a great gap of knowledge. There is no discussion concerning work techniques aimed at integrating coping modes related to treatment and rehabilitation among individuals who were victims of sexual traumas and abuse into the substance abuse context. Furthermore, I believe that there is a lack of professional instruments that could assist the therapist, facilitating, even to the smallest extent, the psychological, traumatic suffering of stress and trauma victims, who are addicted to drugs.

In his book *Treatment and Rehabilitation of Drug Addicts in Israel* (2002), Hovav refers to the establishment of treatment structures for substance abuse victims in Israel, and to the development of diagnosis trends and treatment programs throughout Israel's years of early development. Although the book integrates works by top professionals in the field of substance abuse in Israel, it does not at all address the investigation of how modes of stress, psychological trauma, abuse, and sexual assault connect to substance addiction. Hovav portrays the responsibilities of the addiction treatment department in the Ministry of Welfare, the foundations for the social service's activity in municipal governments, as well as the common treatment principles in substance abuse victim treatment centers operated by the Ministry of Welfare, Ministry of Health, and the penal system. It does not portray any therapeutic, thought-inducing approach regarding the relationship apparently existing between addicts and stress and trauma victims within any of those structures.

In his book, it is interesting to find a discussion on a piece of data from the penal system:

> In Neve Tirza Women's Prison in Israel, housing 167 prisoners [...] approximately seventy percent of the prisoners are substance abusers, and most of them are addicts. Let it be emphasized that [these] prisoners are victims of physical or sexual violence.

Why is it, then, that this piece of data is not sufficient to guide those engaging in the field toward unique therapeutic and professional assistance? Why does facilitation for such treatment methods that integrate treating stress, trauma, abuse, and addiction remain non-existent? Zomer and his colleagues raise the same questions (2005).

The worksheets prepared by Andrea Senderovich (2002) for the Knesset's substance struggle committee demonstrate the relationship of childhood and adolescence sexual abuse and substance abuse. She presents important information yet unpublished as an article or a more significant research publication. In the same document, Senderovich writes, "[...] the issue of the way in which childhood or adolescence sexual abuse and substance abuse in adulthood are related is quite new to [Israeli] professional literature." The studies indicate that among women, the relationship is more significant, ranging from 40 to 80 percent. According to the professional literature she reviewed, "60 to 84 percent of adult women in rehabilitation programs underwent sexual abuse as children [...] substance abuse by sexual abuse victims may be related to the 'self-sedation' process, attempting to cope with the anxiety, depressions, and difficulties resulting from the assault."

Senderovich raises further issues in the paper: "Consequently, it is argued that substance use provides the user with an escape from the rough feelings resulting from past trauma, particularly sexual abuse." Since research findings indicate "many women who experienced sexual abuse in adolescence were raped at an older age and demonstrated a greater tendency to use crack cocaine," Senderovich maintains that "it is a vicious cycle, where an individual uses a substance in order to cope with past trauma. Due to the need to obtain the substance, he is again sexually abused, using substances in order to cope with the new trauma that occurred."

In Chapter Ten, I present the Cycle of Suffering model, constructed in 2004 (Pirani, 2007). I address some other questions raised by Senderovich in Chapters Seven, Eight, and Nine, discussing SUD treatment, as quoted: "Others argue that an approach responding to both physical detoxification and coping with past trauma should be implemented." Senderovich concludes by raising various issues relevant to the topic, one of which raises the following questions: Should substance abuse victims' treatment be separated from addicted women's treatment? Is further research required in relation to SUD treatment in Israel? Additionally, she discusses the approach of Israel's therapeutic, hospitalization models and the managers for those issues, which I will probably address in my next book.

Further review of professional literature in Israel in the field of stress, trauma, and addiction reveals the book by Seligman & Solomon (2004) discussing trauma-related issues induced by abuse events. The book features articles by researchers who specialize in the fields of abuse, trauma, sexual violence, and proposals for handling thereof. The editors raise trauma related issues, discussing those indirectly related to drugs: "There are victims of childhood sexual abuse working in prostitution... drug dealers are well aware that a higher percentage of hard substance abusers were childhood sexual abuse victims." They further state:

[...] among several populations at risk, such as female homeless, female prisoners, prostitutes and female substance addicts, one may notice a rather high percentage (50%-70%) of sexual abuse and incest victims... [...] Approximately sixty percent of incest victims suffer PTSD (Post-Traumatic Syndrome Disorder) symptoms, also demonstrating co-morbidity of psychiatric disorders such as depression, anxiety, phobias, eating disorders, drug addiction, and dissociative disorders.

Gur (2004) indicates even higher rates: "Approximately ninety percent of female delinquent drug addicts that engage in prostitution underwent sexual abuse and/or incest," while Zomer (2004) addresses the role that drugs play in blurring awareness to emotions: "Others would attempt to blur awareness toward emotional distress by consuming alcohol, substances, or by employing other psychological dissociation mechanisms."

Apparently, the way in which stress and past sexual trauma and addiction are connected gradually shows itself to any reader interested in the writings of those investigating this field in Israel. Thus, the question raised by the editors seems convincing:

> Why are issues related to abuse and trauma scarcely included in the professional continued study programs in Israel? Why are therapists excluded from training programs in treatment fields associated with these issues?

While many know the limited scopes of research and employee training in Israel, presented through data associated with the relationship of stress and psychological trauma and substance addictions, I, too, raise the same questions. Even while writing this chapter of the book, I do not possess the answers yet.

Zomer and colleagues (2005) conducted a study in collaboration with Israel's Anti-Drug Authority, Haifa University, and the Israeli Center for Treatment of Child Victims of Sexual Abuse in relation to dissociative disorders among substance abuse victims. The researchers maintain that "this study enhances the understanding that substance abuse is associated, at least partially, with the patients' needs to conceal dissociative, post-traumatic, and psychiatric disorders." The research indicates data important for this chapter's discussion: the PTSD prevalence rate within the rehabilitated population is 61%. This research explored various traumatic experiences the addicts underwent during childhood, comparing its outcomes with a control group consisting of traumatized individuals who were not drug addicts. The traumatic experiences they explored included emotional neglect and abuse by parents and siblings, as well as physical abuse, sexual assault, and incest by siblings, other family members, and those who were not family relatives.

I took great interest in the above research data, since they are related to the clinical and therapeutic knowledge possessed by many treatment professionals. However, the data presented in those studies remain far removed from my feelings regarding the true data in the past two decades as a treatment professional. Those feelings are a direct consequence of the long years of daily encounters, amounting to thousands of drug addicts, therapeutic interventions with hundreds of therapy groups, and supervision of many professionals treating addictions.

Zomer and colleagues (2005) state that approximately thirty-one percent of all drug addicts report sexual abuse, compared to approximately twenty percent within the control group. This datum is significantly lower than the magnitude of the phenomenon to my estimate, based on long years of fieldwork. There is great importance to resuming the investigation of data concerning the rate of sexual abuse victims among the substance addict population in further studies.

In the handbook *Women Treatment Forum*, published by the Israeli Ministry of Labor and Social Welfare, Nevo, Galvan, and Ben Guy (2006) state:

> [...] Most women refer to the beginning of substance abuse as a consequence of a specific life traumatic experience; incest or rape are the most common events resulting in substance abuse among women and female adolescents.

The authors support the data presented in this chapter, and the key issue discussed in this book. They state that girls who underwent sexual abuse as children are strongly predisposed to future substance addiction, "due to the fact that drugs serve to ease the unbearable pain of abuse, constituting the first layer of defense through the process of coping with such trauma."

In his, and the most recent book addressing addiction in Israel, *Addiction and Recovery: Selected Issues in Treating Addicts*, Amnon Michael (2007) devotes discussion to the cycle of addiction. He refers to a progressive stage, where addiction develops when one attempts to remove painful emotions by means of drugs. He also states that one of the reasons for substance addiction is direct harm and sexual or physical abuse experienced by the addict during childhood. Hence, he argues, even the treatment stages involve therapeutic work addressing pain, in relation to context, memories, secrets, and traumas concealed by the client, both from himself and from others, for years, and even decades. It is a shame that the book addresses traumatic reasons for addictions sporadically. Michael states, for instance, that approximately eighty percent of the women in therapy for problems resulting from substance use have a history of childhood sexual and physical abuse. Thus, trauma and violence, he concludes, connect to female addicts; "childhood sexual abuse was found to be highly correlated to substance abuse during adolescence and adulthood."

In that light, why was another step not taken within the book to channel this important information toward a trauma-oriented treatment for addicts or toward research integrating both phenomena? Why does this data address only women, while data from the therapeutic practice also refer to male victims of sexual trauma? Why does the Intake Form, presented by Michael as an appendix to the book (a form available in all substance abuse victim treatment units of local governments, see Appendix 2), omit questions addressing any stress or traumatic events in the client's life? After all, this item of data is vital for future treatment plans addressing addiction. Why, on the other hand, does any simple, initial intake form handed to a soldier seeking counseling by the IDF mental health officer include a cluster of questions concerning traumatic experiences in the soldier's life prior to his enlistment, as well as traumatic experiences in his family's life? As an IDF mental health officer, I am aware that any soldier seeking psychological counseling during military duty will face such questions during his or her first session with the mental health officer.

In October 2007, I conducted a review on the Israel Anti-Drug Authority's website in an attempt to crosscheck several fields: treatment, addictions, and stress and trauma events, in all languages and forums. I was not able to find more than five or six articles. The lack of professional literature in Israel addressing the integration of complex stress situations and their phenomena—namely, PTSD and SUD—is one of the reasons for writing this book. I present several assumptions regarding the lack of material within the professional literature available in Israel:

Studies integrating those phenomena are not sufficiently familiar to the leading researchers in the field of addiction in Israel.

The researchers contributing the professional agenda in the field of victims of addiction in Israel are academics rather than therapists.

They reside with one key professional agenda, the limits of which are hard to break.

A study attempting to identify and investigate the phenomena in question is complicated and expensive.

Treatment integrating both phenomena requires further professional training for the financing mechanisms, and larger budgets for treatment structures, but budgets are non-existent.

At this point, I come across interim insights. The small number of studies addressing the connection of stress and trauma experiences, and substance abuse, as well as the scarce professional literature addressing the issue, all call for further studies in order to establish a professional guideline for clients suffering problems, namely, PTSD and SUD. It would be only professional and proper to conduct further investigations and studies, in order to chart and characterize the apparent connection of stress and trauma events victims and drug addiction in Israel.

The abundant clinical data and professional knowledge among professionals who engage in psychologically treating addicts has nevertheless been gathered in other modes. The Israeli social justice website "Makom," the popular website "Hebrew Psychology," and other websites offer links to forums integrating content related to stress events, PTSD, and SUD in Israel and worldwide.

The first item of data across which I came while scanning Internet search engines in winter 2007, is that the Arab and ultra-Orthodox sectors particularly suffer lack of information regarding sexual assault and abuse. Those sectors bear structural characteristics that induce preserving of secrets within the family, particularly when female abuse is concerned. Furthermore, in both sectors, it is uncommon to support women who share their own suffering with others, thereby breaking the conspiracy of silence associated with those issues. When women in the ultra-Orthodox community share the sexual abuse experience they have had with others, they violate the principle of "family and community wholeness," as stated by Makom. Ultra-Orthodox women who dared to complain about sexual assaults were ex-communicated. Those who left had nowhere to turn. Makom reports a substantial increase in the rate of Haredi women seeking shelter in recent years. Approximately one hundred ultra-Orthodox women have sought shelter each year since the first, and only, shelter for ultra-Orthodox women in Israel opened in 1995.

Makom reports an increase in sexual assault and violent crimes against women in the Arab sector, not resulting from a larger number of assault cases but rather from greater awareness to the prospect that a woman is allowed to report the situation and the option for therapeutic solutions. Thirteen percent of Arab adolescents, aged 14-16, who participated in the study were sexual assault and incest victims. According to Makom, they were schoolgirls, almost all living in an urban community, coming from affluent families.

In seventy percent of the assault cases within the ultra-Orthodox sector, the assailant is a close relative (father, brother, cousin, or grandfather). Forty-seven percent of the assault cases took place in the victim's home, and in twenty-seven percent of the cases, a third party was present. Just as there is a conspiracy of silence in association with those issues in the ultra-Orthodox sector, the same occurs in the Arab sector:

> Many women know their daughters are undergoing sexual abuse in the other room, but they choose to ignore it. Some fear of breaking the family apart and the subsequent shame; others fear they will be forced to bear the burden of economically supporting and providing for the family if the husband is imprisoned (Makom website).

The data are severe and difficult to comprehend. A secret shrouding trauma is not conducive for treatment. Unavailability of treatment may lead to substance use, or use of other dissociative mechanisms, which split thoughts from emotions. When no therapeutic solutions are available, post-trauma symptoms emerge, resulting from traumatic experiences. Those symptoms will be often associated with substance abuse in a later course. The data applies not only to the ultra-Orthodox and Arab sectors, but also to the secular Jewish population, where, likewise, most sexual abuse cases involve a familiar person, and there is a conspiracy of silence in association with assault and abuse incidents.

I write this book because of the abovementioned data, and the hundreds of life stories to which I have been witness throughout my years of work with addicts, who were also victims of stress and trauma.

While the Israeli professional literature review is scarce, in other countries the research material in this area is abundant. The global research offers many articles and abundant professional literature that discuss the way in which damage caused by stress and trauma and psychoactive drug addiction are related (See Ford, 2006; Ouimette & Brown, 2003; Adams & Boscarino, 2005; Foa, Hembree, & Rothbaum (2007); Brothers (2004); Foa et al. (2004), and many others).

I review the current articles addressing the nature of sexual abuse and its prevalence within the population; studies addressing violence and addiction; and articles addressing addiction resulting from stress, trauma, and abuse.

The presentation of those articles and studies is designated mainly for those who are interested in the information, namely, professionals who engage in psychological treatment. Additionally, I wish to portray the extent of damage caused by stress and trauma within the population. The articles indicate the scope of research conducted worldwide concerning the relationship of stress and trauma induced damage and psychoactive drug use.

Brothers (2004) estimates that one in four women, and one in six men have undergone sexual abuse by the age of 18. Other studies indicate similar data:

1. A study comparing female incest victims to female non-victims found that 68% of the group of female incest victims reported rape or rape attempt cases after age 14, compared to 38% in the other group (Ouimette & Brown, 2003).

2. A comparative study examines which group of women is at a higher risk for sexual assault, those who have experienced violence throughout their lives relative to those who have not. They found that the risk of becoming a rape victim was three to four times greater among girls who experienced violence during childhood, relative to girls who did not (Ouimette & Brown, 2003).

3. A comparative study examining the risk among children sexually assaulted during childhood with children free of assault revealed that sexually assaulted children are at a higher risk of physical or sexual assault in adulthood compared with children who were not molested (Newman et al., 1998).

4. A study investigating the characteristics of a violent delinquent group indicated that most violent delinquents experienced physical or sexual abuse during childhood (Groth, 1979; Seghorn, Prentky, & Boucher, 1987).

5. A study aimed at identifying the gender of delinquents who sexually assault children revealed that the significant majority of sexual offenders are men; more than 95 percent assaulted girls, and more than 80 percent assaulted boys. The findings show that most of those men were sexually assaulted as children (Fergusson & Mullen, 1999).

6. In a comparative study investigating the effect of domestic violence on the prospect of children becoming future sexual assault victims, comparing children of a violent domestic setting and children of non-violent domestic setting showed that children of a violent domestic setting would be 24 times more likely to become victims than children of a non-violent domestic setting (Dinzinger, 1996).

7. In a qualitative study investigating abusive characteristics of those sentenced to capital punishment for killing in the United States as of 1987 showed that 12 out of the 14 delinquents tested underwent brutal physical abuse, and in five of those cases, they were sodomized by relatives during childhood (Ouimette & Brown, 2003).

8. Another study investigating convicted murderers revealed that 83.3 percent of the subjects experienced physical and emotional abuse as children, and 32.2 percent were sexually assaulted as children (Blake et al., 1995).

9. In a study investigating female delinquent life and abuse, narratives revealed that more than 75 percent of the delinquent women experienced sexual abuse. Furthermore, the abused women are statistically likely to become victims of sexual and physical abuse in prison as well (Smith-Warner et al., 1998).

10. A study investigating the assumption that sexually assaulted girls would become abusive or assaulting adult women revealed a highly intriguing finding: 80 percent of the women abused as children would assault or abuse their children as adults, within an assault and abuse cycle's framework (Kaufman & Roux, 1987).

Many other articles portray other studies addressing the relationship of post-traumatic experiences and substance abuse:

1. Fifty-five percent of Augusta Trauma Center patients diagnosed with a co-occurrence of mental illnesses and substance abuse also revealed a history of sexual or physical abuse (Greene, Baird, & Kuo, 2000).

2. Anger, suspicion, depression, sleeping disorders, dissociation, sexual deficiency, self-mutilation, and addictions were found to be phenomena characteristic of individuals who underwent sexual abuse as children (Brothers, 2004).

3. Two studies investigated the relationship of substance abuse and previous traumatic experiences. Findings showed that 66 percent of those reporting substance dependency demonstrated PTSD. Additionally, 45 percent of those reporting alcohol dependency demonstrated PTSD. The subjects reported that the trauma preceded the addiction (Girconica et al., 1995a; Girconica et al., 2000b).

4. In an epidemiological study by Chilcoat and Menard (in Ouimette & Brown, 2003), 2.6-10.8 times as many PTSD symptoms were found among substance addicts (particularly opiates and cocaine), relatively to non-addicted trauma victims. Plus the researchers report 1.6-2.9 times more PTSD in epidemiological studies conducted with adults who suffered alcohol or marijuana dependency and other hard drugs.

5. Studies investigated co-occurrence of SUD and PTSD in a suffering individual. Results showed that adults coping with post-traumatic issues are 1.5-4.5 times more likely to suffer an addiction problem (alcohol and substance) than adults without PTSD, that is, individuals suffering post-trauma relate to drug abusers.

6. Chilcoat & Menard (in Ouimette & Brown, 2003) investigated the relationship of post-trauma and substance addiction among adolescents in the United States. The findings indicate that adolescents who suffer PTSD are 1.4-3.2 times more likely to develop an addiction problem than adolescents who do not suffer post-traumatic disorders.

7. While testing post-trauma symptoms prevalence among drug-addicted women who suffered traumatic abuse as children, statistics showed that PTSD prevalence is 30-59 percent among women who suffer chronic addiction problems. The women experienced exposure to traumatic violence such as physical or sexual assault in childhood (Najavits, Weiss, & Shaw, 1997).

8. Fullilove et al. (1993) investigated the prevalence of addiction following post-traumatic experience. They indicate that PTSD-SUD co-occurrence is rather frequent following traumatic violence.

9. According to Najavits (2002), the co-occurrence of post-trauma and addiction is more frequent. Twelve to 34 percent of male addicts are PTSD victims while among female addicts the rates are higher, ranging from 30-59 percent.

Out of 1000 children aged up to 18, 44 undergo abuse every year (Brothers, 2004). This item of data becomes even more significant when we explore the implication of abuse from the viewpoints of males and females. Brothers maintains that the male attitude toward the abuse's effect is more ambivalent. In our professional work at Rothschild 2, this item of data receives special attention and thorough consideration. However, most male patients at Rothschild 2 do report extremely rough abuse in childhood. I present the justification of the fact that men dare or do not dare address abuse in their past more thoroughly in the chapters addressing the therapy and the therapeutic climate we construct at Rothschild 2. The research scope is broad, and we quote only part of it.

Ofer's narrative, in the Life Stories group portrays an abused child, who grew up to become a drug addict. Ofer is a single, 45-year-old man; muscular, short-haired, missing his front teeth, impulsive, acting out, has the air of rough delinquency while his expression cries out of help; an exhausted, suffering gaze; a gaze of a child who seeks love:

> I was four years old when I first saw my mother shoot up, and then faint. I was terrified and cried. I ran to the neighbors, calling out, "Come, hurry, Mom's not feeling well."

> I was born in rehab, where I was raised until I was two. My mother told me that just before her death. I remember going to see Mom that last time at the hospital. I was nine years old then. She hugged me.

*I felt how she loved me and did not want to break apart. She cried...
until she stopped breathing. I remained lost, screaming to heaven for
taking my mother away. All alone, I returned to a violent home, with
a stepfather, a university lecturer. Who would now believe me that a
lecturer was the devil in disguise? Who would believe my stories? My
stepfather would hit me physically and sexually abuse me, and would
be satisfied only when he pushed me into the bathtub and "urinated"
on me so to speak. That was how I interpreted his actions. Why, why
did I have to go through all the suffering and humiliation?*

*I have no recollection of school, the teachers, and other educators.
Perhaps I never strongly connected with them. At home, I would
feel miserable, scared, hungry, dirty—disgusted with the filth that
stuck to me.*

Ofer begins sobbing. One of the group members offers him a tissue,
but he pushes away the extended hand, saying, "I cannot go on."

"We love you, Ofer," the group members tell him, rising to hug
him, one by one.

Research data associating stress, trauma, and post-trauma events
with substance abuse, or, briefly referred to as PTSD+SUD:

10. Dansky and colleagues (Dansky, Saladin, Brady, Kilpatrick, &
    Resnick, 1995) investigated the substance addiction problem
    among women who lived in a battered women shelter. The
    study compared women with a background of sexual abuse,
    who developed post-trauma, with women who did not suffer
    from post-traumatic problems. Findings show that women at
    the battered women's shelter who suffer PTSD were three times
    more likely to have an addiction problem compared with the
    women who did not suffer PTSD.

In the studies reviewed thus far, the researchers indicate that
regardless of gender or cultural background, approximately 90

percent of the patients who abused or currently abuse drugs reported physical or sexual assault in their past. More than 59 percent of them suffer from PTSD (Najavits, Weiss, & Shaw, 1997; Dansky et al., 1995).

Other findings indicate the significant direction that many researchers worldwide have taken in the past decade—the strong relationship among on-going drug addiction and preceding violent abuse and post-trauma symptoms (Najavits, 2002).

11. Dansky et al. (1995) further investigated the prevalence of traumatic backgrounds among female drug-abusing patients, who also suffer post-traumatic experiences, relative to patients who suffer only from post-trauma. Findings show that females treated for PTSD-SUB possess a broad history of early trauma and post-traumatic symptoms more than women who suffer only from PTSD.

12. Ouimette & Brown (2003) summarize the results of epidemiological and addiction therapy studies, proving that PTSD often precedes SUD (in 53-85 percent of the cases), not vice versa. In my opinion, those findings convey a very clear message to therapists as to the strong association of both phenomena and to the fact that traumatic experiences precede substance abuse, thereby requiring a different mode of thinking in the research and therapy fields in Israel.

13. Giaconia et al (2000) investigated what preceded and what follows; alcohol consumption or traumatic experiences. This study took place among a group of 384 18-year-old boys. The research findings indicate that 54 percent reported that alcohol consumption preceded PTSD, while the remaining 46 percent reported the opposite. This data item is an exception for the results of the studies I have thus far reviewed.

14. In another study, Chilcoat & Menard (in Ouimette & Brown, 2003) investigated whether trauma experienced by adolescents would

increase their likelihood to start drinking alcohol, compared with the reversed condition, where adolescents might experience trauma following alcohol consumption. In perspective studies the researchers conducted among middle-class adults (aged 21-35) in support organizations, they revealed that PTSD resulted in four times a greater risk to develop substance use disorder, while the existence of SUD did not increased the risk of PTSD development.

15. Stewart and colleagues (Stewart, Samoluk, Conrod, Pihl, & Dongier, 2000) present similar findings. Many addicts bear a PTSD history. The research occurred among alcohol- and street-substance-consuming women, as well as among army graduates and distress victims. Although SUD may precede PTSD, research does indicate the attempt to cope with PTSD results in development or escalation of SUD. Furthermore, post-trauma and substance use disorder appear to worsen the soul pain and, in the long term, intertwine.

16. The same researchers sought to investigate trauma's prospective effect on substance abuse due to car accident or rape trauma. One of the study's hypotheses investigated whether or not a larger number of PTSD events would emerge in case of substance or alcohol abuse, prior to the traumatic experiences. This study indicates just the opposite, as well: The soul pain preceded the addiction (Stewart et al., 2000).

17. A group of researchers investigated abuse and addiction for several years. Van der Kolk (1987) proves that children who underwent abuse would, as adults, experience guilt, flashbacks, nightmares, various anxieties, depression, alcohol and substance abuse, suffer harsh feelings of humiliation, lack of vitality, and would enact harsh violence. This is the beginning of the traumatic process associated with abuse. Since, in due course without professional

intervention, harsh post-traumatic syndrome sensations develop, which, in many cases, precede substance abuse.

In a comprehensive article, Brady (2004) reviews articles addressing the relationship between post-traumatic stress disorder and substance use disorder:

a) A comparative study on females relative to other females who do not abuse drugs (Cottler, Compton, Mager, Spitznagel, & Janca, 1992)

b) Among alcoholics, the prevalence of PTSD symptoms was found to be 5.2 times greater than non-alcoholics (Foa et al., 1993).

c) Statistics show that on average, 25 percent of those abusing drugs were PTSD victims.

d) A study simultaneous to that by Brown et al. revealed that approximately 42.5 percent of the substance-abusing females were PTSD victims (Dansky, Roitzsch, Brady, & Saladin, 1997).

e) A study investigating addicted females found that 59 percent of those females experience PTSD.

f) Findings show that 20.5 percent of the study's cocaine addicts suffered PTSD (Najavits et al., 1998).

g) In his research, Brady (2004) indicates that PTSD increases the risk to develop substance and alcohol addiction by 4.5 while substance and alcohol addiction increases the risk for trauma only by 1.6.

18. More than two thirds of the men and women in a rehab center reported childhood abuse or neglect (Ouimette & Brown, 2003).

19. Chilcoat and Breslau (1998) investigate the relationship of both phenomena. They maintain the likelihood to identify substance abuse among individuals demonstrating PTSD symptoms is three

times greater than among those who do not demonstrate PTSD symptoms. Helzer and colleagues (Helzer, Robins, & McEvoy, 1987), too, prove in their study that the likelihood for addiction issues among individuals with a PTSD history is 2.2 times greater than among those who do not suffer the disorder. The basis for their study is a sample of 2,943 subjects, and is one of the first studies in the field that relied on such a large test group. Other studies indicate that 20-33% of addict patients have experienced PTSD (Brown, Recupero, & Stout, 1995; Najavits & Gastfriend, 1998).

20. Cottler et al. (1992) investigated to what extent addicts and non-addicts report events of a traumatic character throughout their lives. The findings indicate that addicts experienced and reported traumatic experiences to a greater degree than non-addicts report.

21. Approximately 90 percent of alcoholic women experienced sexual abuse as children or suffered various types of parental violence (Miller, Downs, & Testa, 1993).

22. More than two-thirds of men and women treated for addiction in rehab reported childhood abuse (Ouimette & Brown, 2003). The likelihood of developing an alcohol addiction among sexually abused adolescents was 21 times more than non-abused adolescents.

23. 71 to 90 percent of the female adolescents and 23-42 percent of the adolescents treated by the Mania Addiction Treatment Center reported a sexual abuse history in childhood (Rohsenow, Corbett, & Devine, 1988). There is a twice-greater risk for substance abuse among adolescents abused in childhood compared with those not abused in childhood.

24. Ford (2003) wrote an article addressing therapeutic groups for trauma victims, who were addicted to substances. He indicates several items of data regarding the relationship of trauma events and substance abuse he identified among them: "Adults with substance abuse issues, particularly those abusing opiates, were

found at 2.6 to 10.8 times greater rates, even as PTSD victims, as opposed to non-addicted adults." Another item of data presented by Ford indicates that substance addicts, particularly alcohol, marijuana, and hard drugs such as opiates are of 1.6-2.9 times more likely to become PTSD victims than those who are not addicted to drugs. Women who have experienced a violent trauma are three times more likely to develop a substance addiction than women who have not suffered the same trauma. Among men and women who have been treated for drug addiction, regardless of ethnic origin or cultural background, 90% were found to have reported a history of a violent or sexual assault, while PTSD was identified among 59% of them.

Every Sunday, I encounter a steady stream of life stories, fifty life stories a year, approximately one thousand stories throughout the group therapy process in all my years of work. I meet hundreds of other stories addressing stress and trauma in other therapy groups I facilitate: therapy groups discussing mental pain, traumatic memories, feelings of anger and guilt, asking for a significant figure's forgiveness, and other situations related to identification; an endless flow of mental pain that hundreds of clients discuss with me in therapy at Rothschild 2 Center.

I call Effye, one of the most experienced facilitators, "The Heart Cracker," or "Colonel Mental-Pain Groups." Effye facilitates two weekday groups on Monday and Tuesday mornings. Returning from the weekend, the professional staff arranged clients for Effye's group. They know the group session with Effye will be followed by other group therapy sessions, to sooth the ache, the trauma wounds that had been opened again. Throughout the professional work process at Rothschild 2, we aim to uncover the client's mental pain throughout the week, heal it, and convert it into a narrative clearest to them, turning their past hurt into an existence where, in the moment, the extent of self-blame becomes smaller.

This week, I heard Vera's story, a young woman of 24, who lives unmarried with a partner twice as old as her. The couple has a biological four years old son.

> I was eight when I found my beloved father hung in the garage of our home in the States, in New York. I remember my mouth gaping with fear and shock, like the gaping mouth in Munch's painting *The Scream*. I froze. I fled to the street, calling out to the neighbors, screaming hysterically. I remember nothing more of that day, but from that day on, my life has become an open, unbearably painful wound. "How could you leave me like that, my beloved father?" I have asked.

Vera bursts in tears, causing many group members to shed tears as well. I, too, identify with her. My daughters come to mind, and I feel the urge to run and hug them tightly. She continues:

> The thoughts drove me insane; how just the evening before, you were playing with me, asking me to be a decent student, help Momma. Why did you leave me? I want you to come back. I will protect you. I want you here. I want my Daddy.

Vera bursts into tears again, crying bitterly. To me, she seems to have let go of tremendous distress by sharing her pain with her fellow group members. Nitzan, her closest friend, hugs her, and they cry together. Tatiana gets her a glass of water.

> Before the heroin, I felt as though the sadness, despair, and feeling of helplessness were driving me insane, not leaving me in peace. No, it makes no sense that I will never see you again, Daddy. It makes no sense that I will not be able to hug you again. I had no outlet for that pain. Momma would not discuss it with me, and the school would not address my personal issues, either. Heroin was my lifeline. I allowed my soul some peace thanks to the heroin.

The professional global literature addressing addictions and PTSD is broad and comprehensive. I find the studies support my feeling that, in many cases, trauma precedes substance addictions. An untreated trauma often results in PTSD, which, in turn, often results in substance abuse. This is a vicious cycle that must not be ignored.

At first glance, Ibrahim seems to be a tough criminal. His arms are muscular, tanned, thick, and tattooed, typical of a criminal who served long years of imprisonment. We met a week after his rehabilitation from 30 years of substance addiction. He showed up wearing Bermuda shorts, a tank top, and brown leather sandals; on his right arm, a rough, light blue-green tattoo of a woman in a dress, long hair, and large breasts with the surrounding text "A, A, 3.6." At that time, I could not question him about that. There were other codes tattooed on his right hand's fingers, codes of his gang; a sign looking like the letter C, and next to it, the letter B on his little finger. The letter A is tattooed in the middle of the thumb and next to it a Star of David. Later, I learned of more tattoos on Ibrahim's stomach and back, of which he spoke in therapy. Apparently, Ibrahim tattooed so-called "milestones" on himself, out of longing, despair, sadness, boredom, or identification throughout his long months in prison, signs he will never forget.

Ibrahim seems tough, expressing no emotion or weakness. These are only some of his coping mechanisms, acquired through his years among criminals, constituting a few of the survival modes he has developed. Ibrahim learned that an individual expressing weakness in the world of crime, even for a split second, would immediately become prey. He is 45 years old, divorced; his stocky body demonstrates an obesity tendency; his hair is graying and unkempt. Two months later, I still have difficulty picturing him as an athletic criminal, climbing gutters like a cat. His left eye is scarred; apparently, it miraculously survived a violent episode. The scar stretches from the eyebrow to his ear, and seems to have engraved a path of suffering on his cheek, never wiped away. The little finger is missing from his right hand, and on the first handshake, I recoiled, felt embarrassed, and was even instinctively disgusted.

During my conversations with Ibrahim, I heard expressions unfamiliar among my native Israeli patients, such as "horrors not seen since Napoleon's days." His Palestinian-Israeli rootedness originates from the tales of his great grandfather, who recounted Napoleon's conquests in the Land of Israel. Ibrahim possesses a phenomenal memory. He portrays his childhood and adulthood through vivid, spectacular images, from the appearance of the furniture at his parents' home, his living environment, to how his peers in the village would dress in those days, the natural surroundings where he was hiding as a child, and even the fisherman appearing on the Israeli Lira bill in the 1960s.

"I hate the Muslim more than any Jew could," Ibrahim told me in one of our earliest sessions. "Although I was born a Christian Arab, my identity is Jewish-Israeli by all means. I hate Muslims to death." Ibrahim's words left the wrong impression on me. I thought he was trying to please me, which is a behavior I encounter sometimes among Arab patients. I suspected he was trying to undermine my initial impression of him. Long months of therapy would pass before I understood his passionate hatred toward Muslims.

I remember the face of my first counselor at the children's boarding school in Haifa. You cannot imagine how cruel he was. I will yet tell you of the boarding school.

In SUD treatment, there are those moments when I question myself. Could those episodes have possibly occurred here, in Israel... here, a half-hour away from the heaven where I lived? This is beyond my understanding. All the stories in this book took place here, in Israel, on well-known streets, in towns neighboring the community where I was raised. Who knows how many girls and boys suffer, are depressed or raped as I write, here, on my street, or on nearby streets? Even now, reality deeply strikes me. These days, those who were adolescents at the time when Ibrahim was treated come to therapy. Nothing has changed among native Israelis who still suffer abuse and among their contemporaries who immigrated to Israel from the former Soviet Union. Even now, so much mental suffering and traumatic stress occur in our global human environment. Those suffering victims will often be the ones to hurt the innocents, causing them a great deal of suffering as well. Trauma will yield suffering, which, in turn, will cause pain, and nothing is new under the sun.

Ibrahim recounts:

> *In the village where I was raised, social classes were very clear. At seven, out of intense envy of the sons of the village's rich families, I stole one boy's bicycle. I so wanted a bicycle of my own. I realized what I was doing was wrong, but all I wanted was to take a little ride around the village, and return the bicycle to where it had been, at the market's corner. I had no criminal thoughts. I was merely a poor, jealous village boy. Unfortunately, the fat father of the child whose bicycle I stole, came across me. Seeing me, he told me, "Come along; do not worry."*

I see the first tear in Ibrahim's eye.

> *"Just take me to your father," he said, "then, I will let you go immediately." I was ashamed to take him to my father. He was so wealthy, fancily dressed. I remember his white, ironed, starched shirt, his black pants held by a brown leather belt. How was I to take him to my father, who walks barefoot, whose clothes are torn, smelling of fish?*

> *"Is this your son?" he asked my father. "Which family are you from?" he ridiculed him. He wanted to be certain he was not hurting a child of one of the village's distinguished families. By the time my father*

replied, I had been brutally slapped by the bastard who promised to treat me well. I was in extreme pain. I felt my cheek was on fire. The humiliation of my dejected father, who did not dare respond and cast his eyes down to the ground, was even greater than mine was.

"Don't you dare approach our neighborhood," roared the bastard. My barefoot father's submissive, humiliated gaze has been engraved in my memory for 40 years, and shakes me to this day. I long forgot the slap on the cheek, but have heard and felt the cries of my mother burning alive by lunatic Muslims every day and every night."

Tears of pain flow down Ibrahim's cheeks like rivers gushing from a collapsed dam. For a moment, the tough criminal was, again, a helpless, neglected child, back in his hometown.

These days, I am attending a professional course offered by the Ministry of Welfare. I share my professional thoughts with my fellow students. "This is so obvious, so well known," the other participants said. All participants, experts in various fields of social work, share the same gut feeling. "This is so obvious. I, too, have encountered clients who have shared episodes of similar context. In our social service, too, the abuse victim patients have abused drugs."

In 2008, while giving an exercise to social work students at Haifa University, I asked them to briefly describe their acquaintance with an individual addicted to any drug, and specify the causes and the circumstances prompting substance abuse. The findings did not surprise me. The students witnessed the fact that most addicts have a traumatic history.

Many professionals are familiar with this information. All that is necessary is to gather the findings to a study, which, in turn, will call for an alternative therapeutic approach toward SUD. I am convinced that a comprehensive study will yield an evolution in Israel's treatment policy, convincing policy-makers to allocate more budgets for the early stages of the violent abuse, and into treating individuals such as those of whom I am writing.

In the following chapters, I address the phenomena arising from stress, trauma, and abuse. I portray the characteristics of human responses to stress and trauma, and address symptoms that develop when those harsh emotional conditions remain untreated. Professionals are familiar with the information related to physical, sexual, and emotional abuse of children, adolescents, men, and women. Guidance counselors at schools receive instruction to watch out for unusual behaviors in children, as are educators, social workers, psychologists, school principals, medical staff, and hospital nurses. I know most of them are aware of the high-risk levels typical of those children, due to violent, continuous abuse, stress, violence, and various traumas.

Although professionals pay attention, observe, report to their supervisors, and share the information they hear with other professionals on their encounters with children, adolescents, and women at all intervention levels, the outcome is still far from satisfactory. More and more individuals who come to receive treatment from me, within the framework of the public services, report that professionals who noticed a certain behavioral change in them and referred them to therapeutic intervention were unaware of the problem's future ramifications, thus did not promote the required professional intervention, although they realized the severity of their mental condition. Receiving no other therapeutic solution, many trauma victims resorted to using drugs.

A different intervention "umbrella" is necessary in order to cover the various sources of professional knowledge, moving toward another therapeutic path. A mode of treatment based on the fact that young violence victims experiencing stress, trauma, and abuse might one day develop a substance addiction if we do not know how to assist them through early intervention, as treating stress and trauma victims requires. Many professionals know that the damage suffered by many could worsen if not treated immediately.

Thus, as intervention models for trauma due to terror and combat develop (Zomer & Bleich, 2005), and as intervention methods for abuse situations arise (Seligman & Solomon, 2004), it is necessary to develop models for treating stress and abuse, in order to address a future drug addiction problem, through an extensive professional perspective.

Even if stress and trauma naturally heal eventually, many stress and trauma victims would not be capable to carry the continuous, burdensome suffering (Foa et al., 2004; Seligman & Solomon, 2004; Zomer & Bleich, 2005). Tens of thousands of sexual trauma victims and victims of stress stemming from abuse, with no other available response, will resort to any available aid, one whose depth of destructive effect they are unaware, namely, drugs.

Thousands of children and adolescents, victims of stress and trauma due to physical and sexual abuse, terrorist attacks, exposure to fighting on the Gaza Strip, the Northern border, and the central part of Israel are not yet aware of the post-traumatic symptoms rooting in their soul. We, as professionals are supposed to know that, to foresee it and warn them.

Those thousands of adolescents could suffer in due course from sleep disorders, tantrums and attention deficits, symptoms that trouble their soul. Those children and adolescents, with no other therapeutic response, may at one point in their life resort to the most available cure, namely, drugs. Only a therapeutic "umbrella" covering most symptoms, addressing the destructive so-called "leftovers" of the stress and trauma-damaging effects—only an approach, uniting professional, therapeutic forces will succeed in reducing future damage.

Such an interventional therapeutic "umbrella" might reduce the prospective damage of other stress and trauma victims in the future, an issue I address further in my writing.

The following chapter portrays stress- and trauma-inducing threats on the individual's physical and mental well-being.

CHAPTER THREE

Addiction-Induced Trauma

———————————————————————————————————————

A cat lurked around bunnies. He leaped forward in the blink of an eye, catching a white kit in his mouth, fleeing with it. The kit's cries of fear rang out all along the escape route. The blood drops left no shadow of doubt, as to the fate that had found the bunny.

Long years of treating substance abuse victims within a public service framework have introduced me to an issue that is insufficiently addressed by the public: Many substance abuse victims who approach social services are victims of trauma or other stressful experiences.

In this chapter, I address several issues referring to the professional literature's definition of trauma, portraying the complexity of fear and anxiety with which trauma is intertwined. I focus on the continuous mental pain experienced by sexual trauma victims, who arrive at therapy as substance abusers, and present the narratives of suffering typical to the thousands of patients I have encountered since 1992.

My experience has revealed that the life outlook of adults who have undergone stress and trauma is completely different to others. Their outlook strongly implies the sadness and pain, arousing feelings of compassion, concern, and desire to assist. To me, it appears that sometimes trauma victims feel that others are incapable of understanding their pain. Victims feel that at times people misinterpret the true laughter that rests within them. A trauma victim will cast a reserved, hesitant, disinterested gaze. To me, it often seems as though he feels he has no right to rejoice, to laugh, to be happy.

In the Life Stories therapy group I facilitate on Sunday mornings, the group members take turns in relating each member's life story. I know that not only does the group's process facilitate the individual therapy; it also facilitates re-organizing one's renewed life narrative. I have noticed this, having treated hundreds of individuals. By the very sharing of one's life story with the group, the story-teller prompts and undergoes a process where he reassembles the broken pieces of his life into a fully renewed narrative; a story intertwined with pits of sadness, loneliness, hurt, and suffering; a story that may also contain moments of pleasure, happiness, achievement, and joy.

This week, Marlene had her turn to relate her narrative. Marlene, 24, is a beautiful blonde young woman with large blue eyes. Her gaze radiates utter suffering, fear, and a lack of trust in others.

> *You guys here have trouble understanding how we lived there, in Romania. I was a child at the time tyrant Ceausescu fell, resulting in the collapse of all dictatorial government establishments. My drunken father left home when I was a small child, and I have no recollection of him at all. My mother worked at a meat factory from dawn to dusk. I was alone, always alone... So I spent years in poverty. I attended only a few social gatherings, I rarely celebrated holidays or parties. I always excelled in school; I loved school, the teachers, getting together with my friends, but now I recall the most terrible day of my life. It pops into my mind and overwhelms me. One day, at school recess, a friend invited me to another friend's parents'*

place. It was a simple get together we would often hold; we would
meet secretly, drink some Vodka and feel daring. I was so naïve.
That friend's parents went away on vacation and I had no idea. I
entered the apartment and they immediately set on me, those four
monsters. They dragged me into one of the bedrooms. I was kicking,
and screaming, which got me more hitting and slapping.

Marlene begins trembling and crying. Esti bends forward to her,
patting her shoulder and Marlene continues:

I had never been hit by anybody before. I was shocked, paralyzed with
fear. The boys asked me to undress in front of them. I refused. I was so
embarrassed. I was only 14. Nobody had ever seen me nude. I refused,
trying to flee, but those monsters seized me, their mouths stinking
of alcohol. They pulled down my pants, my panties, ripping off my
shirt and bra. Suddenly, I found myself lying on the floor before them,
naked and ashamed. Those gross guys had octopus' hands, they were
all over me. I tried to run again, I cried, I begged. Nothing helped.
They undressed as well. I remember shutting my eyes, disconnecting
from the views and sensations... they raped me, one after the other,
time and time again, moaning, stinking, touching me over and over
again, violently squeezing my body and my breasts. Everything reeked
of alcohol, my vomit, their smells of sperm and sweat. I disconnected
myself. It happened to "her," rather than to "me."

Since then, I started skipping school, roaming the streets. My mother
didn't know and, in fact, nobody really paid attention to me. Policemen
who busted me on the street would rape me in their car, throwing
me battered, naked, and humiliated in public parks. I was cold and
hungry. I started stopping cars on the road, giving my body for a
few minutes of sitting in a heated place, for a little bit of money. The

drivers would hit me, fulfilling all their perverted thoughts on me, abusing me. All Romanian men are perverts, I felt. I would disconnect my thoughts from my body, flying far away, disconnecting from the humiliation and pain. I remember the men who had to hit me so they could come; so obnoxious, nobodies. What right did they have to hit a 15-year-old girl just to come? Over time, I started drinking. I would drink myself senseless. I wanted to put an end to the feelings of humiliation and disgust. At times, I would wake up in the morning, bleeding in some stranger's home or lying on the street, dressed or naked, clothes ripped, not knowing what I had been through... preferring not to know. Later I learned how to use drugs; heroin. I was instantly addicted. I was ready to get stoned so I wouldn't feel. My body was wounded, bruised and infected. My clothes stank. I was kidnapped and forced into prostitution in Bucharest. That was sickening.

Marlene is trembling and crying. Her fellow group members are wrapping her in hugs. "You are a hero. You are strong. You are a winner. We love you." Marlene concludes:

I immigrated to Israel. It was only then that I finally went into rehab. I had a difficult time without drugs. It was much harder to score here. Thank you for listening to me. I have never told anyone this story. I love you... I need you.

Anyone can start off having a good day, when suddenly it is ruined by an accident, an event, or even by a conversation delivering difficult news. Three hours later, nothing will be the same again...; the series of beliefs that a certain individual possessed up to that traumatic experience, can be shattered (Williams & Poijula, 2002).

And the king trembled, and he went up to the upper chamber of the gate, and wept; and thus he said, as he went, "O' my son Absalom, my son, my son Absalom! Would I have died in your stead, O' Absalom my son, my son!" (Samuel II 19:1)

While he was yet speaking, there came also another, and said, Thy sons and thy daughters were eating and drinking wine in their eldest brother's house:

And, behold, there came a great wind from the wilderness, and smote the four corners of the house, and it fell on the young men, and they are dead; and I only am escaped alone to tell thee. (Job 1:18-19)

In extremely stressful situations that cause mental trauma, one experiences an emergency condition, which is a mental condition that damages one's life sequence and thinking patterns. When that sequence, or unity, is damaged, one may notice physical and emotional stress reactions that are strongly associated. According to Foa and colleagues (2004), most people return to full performance following a stressful experience. The common assumption is that only ten percent will develop a post-traumatic syndrome. Through my clinical experience, I witness a different reality. Thus, I am interested in investigating this statistical item of data. Because of the traumatic experience's severity, the victim's usually young age, the recurrence, and that most assaults are sexual, most victims who come to Rothschild 2 are those whose innate healing powers failed them. Later I address the causes affecting the trauma, its preceding causes, and the consequential causes.

Four dimensions portray the relative human reaction to trauma: physical, emotional, cognitive, and behavioral. I specify the main reactions as:

Physical Reactions	Emotional Reactions	Cognitive Reactions	Behavioral Reactions
Palpitations	Shock	Confusion	Seclusion
A Feeling of Suffocation	Fear	Memory Difficulties	Hostility and Aggression
Various Aches	Anger	Disorientation	Alienation
Diarrhea	Guilt	Deficient Attention	Performance Difficulties
Fatigue	Apathy and Dissociation	Decision Making Difficulties	Alcohol and Substance Abuse
Changes in Appetite	Helplessness	Apprehension	
Dizziness	Anxiety	Loss of Trust	
Weakness	Depression		

Figure 1: Four Dimensions to Human Reaction to Trauma

A conversation with Eran exhibits an anxiety attack of a PTSD victim, years after the experience:

Today it struck me. Actually, it struck me yesterday... the conference call, intended to arrange a meeting for me with two department heads in the factory, throwing me back six years. I feel how all the blood in my body leaves the legs. I black out. I am unable to think logically. At such a moment, logic is gone. What is going on? What do they have to say to me? What are they up to? Who ratted this time? They are trying to kick me out of the police... Thousands of irrational thoughts wash over me, they come and go like sea waves, choking me, threatening to wash over me... I'm short of breath; my heart beats stronger and faster. Stress runs through me. I had learned that in those moments, I should breathe deeply, inhale air into my lungs, slowly release, assuming that I remember to do it. I must try to calm the raging sympathetic nervous system of my body. Nothing. I blackout. I feel tremendous discomfort in my chest and my legs are heavy. A new employee in the department approaches me, asking why I am so pale... even she feels it. Who can I lean on now? Two childhood friends come to mind. They will always love me; my sons, my wife... that's it, I'm done...

Like a fisherman pulling a fish caught in the net, I remember the conversations with my therapists, held after the trauma I experienced:

"You know you will not be hurt."

"That's right. I know."

"What is coming to your mind now, try to tell me, Eran. Try to share your thoughts with me."

"I remember the phone conversation when they summoned me for the police interrogation. I am as terrified as I was then."

"You know, Eran, you are not being summoned for interrogation. The intention was to schedule a work meeting."

"This is not the knowledge, not the thought, but the feeling—the body remembers its reaction at the time of the trauma. I cannot control it. I try to control it, or I think I manage, but I don't. I feel the discomfort."

"The sympathetic nervous system responds to noise, to a clue—it is a momentary reminder for the anxiety you experienced. Your physiological system did not forget the "fight or flight" reaction. A physical reaction discharges neurotransmitters and hormones at moments of danger...

"Eran, your nervous system is still very vulnerable, extremely sensitive. Deep breathing can help calm your body systems preparing to fight. The medications prescribed by your psychiatrist may also calm the danger-related physical reactions... I remember you were following

well-arranged medical instructions that allowed you to count on benzodiazepines for tranquilization for several days. The treatment was of such great assistance to you in the past..."

"Experiencing those threatening sensations again deeply frustrates me. I draw inside myself. Just this morning I scheduled a movie date with friends. I couldn't care less about it now. I want to go home, to bed. My bed is calling me."

The meaning of the Greek word "trauma" is "a wound" or "injury" (Zomer & Bleich, 2005), namely, "damage to living tissue caused by an external force." According to the authors, the metaphor in this context is "a psychological wound or injury, a wound caused by an external stress event, which is perceived by the individual as an actual threat to his life or to his physical and mental wholeness."

"The moment a trauma event takes place, the victim's main behavior is geared toward survival," (Shalev et al. 2002). The more trauma victims I meet, the greater my astonishment over the mental strength they employ in order to survive those events. I have seen individuals whose whole existence shattered because of continuous sexual abuse or a sudden loss, individuals who emerge from the ruins of their lives broken and bereaved. For months, their nights are full of nightmares. Every morning, meeting a new day involves an encounter with waves of fear, anxiety, despair, and dejection. Sometimes, they wish to die in order to set themselves free of the suffering. They survived thanks to tremendous psychological strength, an ability to repress, or through substance abuse.

Psychological trauma may be an experience resulting from a terrorist bombing, car accident, earthquake, plane crash, violent robbery – experienced directly by somebody, or even exposure to an event taking place nearby (Williams & Poijula, 2002). Contrary to a physical trauma, which is determined by objective components only, Zomer and colleagues (2005) state that "psychological trauma is induced, first and foremost, by a subjective feeling of the trauma's objective characteristics." That is, the more threatening the individual perceives the event, and the more he perceives himself as helpless, the higher his risk to experience trauma.

Even if I stop viewing it through the therapist's or the researcher's eye, I fail to see how such psychological suffering could be measured: the intensity of the consistent anxiety; the paralyzing fear, the victim feeling as though his life and body are threatened by another are all harsh feelings. How could one quantify psychological sensation into a concept of experienced trauma that one has not experienced and therefore cannot understand? The reader might raise this question as well.

By 9 a.m. on Sundays, I'm updated on the major happenings that the first morning group of patients has gone through on the weekend. Following a brief morning round at the treatment center divisions, I take urine samples from the group patients for drug testing. Simultaneously, the staff and the clients look after the house, tidying it up, feeding the animals, and have the first cup of coffee.

The client urinalysis routinely takes place on Sunday and Wednesday mornings and Sunday, Tuesday, and Thursday afternoons. The analysis facilitates the fulfillment of the following two key professional goals, constituting the guidelines of each workweek:

1. To monitor and investigate my patients' being drug-free while they participate in the therapeutic program

2. To keep up a brief, personal conference, so to speak, with each client, prior to them entering the drug screening, or following it

At 9 a.m., I meet Caryn for a therapeutic session. The session is part of a comprehensive therapeutic plan, provided for Caryn as a trauma victim and a drug addict. Caryn, a single female, only 19 years of age has received treatment at the Rothschild 2 Center for approximately four months. She has been clean for approximately eleven months. Her life has been full of suffering, trauma, and humiliation. Caryn was sexually assaulted in the bathroom of a dance club in Haifa approximately two years ago. A unfamiliar young man followed her into the bathroom and forced her to give him oral sex. Caryn remembers trying to resist, but nobody heard her scream nor came to help. The act was quick, accompanied by loud trance music in the background. The guy's sweaty odor mixed with the smell of soap in the bathroom, and her first ever experience with the smell of ejaculated sperm. To this day, Caryn has been unable to forgive her friend who accompanied her to the bathroom, but failed to notice her delayed return.

During the session, I question Caryn about the other goings on in her life, outside the center's therapeutic structure and her work as a waitress two nights a week. Caryn replies she is embarrassed to share, and I feel that she seeks my help in recounting the incident, thereby stopping her from continuing to go downhill.

> "Caryn, we have addressed many issues by now. I have a feeling that you are carrying a heavy burden on your shoulders. I believe you can share the secret, or secrets, with me because to me they seem to pull you down."

> "I'm ashamed, but I'd rather share it with you... I have been with five men in the past few days, although only one of them is my boyfriend. I feel like a nymphomaniac."

> "Nymphomaniac is a broad term...Why do you feel that way?"

> "Because I don't even like them; I know what I do is vulgar. I give them a blowjob within minutes. It's like a hobby."

> "What kind of benefits do you get from your so-called 'hobby'? Love? Attention? Power? Possession? Interest? Control? What is it...? Why not try to describe to me how you feel."

"I do not know. I told you. Maybe it's some hobby I started. When a man comes, he is this small." (She gestures with her hand to demonstrate a small object or creature.)

"And if he is small, how do you feel about that?"

"I don't know. Perhaps I feel strong. They want me. They are attracted to me. They say I am something special..."

"What do you think of yourself afterward? What do you think they think of you?"

"I don't know. I feel it's vulgar, but this is my way of coping with things..."

"What have you overcome? In our sessions, I get the impression you are a talented writer and artist. I think you should be appreciated for your good qualities."

"I want somebody to love me, to want me. I'm afraid of men..."'

"You said giving men blowjobs helps you cope..."

"I am coping with the episode in the bathroom. I was very scared back then, where he assaulted me. That was where I was helpless. Now I am the one who controls them. Now, if I stop, they will beg me to go on. Now, many of my friends wouldn't dare do what I do."

The research related to trauma victims should continue its attempts to portray concepts that it seeks to understand, as Zomer & Bleich (2005) maintain. The researchers address new studies in the traumatic experience field, arguing that the term "traumatic experience" is too broad, full of inner contradictions and only a few commonalities. They further state that an individual episode is quite different from a community episode. Thus it is necessary to find a concept demonstrating the difference among an event resulting from a natural adversity (such as an earthquake or hurricane), a human-related event (rape, robbery, or a terrorist act), and an accidental event, such as a car accident or a helicopter crash. The scholars mention other ways to distinguish a one-time stress episode and a continuous traumatic episode. Terr (1991), Burke (1991), and Wilson (1994) also addressed those modes of distinguishing one trauma from another. Terr maintains that Type 1 trauma (a one-time episode) is usually unexpected, out of the daily human stress domain. They differ from Type 2 trauma, which is recurrent, as in continuous abuse against children, women, and men.

Terr also maintains that Type 1 episodes may induce developing post-traumatic stress disorder while Type 2 trauma episodes may induce developing PTSD, dissociation symptoms, and even inconsolable feelings of sadness (further discussed in Chapter Four). I mention these studies since most clients coming for treatment with me at Rothschild 2 belong to one of the traumatic episode categories defined by Terr as Type 1 or Type 2. They seek treatment as drug addicts, but throughout the treatment, we find many have suffered harsh, continuous sexual trauma episodes as children.

Beck (1992) presents another trauma definition, a Type 3 episode. He states this type of stress is characteristic of chaotic relationships, which induce incessant anxiety, characterized by a high degree of inconsistency, resulting in a difficulty to predict any regularity. To this group, I categorize clients from families where chaos and dysfunction reigned. The parents in such families did not notice the distress signs conveyed by the child trauma victim, and were too preoccupied to understand him or her. Furthermore, physical violence was a common mode of upbringing. Such a lifestyle, which lasts for years, may lead the child to suffer particularly rough psychological crises.

Wilson (1994) proposes to define Type 4 traumas as situations inducing a high degree of consistent uncertainty requiring adaptation to the consistent stress situations. He maintains those situations could be consistent with the ongoing terrorist attacks experienced by a certain population, or the threat of terrorist acts directed at the civilian population. Such stress events may escalate tension, apprehension or sadness. In recent years, we witness similar situations in Sderot, a town in southern Israel. Dr. Roni Berger, with whom I have met this year, states that Sderot residents are under constant psychological tension because of the Qassam rockets, impossible to anticipate. Residents of the border settlements and other towns in Israel have experienced similar situations, such as ongoing terrorist attacks. What is the fate of their future psychological lives? What will be the state of mental health of Sderot resident in years to come?

I am well aware that predictions are quite risky. Early diagnosis "may limit the scope of vision, and even turn out to be a self-fulfilling prophecy" (Yalom 2002). However, I immediately question this context, as do many other professionals: How many PTSD victims from those communities will we identify in years to come? Without immediate professional treatment provided to trauma victims, what will be the fate of those living in the conflict areas? I am aware that many researchers in the behavioral sciences in Israel investigate such psychological effects on Israeli society, in communities struck by continuous terrorist violence (see Zomer & Bleich, 2005) and under abusive conditions (see Seligman & Solomon, 2004). Thus far, I have reviewed the causes for stress situations. Now I address the causes affecting the individual's response to those situations.

Trauma-Precedent Factors

Many factors may affect the individual's response to traumatic experiences (Williams & Poijula 2002). Among the factors preceding the trauma, they document the individual's age, extent of preparedness for the experience; the scope of destruction and/or previous exposure to trauma or depression or anxiety preceding the experience; family stability and socio-economic status; previous issues with legal authorities, academic failures, social support, suicidal behavior to which he or she was exposed as a child, etc. The fact that females are more prone to PTSD than males, as are adolescents and young adults up to age 25, the geographical proximity to trauma, the degree of exposure to trauma, and the duration of the threat sensation all inform the therapist. Shalev and colleagues (2002) also refer to the factors that fulfill a role prior to the traumatic experience. They state that "lack of social support and presence of secondary stress factors are key risk conditions for post-traumatic stress disorder (PTSD) development." Williams and Poijula (2002) also indicate the events that affect the victim following the traumatic experience. They argue that the latter fulfills a significant role in determining whether psychological trauma will develop.

Post-Trauma Related Factors

Lack of decent social support; lack of parental support, inability to act in regard to the abusive event, sinking into self-pity and self-neglect; passivity instead of activity, and inability to draw meaning out of the suffering are all factors to consider in the therapeutic intervention sessions with the clients.

To some traumatic experiences, the individual will respond with great extremity within the first few days following the trauma, as maintained by Williams & Poijula (2002). Those responses may yield an acute stress disorder (ASD) (see also Zomer & Bleich, 2005). The post-traumatic syndrome combines with dissociation phenomena, resulting in an acute stress disorder (broadly discussed in Chapter Seven). For example, one might experience reactions of great fear resulting from the traumatic experience; a feeling of helplessness or terror; loss of feeling; dissociation or lack of emotional response, constriction in one's awareness of others' presence; a feeling of alienation and withdrawal from one's familiar surroundings, forgetting the event or parts thereof. Other experiences include a feeling of relentless clinging to life associated with the traumatic experiences—dreams, thoughts, and flashbacks—persistent avoidance of experiences resembling the trauma, over-alertness, fear and weakness both in life functions and life tasks. I find it important to mention those phenomena related to traumatic experiences, since they occur within the first few days following the trauma, and may partly appear in the post-traumatic stress disorder, discussed in the following chapter.

When examining the victim, from the moment the traumatic experience occurred, it is common to define the responses observed from the first week through the fourth week as initial responses. The acute stress response is observable from the second through the fourth week. Depression and anxiety responses are observable from the fourth week and even up to six months following the event. Chronic post-traumatic responses are observable from the third month after the event (Foa et al. 2004). However, since the stress event was not a one-time event for most of the victims I encounter at Rothschild 2, and most of them didn't receive treatment due to concealment, shame, terror, or a feeling of threat, I assess the clients' post-traumatic situations as more severe. Another study is required to confirm these assumptions.

Only a few studies in Israel investigated trauma resulting from violence and abuse in connection with substance addiction issues, although rather broad professional literature available in Israel explores psychological trauma resulting from military combat, terrorist suicide bombings, and car accidents (Zomer & Bleich; Shalev et al., 2002; Seligman & Solomon, 2004). Various studies indicate the extent to which an individual who is not in a constant state of military battle will be predisposed to a personal adversity or to another traumatic experience.

In a study investigating 1007 subjects, 384 replied affirmatively when questioned if they had ever been exposed to any trauma in their lives. This item of data reveals that 39.1% of the subjects reported some traumatic experience in their lives (Breslau, Davis, Andreski, & Peterson, 1991).

> Abuse may also occur in a military boot camp, or in any other military environment; the problem may be induced due to situations where a so-called true man is expected to withstand the physical and psychological suffering, no complaints acceptable (Brothers 2004).

Out of all rape cases in the United States, the summaries cited in the book by Foa and Rothbaum (1998) reveal that 24 percent of the female victims will develop a post-traumatic stress disorder, and 3.4 percent of them will develop a complex post-trauma. Thus, they state, 1.5 to six million women in the United States suffer post-traumatic disorder following a rape and/or sexual assault. The huge scope of this data renders it hard to conceive, truly incredible. This is probably Israel's victim rate as well, including many men who have been sexual assault victims, not mentioned in the book.

Ouimette & Brown (2003) refer to the trauma victim rate in the whole population, thereby responding to the comment I previously raised. The researchers state that five percent of the men and 10.4 percent of the women, and, on average, approximately 7.8 percent of the whole U.S. population have experienced trauma in their lives. Moreover, many of those who experience trauma may develop post-traumatic phenomena.

Kessler, Sonnega, Bromet, Hughes, & Nelson (1995) argue that events of higher risk for trauma development of post-traumatic symptoms need categorization. They maintain that rape is the traumatic experience whose victims are of the highest risk to develop a trauma (65 percent of men raped and 45 percent of the women). In that study, the researchers reported that out of 5877 subjects, five percent of the men and ten percent of the women experienced trauma. The researchers went even further, attempting to estimate the amount of time it would take before the trauma victim experienced relief. They claim that a victim who experienced trauma and received treatment would experience relief within three years, while an individual left untreated would experience similar relief within five years.

I assume many of the addicts who come to Rothschild 2 have self-medicated with drugs while going untreated. The relief among them shows during treatment, many years later.

In a study addressing 2000 U.S. adults, Finkelhor (1987) found that 27 percent of the women and 16 percent of the men survived a sexual assault in childhood. Many of us in the psychological trauma field share the view that childhood sexual assault is always a psychologically traumatic experience. Sexual assault victims constitute the largest sector among PTSD patients with 60 percent of sexual assault victims meeting the PTSD criteria at some point in their lives (Brothers 2004). Generally, relatives sexually abuse women, while strangers usually sexually abuse men (Ouimette & Brown, 2003). These events are common. In my years of work with drug addicts in Israel, too, I have met thousands of sexual abuse victims.

Seligman and Solomon (2004) indicate that one in six boys up to age 16 has experienced direct sexual contact with an adult or with an older child. This harsh data combined with the previous research data I presented in the epidemiology chapter, and many others, enhance my understanding of the prevalence of damage to the population from civilian trauma. Ouimette and Brown (2003) further state that the greatest risk of developing a trauma comes from rape. Trauma may develop among approximately 60 percent of the men raped and among approximately 40 percent of the women raped. The majority will develop a post-traumatic stress disorder if not treated immediately. Further harsh factors affecting the development of trauma and post-trauma are military fighting episodes among men and other sexual assaults among women. A study addressing adolescents (Ouimette & Brown, 2003), indicated that approximately two percent of the boys and ten percent of the girls experienced trauma. The study indicates than during adolescence, the number of women who experienced trauma was five times greater than the number of men who experienced the same. This is a severe statistic—serious data needing serious attention.

In their book, Foa and colleagues (2007) discuss their anxiety disorder model they developed in 1985. The discussion addressing anxiety and trauma constitutes a key component here, and particularly in this chapter. Both are strongly associated with powerful, complex processes. It is commonly thought that post-traumatic stress disorder occurs due to trauma, which in psychological terms is defined as an anxiety disorder (ICD-10, 2002). Again, it is clear that a stress event induces a psychological response prompting other episodes: somatic responses, psychological responses, and psychological trauma. Trauma also consists of components stemming from the extreme fear structure. Hence, familiarity with various accounts of fear response is highly important in this context, according to Foa and colleagues (2007). Feelings of fear appear in the brain as a cognitive structure, and as an apparent plan to avoid danger. The fear response comprises four stages:

1. Fear-inducing stimulus, for example, encountering a wild bear

2. An increased heart rate suggests measurement for a fear response

3. The meaning attributed to the bear (scary), the meaning attributed to the fear

4. The meaning attributed leads to the fear response – one should flee from the bear

In this account, the victims' psychological trauma and emotional response fulfill a major role in treatment. In addition, the responses are imperative to planning therapeutic intervention for addicts who are also trauma victims. Where does the root problem lie? It is when the cognitive mechanism for the fear response keeps operating in the individual, even when the threat is gone. This is the point when the post-traumatic episodes usually emerge, needing immediate treatment. Chapters Seven through Nine discuss treatment methods and I broadly address the modes of coping with memories from traumatic situations. The fear response's cognitive structure becomes pathological in the following cases (Foa et al. 2007):

1. When it is associated with stimuli that do not reflect reality

2. When pathological responses emerge and those stimuli are absent

3. When the phenomena yield a maladaptive behavior

4. A harmless episode is erroneously perceived as threatening

I encounter the above situations in my daily work. They support the theoretical knowledge I possess regarding the pathological fear response among trauma victims. Many colleagues of mine could also bring their findings from their therapeutic-clinical work, confirming the reality of those situations.

There is a fierce struggle going on between Kamma, the Rothschild 2 resident dog and Choco, my family dog. Choco comes to work with me every day, returning home in the evening. Kamma is jealous. I have sensed this from the first moment. After all, little Choco benefits from a night's sleep covered in a down blanket, in a warm home where she is a member of the family while Kamma remains behind to guard Rothschild 2 every evening, alone, without a family, smells of cooking, or a down blanket.

When Choco comes to work with me, full of energy, joy, and excitement, Kamma bares her teeth, barking to warn Choco, "This is my territory. Beware of the fence borderline." One morning, when cheeky little Choco crossed the so-called red line marking Kamma's territory, Kamma set on her, furiously biting her in an outburst of continuous frustration. Little Choco fled, screaming in fear, her chopped tail between her legs, seeking a hideout. Her body was trembling; her cries – heartbreaking. Long months would pass before she dared even to look at Kamma over the fence.

Marlene's life story and the stories of many others demonstrate to some extent the feelings of a trauma victim. Through Marlene's story, and the life stories of individuals I have treated, I, too, clearly experience the intensity of the psychological suffering that comes from stress and traumatic episodes.

Sexual abuse victims often engage in self-protection rather than focusing on learning how to cooperate with others. Consequently, as Marlene's story demonstrates, they channel their behavior toward subsidizing their lack of confidence, turning their immediate world into a safer place (Brothers, 2004). The psychological trauma is undoubtedly an adversity for the helpless individual.

Marlene's story is the story of a domestic traumatic experience victim. As a trauma victim, helpless Marlene faced a force stronger than she was, as indicated by Prince (1995) and Herman (1992). Not only did the traumatic experiences pose a threat to her life and her physical well-being, they also involved a close, personal encounter with violence and death. Marlene encountered a force stronger than she was, the force of the boys abusing her, humiliating her, hitting her, and raping her, while she faced them, helpless.

Trauma survivors often experience an intense feeling of alienation toward others and the world in general, according to Brothers (2004), who further states that 80 percent of the childhood sexual abuse victims experience certain difficulties related to intercourse in adulthood. Trauma is a rough experience stemming from the episode, or several episodes, or from the fact that the victim witnessed an episode or episodes, involving death or severe damage, or a threat of death, severe damage, or even the threat to one's or another's physical well-being (Foa et al., 2004).

In a book edited by Munitz (2003), he mentions the subjective psychological aspect affecting the trauma victim. The concept of traumatic experience, he maintains, refers to a physical or psychological episode whose actual physical damage component may be of no objective significance, but appears to the victim as endangering his safety, psychological well-being, dignity, health, and sometimes his life.

> The most basic needs of trust, openness, intimacy, mutuality, and closeness are not answered, or they induce frustration among sexual trauma victims. The survivor experiences alienation and detaches from her physical self, and her body becomes an object serving others (Brothers, 2004).

Parental violence is another type of violence where children experience domestic trauma. Such violence threatens the child's sense of existence (Katzenelson, 1998). The constriction of his feelings, the emotional isolation, and avoidance lead the battered child to employ initial defense mechanisms of splitting, denial, projections, and trauma restoration (Groth, 1979).

Various psychological and physical factors could induce a "life threat" and Type I trauma.

Physical Violence	Sexual Assault	Sexual Assault by the Father	Verbal Violence	Extreme Emotional Deprivation
A drunk and violent parent	Neglect	Abuse by peers	Terror suicide bombing	Natural adversity
Personal coding for trauma	Eating induced issues		Assault by mother	ADHD and its implications

TRAUMA

Figure 2: Various stressors that could induce a sense of extreme threat and trauma

79

"It is likely that it never occurred to my father that his ass-kicking would leave my soul scarred by terror," Menny relates to me. To this day, his walk is tense, his shoulders hunched, his steps hesitant. I look at him and see a terrified child who trusts no one. Menny jumps abruptly on hearing loud noises, objects falling to the ground, or on hearing voices from the nearby building site. There are moments when even the suddenness of a phone call makes him leap with fear. "The normal reaction to acts of horror damaging the individual is to try and erase them from the mind," writes Herman (1992). Based on conversations with many clients, I have learned that it is extremely difficult to manage, which most trauma victims I have met are not able to do. How difficult it is for Alex, a drug addict and criminal, to come forward and tell me of his childhood. As a child, Alex was scared to death of the sound of the house keys jingling, implying the return home of his drunk father.

Trauma is a "stress inducing event or situation, short term or continuous, which is exceptionally threatening or catastrophic by nature and may induce significant distress to almost anyone" (ICD-10, 2002). The professional literature assumes that the traumatic experiences usually involve harsh feelings of threat to life or physical well-being, as maintained by Herman (1992). Some of the events are experienced as intrusive memories, a feeling of being petrified, emotional numbness, disconnection from others, lack of responsiveness to one's surroundings, and nightmares. Other events of that time manifest as hyperarousal, including impulse control disorders, compulsive fears from which the client wishes to withdraw and even escape (Munitz, 2003).

I remembered Yair well. He was 40 years old when he came to me for treatment, married and a father of three, addicted to drugs for 24 years at the time. He told me how much he hated his living room couch, loathed it, unable to look at it anymore. The couch is the same couch where he had sat every night for 20 years because of the nightmares torturing him. The traumatic memories constantly invaded Yair's life.

Sleeping difficulties may occur for many reasons, including fear of abuse at night, resulting in a continuous pattern of nocturnal over-alertness, as maintained by Courtois (2004). Long years of sessions with many clients have taught me that the intensity of sexual abuse is the roughest, thus sexual violence bears the most far-reaching ramifications on the victims' psychological, social, and interpersonal functioning. In the short term, immediately following the sexual abuse, the most common symptoms are anxiety, sleeping disorders, nightmares, attention deficits, crying outbursts, nausea, paranoia, physiological arousal, and impotence (Krystal, 1978; Katzenelson, 1998; Berman, 2003). In the long term, the most prevalent responses are depression, eating disorders, low self-esteem, self-blame, helplessness, somatization, and self-abuse inclusive of drug and alcohol addiction. One of the most common and harsh results is PTSD (Hendin & Hass, 1991; Berman, 2003).

Different individuals develop different responses to overcome the unbearable sensations, coping by means of defense mechanisms suiting each individual's personality (Terr, 1991). The mechanisms facilitate the individual to reduce the anxiety, depression, and psychological suffering resulting from trauma he underwent, sensations with which he, having no mental strength, is unable to cope.

Among the professionals treating stress and trauma, the common assumption is that the individual possesses various modes of coping with such episodes:

a) A common way to curb anxiety, which is associated with sexual abuse victims' interpersonal relations, is to leave them far removed, formal, and lacking emotion as much as possible, according to Seligman & Solomon (2004).

b) Another way is developing a pessimistic life theory guided by a total mistrust of anyone. The following two negative beliefs are characteristic of women who will develop PTSD because of a trauma (Foa & Rothbaum, 1998): 1) The world is unsafe and dangerous; 2) Humanity in general, and the victim in particular, are deficient, undeserving individuals.

c) A third mode is avoidance. We observe a large number of situations involving avoidance among violent assault survivors (Foa & Rothbaum, 1998). The victim views a stranger (who resembles the aggressor in some way) as the aggressor, or an individual standing anywhere near him as threatening. Even a random touch by a stranger may restore fears in the victim. Other stressors include walking alone on the street, staying home alone, entering a vehicle alone at night, conversing with a stranger, a person stopping a vehicle, walking at night with a friend, reading news or watching a report of violent assault on television, encountering the name or the picture of a victim on the news, walking to the building/apartment/street where the assault took place, sexual or intimate situations, and even clothes that remind the victim of the assault (also see Chapter Seven).

When Lynn wanted to visit her mother in the United States again, she knew she would have to pass by the school where she experienced the first rape while walking down the street. While riding the bus on the street leading to her home, she knew she would pass by the cemetery where her best friend lay buried; she had committed suicide following their rape. Her mother's home, too, has many memories associated with it. It's where her stepfather abused her, a place where every photograph, every piece of furniture, smells of cooking, and the smell of the home all reminded her of her life's horrors.

d) A fourth mode of coping portrayed by therapists: Many abuse victims develop reactions that sometimes resemble "concentration camp syndrome," and, as Prince (1995) indicates, this syndrome involves embracing an extreme survival mechanism that allows the individual to channel all of his mental and physical strengths toward survival. Channeling one's energy to other paths appears as a waste of mental energy (see also Pirani, 2005).

Living with such psychological conditions would be extremely difficult in the long term. One's soul cries for help, repression, or relief from drug use. While writing this book, I can assume that thanks to survival mechanisms, many people in the world are able to live and survive: sexual trauma victims, victims of domestic violence, citizens of countries under tyrannical governments, and long-term prisoners. Under such psychological conditions, such terror, one misstep or misspoken word might induce destruction and death. This is terror; this is fear. This is the victim's helpless state.

Those who live in terror manage to survive without giving way to the psychological pain. This is the power of psychological survival. Thinking back on the statement made by Williams and Poijula (2002), I agree to the notion that an individual's response to a traumatic situation or to an intensely stressful situation cannot anticipated, because it depends on many factors, as stated by Munitz (2003) as well. The traumatic situation and its duration effect; the individual's physical condition and resilience while being hurt; his predisposition in terms of personal strength and maturity; the social support received during the traumatic period; the intensity of the inner conflicts induced by the traumatic situation; and the psychological meaning the victim attributes to the trauma experienced, consciously or unconsciously.

e) Many people, mostly men, will learn a fifth coping pattern, namely, expressing anger toward their trauma experiences. Anger is one of the only emotional responses accessible to men, and the only emotion that many men suffering sexual abuse are capable of expressing is rage, as argued by Seligman and Solomon (2004). Yet they indicate that in many cases, feelings of sadness, loss, and despair underlie the expression of anger and rage. Those are the feelings we at Rothschild 2 attempt to uncover.

Here I address the various causes and circumstances affecting the emergence of a psychological trauma (See Figure 2). The aggressor-victim relationship appears particularly complicated when the aggressor threatens the victim's life on the one hand, and grants him life on the other hand by not killing him (Prince, 1995; Kulka et al., 1990). This distortion incurs further guilt in the victim.

The memory of the traumatic experience catches Alex in events associatively linked to that event. As a child, Alex saw in his angry father's eyes the rage about to burst. Ever since, any gathering or Friday night dinner could have potentially become violent, possibly reigniting the trauma he experienced. There were moments when he had feared being wounded or killed from the beatings, but Alex also had other moments, when he admired his father, even loved him; these are distorted emotions.

In my therapeutic work, I realize repeatedly that most clients coming to Rothschild 2 are affected by childhood traumatic experiences, mainly sexual assault. I highlight this as a fact, a reality I have discovered with my patients. Professionals in the psychological therapy field have become more familiar with the intensity of the damage caused to an individual in general and a child in particular because of sexual abuse. We find this notion extremely difficult. Rape is a type of violence that crosses all boundaries of both the physical and psychological self.

Imposing a sexual act on someone leaves the victim with a highly traumatic memory (Lazar & Cwikel, 1992; Eylon, 1983).

Shoshi recounts: "I cannot understand why, for a whole year, my parents did not notice what I was going through. I cannot understand such a feeling. It shatters me from the inside."

I proceed by indicating that other post-traumatic responses such as anxiety, phobias, depression, and sexual dysfunction may occur among both male and female victims of sexual assault within five years of the occurrence, and even 30 years thereafter, as maintained by Lazar & Cwikel (1992). I address the matter in the chapter discussing post-trauma (Chapter Four). Sex crimes severely damage the human foundations of psychological strength, and the psychological ramifications of victimhood, both psychologically and physiologically speaking, are extremely harsh (Katzenelson, 1998). One can see how most sexual assault victims suffer long years of trauma (Etgar, 1999; Terr, 1991).

Of all sex crimes, incest is the most severe traumatic experience, bearing harsh psychological implications on the inner being of the boy or girl, as stated by Seligman and Solomon (2004). The experience may reverberate in the victims' souls throughout their lives.

As in any traumatic occurrence, and to an even greater degree of extremity, incest is an experience that shatters the regular coping system that instills a sense of control, connection, and meaning within the individual. This is a most unusual traumatic occurrence, as it takes place precisely within an intimate parent-child relationship, or other relationship with relatives. Incest is a violent act even when it involves no physical pain simply because of the shattering of the body's limits, the threat to the body, and the domination (Seligman & Solomon, 2004). In my therapeutic work, I assume—based on the knowledge that the effects of sexual assault and rape are more severe when taking place in childhood—a child who experiences constant abuse learns to be cautious of potential aggressors everywhere.

According to Seligman and Solomon (2004), the child is likely to develop profound difficulties in making future connections and forming interpersonal relationships.

Battered Children

Many professionals will agree with the statement that battered children live in constant trauma, leaving a deep impression on their psychological development (Katzenelson, 1998). This type of trauma may cause harsh psychological damage, which becomes part of their personality as they mature. The physical abuse affects the child's emotional and behavioral functioning (Finzi, Shnit, & Weizman, 1999; Groth, 1979). Even if decades pass, the horrific experience the child undergoes remains in the child's memory forever.

The severity of sexual abuse in children is determined by the victim's age, duration, severity of forcefulness and violence, false pretenses to the child, the presence of somatic anxiety, the number of aggressors, whether or not the abuse is revealed to others, deprivation of treatment, and the child-aggressor relationship, that is parent or stranger (Seligman & Solomon, 2004).

For decades, Itzhak lived with the assault he experienced as a child. Thirty-five years later, he recounts:

> The moment I was sexually assaulted by five older children from the neighborhood, who tormented me and humiliated me—came unimaginable fear and the questions: Why me? Why did they do that to *me*? Why didn't I hit them? Why didn't I run?

Incest

Some variables have a greater effect on the degree of the sexually assaulted child's reaction, as maintained by Courtois (2005). Generally, incest results in more severe outcomes if it begins at a time when the child is very young or in his early teens. Many factors determine the extent of the damage, including if the incest is continuous, forceful or violent; if it involves false pretenses or training the child to become an active party, so to speak. Other severe factors determine outcomes: if the child is told they are to blame, if the abuse involves physical penetration, or if it involves both the parent and the child or other relatives. Particularly difficult is the situation where the abuse is revealed and reported but does not stop; or, if there is some intervention, which is traumatizing in itself, and it is ineffective, and the abuse continues.

In order to cope with the psychological pain and humiliation connected with traumatic abuse, the abused child tends to disconnect himself from the painful emotion, denying it and isolating himself from it. The child depreciates himself, assuming the burden of blame. This process dulls the child's emotions toward himself and those around him. The child often becomes tense with every emotion (Finzi et al., 1999; Gorth, 1990; Terr, 1991), as implied by Sima's words: "It is only now I realize how much I deprived myself of experiencing emotions, ever since that terrible event I went through."

"We notice that children suffering sexual and physical abuse live in the shadow of daily terror; they live an ongoing trauma. A violent parenting style is, too, a threat to the child's well-being and life, damaging his resilience," assert Finzi and colleagues (1999), who further state that domestic sexual abuse is an extremely severe type of violence. The sexual abuse affects the family life in unique ways. The family members mature in a disturbed family climate. Sometimes the parents appear as dangerous, cruel, indifferent, neglectful, and untrustworthy. The key cause for severe emotional injury and consequent permanent damage to clients is abuse of a sexual nature, domestic incest, and other assaults of sexual nature (Warshaw et al., 1988; Groth, 1979). Incest has a devastating impact on the victim's mental health, their quality of life, and development (Finzi et al., 1999; Eylon, 1983; Katzenelson, 1998).

Sunday is a long day, divided into two parts: From 8 a.m. - 2 p.m. I am involved in the activity of the Urban Outpatient Care Center.

At 2 p.m. the Outpatient Care Center staff assembles for a meeting where we discuss the various requests submitted to us by clients, namely, accompanying them to court arraignments, meetings with social services, urgent medical examinations, etc. Sometimes, we invite a member from the Outpatient Care Group who we believe requires further attention. This meeting also includes Effye, who still works at the rehab hospital run by the Ministry of Health in Jaffa. Throughout the year, the professional staff and I meet with increasing information regarding civilian misfortune causing trauma, situations where others damage an individual.

Prince (1995) specifies seven main factors affecting the intensity of the psychological damage due to trauma resulting from child sexual abuse:

1. The child's age at the onset of abuse

2. The duration of abuse

3. The degree of violence or violent threat imposed on the child

4. The age difference between the victim and aggressor

5. The specific family victim-aggressor relationship

6. A lack of protective parental figures

7. The extent to which secrecy was maintained regarding the occurrence, or the extent to which it was openly discussed

Aside from the initial damage caused by sexual trauma in children, Prince further states a secondary damage. The secondary trauma may result from intervention of professionals or representatives of various institutes, institutional conflicts, conflicts of different professionals, and, due to conflicts between the therapeutic and legal institutes and children's psychological and protection-related needs, the general factors may intensify the psychological damage the abused child suffers. A secondary trauma may also stem from trauma victims' responses, which often receive rejection, punishment, or further abuse through victim-like behavior or abnormal sexual behavior. One study indicates that a high degree of depression and anxiety variables as negative qualities is quite prominent (Finzi and colleagues, 1999).

Children harmed by parental violence experience a threatening parental setting. I often realize that among my patients, this experience, combined with a previous sexual assault experience, forces the child to bury the secret deep inside. The parents are those closest to the child in his early years. They are supposed to protect him and provide for all his needs. They are supposed to notice any change in his mood or behavior.

Attachment theory demonstrates the ramifications on the child's functioning because of his parent-child experiences. It is a common assumption that the abused child will fail to form interpersonal relationships, arguing that he is likely to develop some psychopathology at a later stage of life (Bowlby, 1988). A child living under parental threat will adopt another strategy for coping with trauma such as avoidance strategy, denying anger at the parents, and later in life he is likely to develop emotional indifference, submissiveness, and even regard others as threatening and aggressive (Ainsworth, 1989).

As previously mentioned, abusive violence from either parent is one of the harshest types of abuse for a child. Erickson (in Finzi et al., 1999) believes a child who experienced parental violence not only learns the victim role, but also the aggressor role, the one which turns others into victims.

In absolute pain, Tommy illustrates how he turned from a victim into an aggressor:

> Years later, I took revenge on the children of one of my aggressors. I felt as though I was taking revenge on him. I hurt them just the

way he had hurt me. Their terrified gaze traumatized me just as much as the moments of the assault I had experienced.

Shlomit Cohen (2001) cites the psychoanalytical approach for understanding the trauma a child goes through in abuse. Cohen argues that the significance of the abuse resulting from child neglect or abuse may be better understood if not only the abuse be viewed externally (namely, by assessing the abusive parties – the behavior of the parents or any other figures), but also the child's subjective experience regarding himself and what he is experiencing. The outcomes of social developmental risk relate to the structure of the child's systems of coping with the world and with individuals with whom he interacts, Cohen states, and those are grave outcomes. The abused child develops defense mechanisms to face unbearable psychological pain. These defense mechanisms distort his psychological reality and his relations with the world. In my work, I realize that substance abuse is one of the coping mechanisms adopted by the child who does not receive professional treatment.

Coping with trauma narrative is insufficient, and the professional staff needs to collect additional important information to fully grasp the intensity of trauma's damage. It is necessary to explore the individual's condition at the time of trauma, and the strength available to his "self" at the time. It is necessary to question if the individual was tired or physically exhausted due to illness, what his employment situation was at the time and whether or not he was satisfied, if his family life was satisfactory, and the level of his self-esteem. During the traumatic experience, if most of the individual's energy is channeled toward overcoming a severe psychological experience such as an illness or the death of a loved one, then those circumstantial, existential factors, though not part of the traumatic experience, may determine his ability to withstand the trauma and if it leads to harsh psychological outcomes (Munitz, 2003). I address this subject further in the chapter discussing post-trauma.

Herman writes: "In the 1970s, it was recognized that the most common post-traumatic disorders are not the war-related ones among men, but those characterizing women in civilian life," (1992). I modify this with the claim that her statement applies to both men and women in civil life. In the past two decades, almost any drug addict, male or female, arriving at my treatment center has suffered an untreated personal trauma. Rape trauma syndrome devastates male sexual trauma victims, just as it does among female rape victims.

Jonny felt hurt and ashamed because of the abuse he suffered as a child by his adult neighbor. His helpless, submissive, and collaborative behavior, and the fact that, as a man, he did not stop the aggressor, and didn't save himself from additional assault. Jonny's trauma was left untreated. None of those closest to him noticed his distress. As a child, he had neither friends nor the mental strength to seek help. For many years, Jonny could not handle the feeling that he chose not to react, simply assuming he would not be able to fight or flee. In the past, whenever Jonny experienced such terrible feelings, substance abuse was his only escape.

Many studies portray situations where the client, as a child, exhibited dissociative and trance mechanisms, serving to bury the traumatic memories (Herman, 1992; Bar-Guy & Shalev, 2001; ICD-10, 2002). In the professional literature on trauma, we commonly notice the main symptoms known in post-traumatic stress disorder conditions as intrusion, hyperarousal, and constriction (Herman, 1992).

I discuss these symptoms in a broader context in the chapter addressing post-trauma, though it is important to portray the key symptoms, which happen for an individual experiencing trauma; the so-called psychological constriction draws the traumatic memories away from the mind. In the early stages of treatment, I frequently encounter individuals who suppressed the event from their mind, and they do not remember experiencing adversity, stress, or trauma. These individuals recall the trauma when the therapeutic setting is safe and expose themselves to the memory while recruiting renewed psychological strength to cope.

The feeling of intrusion is a dominant feeling in post-traumatic stress disorder. This feeling is often manifested by an intense fear response and sleeping disorder. Intrusion involves symptoms and signs of anxiety, depression, sadness, loss, helplessness, emotional dissociation, hostility toward others, inability to experience happiness and love, and even bursts of rage. Under these circumstances, suicidal thoughts are inevitable and consuming drugs or alcohol excessively complicates the situation even further. The thoughts—constricted at one stage of trauma processing—remain unconscious, threatening to erupt and penetrate into the conscious. This is a different and concealed, repressed, or denied energy, implying a psychological pain unable to discharge. I portray these phenomena in relation to a patient, Aaron, in Chapter Four.

The third factor is hyperarousal, which exhausts the individual's limited psychological energy. A hyperaroused individual is constantly alert and tense for months and even for years. He or she awakens many times throughout the night (some oversleep), is over suspicious, restless, alarmed by external noises, has trouble expressing himself or herself, and sometimes, has interpersonal dysfunction.

The effect of the traumatic experience does not end due to intrapsychic influences. Damage to interpersonal relationships occurs when the victims doubt basic human relations. Many clients have related extreme crisis in their lives—physical abuse, sexual abuse, exposure to terrorist bombings, and even verbal violence—due to which they lose basic trust in others. Under these extreme conditions, the clients, trauma victims, feel emptiness, a tremendous sense of damage, and lack of self-esteem. Herman (1992) illustrates this by claiming that an individual feels "more dead than alive."

Disconnecting from reality in a traumatic experience is a mechanism typical of trauma. Some therapists assume that dissociation acts as morphine. In this context, its significance relates to perceiving the pain as detached from the perceptions of emotion (Atkinson, 1990; Herman, 1992; Munitz, 1994), (see Chapter Seven). We recognize the emotional detachment, the apathy, the inability to experience human feelings, and even restlessness and discomfort in Marlene's and Nitzan's stories, cited later on in this chapter.

When I questioned Ami, a 29-year-old single man, a drug addict for approximately thirteen years, if the words of a fellow group member had hurt him, he replied, "No. I cannot experience any emotions at all. Ever since I saw my best friend murdered in front of me, I have not experienced emotional sensations. I want to be able to feel again." Titiana illustrated her experience similarly, saying, "My brother sexually abused me for years, and also put me at his friends' disposal as a love doll, as a game. Ever since, I have lost interest in my emotions."

Ami and Titiana have detached themselves from emotions, as have many addicts who are stress and trauma victims. A trauma victim may disconnect himself from his painful emotions and memories, both by means of a dissociative psychological mechanism and by means of substance. Heroin and other drugs disrupt the user's emotional sensations, succeeding for a while where other defense mechanisms have failed. In a later course, this so-called "help" poses obstacles.

Some approaches refer to the drug as symbolizing a container, so to speak, absorbing the otherwise uncontainable intense emotions (Amali, 1995). This assumption exists in various therapeutic aspects, and through the therapeutic process, the patient undergoes a gradual change in terms of feelings. Those who come for treatment at Rothschild 2 Center bear an indescribable psychological pain, some of them for many years. This psychological pain is discussed to a lesser extent in the wider public, and sometimes even among professionals treating drug addiction. I notice repeatedly how the visible symptoms such as drug abuse reveal themselves through the therapeutic process as somatic, emotional, or behavioral traces from an earlier traumatic damage. Most clients coming for treatment at Rothschild 2 Center fail to forget their horrific experiences, although they denied them for years. Some do not experience the psychological pain exactly because of the lengthy substance abuse.

At what point in treatment could we assist those who rely on drugs as an escape? This is a sensitive professional issue, the approach to which raises concerns among many therapists. Herman (1992) states, "My clinical experience has proven to me that it is only when the client is capable of addressing his painful story that he may begin the psychological recovery process." Addressing the traumatic experience may be a long, frustrating therapeutic process, with the client sometimes unable to relive the experience, as he strongly resists recalling it. In cases of severe psychological stress, the psychological and physiological reactions strongly connect. Understanding the different modes in which an individual responds to them, as well as understanding the deep-rooted symptoms assimilated into the trauma victim's soul, fulfill a highly important role in the intended therapeutic process. The stress reaction involves both psychological and physiological components and may last long after the traumatic experience has ended (Hendin & Haas, 1991; Tiano, 1998).

Responding to stress situations involves neurotransmitters in the brain. In terms of the somatic effects, it is important to be familiar with a drug's neurophysiological influence on the brain, thus on feeling. Opiate addiction has a neurophysiological influence on stress, also identified in other drugs used by the clients treated at Rothschild 2 and in varied addictions under which they suffer. Opiates succeed in lowering the levels of anxiety and tension, facilitating the dulling of emotions. Thus, opiates are the most popular substance among drug addicts who are also trauma victims. Other substances may induce an illusory sense of power and confidence, social abilities, and even influence various states of awareness (further discussed in Chapter Five). Among the SUD patients there is long term anxiety stemming from recalling the horrific acts they underwent; an unbearably painful recollection for them. Thus, they have developed various psychological defense mechanisms in order to evade it, overcome it, and defend themselves from it (Kagan, Conger, and Mason, 1979; Bert & Ostroff, 1985).

Another psychological defense mechanism is repression. Many patients repress the traumatic memories for many years. This psychological act requires a great deal of constant psychological effort (Krystal, 1978). I compare the channeling of psychological energy required to channeling the physical energy required to submerge a ball full of air under the water (see Figure 5, Chapter Seven).

Repression is a basic psychological defense mechanism where the patient manages to draw harsh memories away from his mind. Breaking the cycle of defensive repression is not simple, since the defense guards the client's mind and keeps traumatic memories hidden. Any movement away from psychological fixation requires different psychological energies. This demands a therapeutic setting that allows gradual reduction of anxiety and providing the client with abundant psychological support (Pirani, 2005).

Denial is another psychological defense mechanism where the patient refers to facts that are obviously non-existent in reality (Kagan et al., 1979). Some patients deny their behavioral patterns, mental awareness, or biological age. Others deny feelings, and some justify horrific acts they commit or those done to them. These mechanisms are primitive, but apparently very effective in the early stages of psychological survival after traumatic experience.

Sometimes, sexual abuse victims perceive admitting the abuse to various parties such as social workers and physicians as ineffective and even detrimental. From the findings, I've learned that integrating severe abuse characteristics, along with the difficulty in revealing the abuse soon after its occurrence, intensifies the severity of the trauma's psychological and physiological implications. These findings emphasize the necessity for the investigative process to be less threatening (Herman, 1992; Berman, 2003). As long as the client bears the secret of the horrific events that he experienced, his visible responses are usually symptoms of past events (Yalom, 2002; Herman, 1992). Some clients respond with sudden rage or outbursts with an intensity that seems unreasonable in relation to the preceding events. Others report difficulties falling asleep, recurrent awakening at night, emotional indifference towards those around them, various affective phenomena, depression, and a sensation of anxiety (Natal Trauma Center for Victims of Terror and War, 2003). These sensations are a daily burden. A significant percentage of those who could not survive the psychological suffering and wanted to die indeed died due to unnatural causes. Others spend years living in indescribable psychological suffering. Their lives have been destroyed and the damage they experienced has caused further pain to their families, children, other innocents, and those around them (Katzenelson, 1998).

Harsh feelings overcame me when I heard the story of Nitzan, a 27-year-old single, blue-eyed woman, with short hair. Nitzan came to the therapeutic center dressed as a religious woman. "This way, I guard myself from men's chauvinistic behavior," she told me in therapy.

I was raised in an impoverished family, in Ashdod; an ordinary family—I am the oldest daughter. I remember my mother working hard and turning in early. It was a sad home without joy, without music... no home cooking. Now I realize my mother suffered from years of depression. My parents divorced when I was three. I remember the loneliness, sadness, and envy. I envied my classmates. They had somebody to call "Daddy." My mother started to bring men over. I felt left out and scared. I did not come close to the strangers. One of them did try to get closer to me, though. I was eight or nine. He wanted to play with me, to go out with me to the playground; he showered me with candy and gifts. At some point, he started to touch me. When I went into the shower, he came to help me. I was ashamed and did not understand what was going on. Initially, he would soap my back, and dry me with the towel. Ever so slowly, his touching became more intrusive. I did not understand. He was not my father. It was unpleasant. It hurt. Then, he began to undress, too. His penis was so big and scary; I had never seen a naked man before. He asked me to soap him, too. He would rub himself against me, moan and suddenly stop, like fainting. I cried for him to stop. My mother wouldn't arrive until the evening— I think she had no idea. She never asked how I was, or noticed my distress; she didn't see my grades dropping, my significant weight loss. Actually, she didn't notice anything. I hate her. I hate her to this day. I was afraid to stay home alone. I never wanted to shower. He threatened me, warning me not to tell anyone.

Nitzan begins to cry the cry of profound relief. Shelly, her fellow group member, brings her a glass of water and a tissue, then she continues:

Since then, my life has never been the same. It has been ruined. I experienced waves of anxiety when I heard his cough from upstairs. His mouth stank of cigarettes. I would withdraw, ignoring his touch, the tattoo on his arm, his nauseating moaning sounds. I would close my eyes, waiting for him to finish touching me. I began running away from home, spending long hours on the street. The cats were my closest friends. Can you believe it? The cats. Seeking human company, I approached a street gang, people who readily accepted me; people who also radiated distress and suffering due to violence.

In their eyes, I was able to recognize the helplessness. This is where I met alcohol. I felt as though it helped me for a few hours, easing the feelings of sadness and depression. I escaped from my feelings and myself. The boys in the gang took advantage of my helplessness. I would awaken from my drunken stupor surrounded by naked boys, smeared in dry semen... so gross. I have no idea what I had gone through there. I realized I was growing more and more popular. The rumor soon spread that I was good at giving blowjobs. Guys courted me; asked me out for drinks. Where was my mother through all that; where the hell was she?

Nitzan bursts into tears, her body shaking. Marlene, who sits next to her, holds her shoulder. Nitzan flinches, still deep in her life story.

I can't go on. I need to stop.

The group honors her request, telling her: "We love you. You are brave. You have found the courage and the strength to recount the stories of your life." The females in the group rise, one at a time, to hug Nitzan, offering her a tight, loving, feminine hug.

I am happy to be here with you. I have never been clean from drugs.

One day in the winter of 2005, Adi left me her journal—*A Junkie's Journal*:

The strong, blue light blinds my eyes. The loud noise threatens to tear my eardrum. I sit in a white, scary strange room, trembling with cold and fear. Why, why me of all people? I have suffered so much in my life – worry, fear, disappointment, and total exploitation. The door opens and a tall, healthy-looking man enters. I knew he was one of them. I knew he was a cop. His body is firm; his arms are strong and threatening.

"Drugs? What does a girl like you have to do with drugs?" he questioned in a friendly tone. "And how do you get money for these drugs? We checked and you don't have a record."

I told him about myself, the fears, how I came to use and how I used sex to get drug money. The cop told me I had better not mess with the police, and that he could help me out of the station, if I agree to spend the night with him. I agreed.

It's nighttime and it's pouring rain. The Halissa neighborhood in Haifa is entirely flooded. This winter is extremely harsh. I live in a ruined tin storage house I got from an old man in return for some action. It's located in an orchard of fruit trees; I thought living near my dealer would be convenient. The rain drips through the holes in the tin roof and I'm cold on this wet bed. There's no electricity, and there's a dirt floor. I awake from the thunder and dampness. I am scared. Maybe this is my last day. I'll die in this bin. The local papers will write about another junkie who was found dead. I cannot leave the ruin. My surroundings are totally flooded. The rain is pouring. I have drugs. If I use, then I will relax. But how? I am afraid to get the drugs wet. This is what I've got for the morning. I am cold, lying, trembling with cold until the morning comes. I need a hit.

Damn it! Use again to go to the bank to look supposedly calm.

Damn it! Use again to go to the grocery store without shaking.

Damn it! Use again to be able to walk alone at night.

Damn it! Use again so I can sleep peacefully.

Damn it! Use again to feel self-confident.

Damn it! Use again to not feel fear, not to be angry, love, or feel.

Damn it! Use again to feel like a normal person.

Yes! Friday is here. Today is pampering day. Today I'll feel like a queen. Today is not just drugs. Today she and I will go to get some crystal—the drug of kings. Today I will be in heaven. I will forget everything. I am on the top of the world. Who can hurt me? I showered, I dressed. True, I have worn the same clothes for a month, but who cares? All they care about is what is underneath the clothes. Today is Friday. I should hit the road to catch as many clients as I can.

I left rehab. I tried. I really did. Three days without using. When I first came to rehab, I was taken there by a cab driver, a friend of the owner's. He said I would feel no pain, that their treatments are powerful and helpful,

"Three days and you'll sleep like a baby."

I brought him all the drug leftovers I had. Enough of that; I am tired of using. I'm sick of sucking strangers for 50 Shekels. Maybe now I'll be able to start a new life, without parents to mess my life up. I got a single room. "There are no females at the center today," I was told. Everybody loves me, encourages me, and applauds me. How nice! When I threw the drugs I had into a bowl of water, all the men rejoiced. How wonderful. In just a few days, I'll be normal, my soul will be free. What a nice group of people. "Would you like some more tea?"; "Would you like something to eat?" I preferred to go into the room, receive the treatment, and turn in. The superintendent on duty helped me make the bed, told me he would be in charge of me throughout the treatment. He made me a cup of tea and gave me the treatment. I went to bed. I awoke in the middle of the night in withdrawal. I went to the office, where he was sitting. He told me to go to my room, and soon he would be coming to give me another treatment. I lay in bed, trembling and sweating. He gave me pills, sat next to me, waiting for me to fall back asleep. The pills kicked in. I felt calmer. Soon I'll sleep. He got into my bed. I couldn't move or speak. The pills are kicking in. I crashed. After three days in rehab—for the first time in my life—I escaped to the drugs again.

The following chapter will address the development of post-traumatic stress disorder, PTSD, which is a psychological outcome of the traumatic damage portrayed in this chapter.

Chapter Four

Addiction-Induced Post-Traumatic Syndrome

When Yossi first came to Rothschild 2, Kamma barked at him, baring his teeth. Yossi started kicking the dog, who has not forgotten that. When Yossi returned, Kamma's hair stood on end, she bared her teeth, barking and threatening to bite him.

Post-traumatic stress disorder (PTSD) is "a delayed and/or continuous response to a stressful event or condition (short term or continuous), typically threatening or exceptionally catastrophic, potentially causing significant distress to almost anyone (ICD-10, 2002). Judith Herman (1992) first mentioned post-traumatic stress disorder in the mainstream. Ever since, many researchers and authors have investigated its symptoms in various contexts, even in association with drug addiction issues.

I assume the discussion in this chapter might raise many questions among professionals and researchers. Many will question the diagnosis for Rothschild 2 Treatment Center patients, who are now clean from drugs, who indeed suffer from PTSD. Who ruled that the addicts with whom I work have PTSD? These questions are indeed complex for several reasons:

1. For most patients, the stressful or traumatic experience occurred years ago.
2. Most patients have not (yet) received a PTSD diagnosis.
3. Most of my patients declare that their main issue is drug addiction.
4. Most professionals working with drug abuse victims do not have the tools to identify and assess PTSD.

> Thus, I address what I have witnessed and heard in thousands of therapeutic sessions. I would love to be assisted by behavioral sciences researchers and professionals, who will be interested in investigating the assumption regarding the relationship of stress and trauma's impact and addictions. The global literature defines this as trauma and substance abuse comorbid disorder.

Since the entire Rothschild 2 staff is present only one day a week, we hold our professional staff meetings on Mondays. We sit for a general update, informing the staff members, who missed the events that had occurred the previous week, on which of the clients had entered therapeutic work; who had reported feelings of crisis during the weekend; who had returned stronger, and other important news. While we gather for a staff meeting, the clients are in a psychodrama group session with Dafna and Inbar.

In the weekly staff meeting, we generally discuss two clients. The staff listens to a review on the therapeutic process each has undergone by the professional managing the case. The staff analyzes the information received, professionally assessing an intervention directive for the client. Then the client joins us for a short conference. The staff's decisions are made when the client leaves the room.

Understanding the traumatic experience and what variables induce a post-traumatic disorder episode are essential knowledge for trauma practitioners. This is not enough, though. The variables influencing PTSD development should include other components as well, Williams and Poijula (2002) indicate three broad risk factors influencing PTSD development:

1. Pre-trauma
2. Trauma
3. Post-trauma

I detail significant variables affecting each broad risk factor, 1-3:

Pre-Trauma Factors

- exposure to hostile events prior to the trauma
- preceding depression or anxiety
- ineffective coping abilities
- family instability, socioeconomic issues, violence and fears
- previous issues with the authorities
- academic underachievement
- lack of social support, particularly in difficult situations
- suicidal tendencies in childhood
- the fact the women are more predisposed to PTSD than men, and the fact that adolescents up to age 25 are more predisposed to trauma than adults
- some families are less resilient to trauma

Various studies will indicate that the variables above fulfill a clear role in PTSD development. In Israel, people are highly predisposed to stress events due to war situations and terror events, as indicated by various support organizations, such as Natal Trauma Center (2002), so we naturally consider this additional factor.

Trauma Factors

- geographic proximity to the event
- the degree of exposure to the event (the greater the exposure, the more likely to develop PTSD)
- the significance the individual attributes to traumatic experiences
- previous victimhood or previous exposure to traumatic experiences
- duration of the trauma, the extent of its brutality and horror
- I see fit to mention here, too, the continuous exposure to stress events due to war events and terrorist attacks.

Post-Trauma Factors

- lack of social support
- inability to act regarding the events
- wallowing in self-pity and self-neglect
- passivity instead of activity
- inability to draw significance from suffering
- ASD (Acute Stress Disorder) and physical arousal such as high blood pressure

I address these components, which increase the risk for PTSD development, in the chapters discussing treatment, namely Chapters Seven through Nine, because understanding them also influences the selection of treatment modes suitable to the type of psychological damage.

To be fair, toward the broader discussion addressing PTSD-related issues, I suggest that the assumptions addressed by this book also apply to events of terror, violence, and war to which residents of other areas of the world have been exposed in recent years.

Michael (2007) addresses the issue that many professionals have studied a connection between PTSD and drug abuse since the 1980s. Those studies indicate a high prevalence of childhood sexual abuse among substance addicts; approximately eighty percent among female drug addicts and 50% among addicted men, as indicated in Chapter Two.

The outcomes of the complex life stories of those who seek help at Rothschild 2 reinforce and even confirm the common knowledge presented in the literature, according to which, an untreated traumatic experience may turn into a post-traumatic disorder.

According to the ICD-10 (2002), the symptoms typical to post-traumatic stress disorder are:

> Episodes where an individual re-lives the trauma through intrusive memories or dreams associated with feelings of stagnation and emotional dullness, disconnection from others, lack of responsiveness to the surroundings, the ability to draw pleasure and avoidance of activity and situations resembling the trauma (p. 161).

A detailed portrayal of post-traumatic stress disorder in Foa and colleagues (2004, pp. 19-20) consists of:

A. Exposure to an event bearing the following two characteristics:

1. Exposure to a trauma where an individual has experienced, or has witnessed life threatening or severe injury, or, alternately, a threat to the individual's or the physical well-being of another party.

2. The individual reaction involved intensive fear, helplessness, or terror.

B. The traumatic experience recurs in one or more of the five following ways:

1. Memories, images, recurrent intrusive thoughts and perceptions of troubling intensity

2. Recurrent nightmares of the event

3. Behaving or feeling as though the event is occurring at the moment

4. Intensive psychological distress while being exposed to stimuli reminding of the trauma or parts thereof

5. Physiological arousal while being exposed to stimuli reminiscent of the trauma or parts thereof

C. Persistent, continuous avoidance of stimuli reminding of the trauma and general dullness of reactions not present prior to the trauma (three characteristics or more):

1. Attempts to avoid thoughts, feelings, or conversations related to the trauma

2. Attempt to avoid places, people, or activities reminding of the trauma

3. Inability to recall important parts of the trauma (not resulting from loss of consciousness)

4. Significant decline in interest and engagement in meaningful activities

5. A feeling of detachment and alienation from others

6. A narrow range of emotions (for example, inability to feel love)

7. Inability to see the future (no anticipation for a career, marriage, children, or a normal life cycle)

D. Consistent hyperarousal symptoms not present prior to the trauma (two characteristics or more):

1. Difficulty falling asleep and sleeping

2. Irritability and tantrums

3. Difficulty concentrating

4. Increased tension

5. Exaggerated fear reaction

E. Symptoms in clauses B, C, and D last longer than one month.

F. The disorder results in a significant difficulty to function, such as declined performance in the individual, family, and employment aspect.

According to Perry (2002), a high rate of those exposed to a traumatic experience suffer post-traumatic symptoms in the first few weeks following the event. The victim rate may reach 92 percent among rape victims, with many of them developing chronic post-traumatic syndrome, which may last many years.

Post-traumatic disorder's core is defined in the second clause of DSM-IV:

> Intrusive memories of the traumatic experiences, emerging in various modes onto one's consciousness. The event's memories return as nightmares or flashbacks during the day or in response to stimuli reminiscent of the trauma.

In many ways, the traumatic memories are an experience relived, as indicated by many researchers in post-trauma research. "The memories emerge uncontrollably, without any ability to stop them. Those memories arouse intense emotional, unregulated reactions," state Perry (2002) and Najavits (2002).

Alex's death, which I address later, is a story of coping with associated loss: "It is only yesterday that Alex was here, I can't believe it. Only the day before yesterday I saw him at urinalysis"; "Who, who is Alex? I can't recall the way he looks"; "His poor mother"; "He only began his academic studies. What a pity." Those are a few of the responses that come to mind as I recall the moment when I told the group members of Alex's death: first-response-to-loss-coping responses, responses of denial and repression, coping with the unbearable lightness with which a fellow group member is suddenly gone.

The emotional traumatic experience is so difficult that various researchers attempt to portray it in various modes. Hertzano-Letty and Toder (2006) write of post-traumatic disorder as a "never ending death." They perceive the trauma experience among patients who develop PTSD as an experience that remained unprocessed, thus they define it as an "unfinished business" drawing away all of a person's strength. The approach taken by Hertzano-Letty and Toder conveys the clear feeling that the trauma may "leave an impression in a person's soul to be engraved forever," as horror followed by a void—a rather powerful definition portraying the psychological suffering experienced by stress and trauma victims. The neverending death is equivalent to unfinished business; to a psychological state where an individual experiences death without dying, a situation to which many patients refer to as "living death," or "living without vitality." The situation where one experiences an unfinished death is a tremendous, attractive pattern, as stated by Hertzano-Letty and Toder, which deprives an individual of any ability to turn it into a resolved experience, thus demanding its solution, over and over again. The tremendous difficulty the suffering individual experiences can force him to sacrifice another element of his life.

The repetition in trauma is a constant experience to relive the trauma in order to resolve it. It is a situation often encountered by trauma treatment professionals. Indeed, those who have not encountered post-trauma patients have trouble imagining the intensity of the psychological experience. The "black hole" metaphor (which is mentioned in Chapter Seven and presented by Bion, 1970, in Rosenwasser & Nathan, 1997), as stated by Hertzano-Letty & Toder

(2006), was presented in order to illustrate the catastrophic experience in infancy, which, by its intensity may induce deficiency states and even psychotic states. I quote this theoretical view here in order to illustrate the traumatic experience's intensity and its prospective outcomes for stress and trauma event victims. "Falling into the black hole" portrays the coping with trauma as a highly intense process, to which the victim is extremely close. Death's power of attraction, as maintained by Hertzano-Letty and Toder, is tremendous.

> Every day, every night, the victim experiences death's awesome power of attraction; illusions, memories, dreams, and images, all those impose themselves on the individual, reminding him over and over again of death's or the threat of death's proximity.

This is the rough experience of many trauma victims. "The PTSD victim is drawn by death's extreme power of attraction, but for innermost reasons, he exerts a counter-force against its power of attraction." The authors assume this is the power of dissociation. Dissociation is a situation where some of the overall psychological functions split from other personality parts under heavy psychological pressure (Nadler, 2002).

I address the treatments available for those states in several chapters to follow. Here I want to say that the treatment clearly requires to gently touch the wound of trauma in a way not to shatter the defenses protecting the victim, stopping him from falling into the black hole of common defenses: full repression of the traumatic experience, dissociation, and drug abuse.

We seek to provide the client with a different kind of treatment that circumvents those defensive mechanisms, a treatment to facilitate him or her to live differently with the trauma's awful memories, arousing the feeling of emotions, rather than the dissociation and repression. "Living" means to continue to hope, expect, create and desire to progress, plan, aspire, feel and engage dreams—side-by-side with the unforgotten memory of the traumatic experience.

The following is the story of Uri, a 48-year-old married man and a father of five, who has been addicted to drugs since age 17.

> *I stopped using when I managed to ask God why I deserve to continue suffering... When I was born, my parents were approaching old age. I was the eldest, followed by my autistic brother. From the moment he was born, my parents lost any desire to live and fight, that is how I felt. My home was gloomy, sad, destroyed. My autistic brother would blow up and throw tantrums whenever we didn't understand what he needed – screaming, biting, shattering and breaking stuff around him. My parents were bereft, primitive. Neither knew how to control my brother, but refused to leave him in the care of those who could. I believe shame gnawed at them. I was constantly nauseous. Tension, fear, and anxiety hung in the air at home. I had the responsibility of an adult. Wherever my brother was, he was left in my care... at the playground. As a child, I didn't understand I was meant to watch over him and supervise his every action. My brother ran into the road and was run over by a car, and killed. To this day, I remember how I chased him. I held him and heard the horrific sound of the blow over and over, I saw the streams of blood...*

Uri wipes his tears.

> *I felt terrible guilt. I failed to watch my brother. I failed to fulfill my parents' expectations. It is because of me that my brother died. My parents' can't really look at me to this day. "Why didn't you keep an eye out for him? You are irresponsible. What kind of an oldest brother are you?" my mother cried, hitting herself. Father withdrew into himself and went silent.*

> *Prior to the accident, I couldn't invite friends over. I was ashamed of my brother—I feared his reactions. The house was like a ghost*

house. I never had a brother I could play with, I had no parents to speak to. Now I know I did love him. I didn't know it back then. My parents overlooked me. I was a talented, smart, successful child, but they didn't enroll me in any extra-curricular activities, didn't buy me toys, didn't let me develop and grow. My parents spent all their money and meager property on attempts to heal my brother from autism, and neglected me.

At 17, I decided I didn't want to be poor and miserable, and would do anything to earn money to become independent. I wanted money to make up for my suffering. I didn't know money couldn't make up for the emotional neglect, psychological suffering, and loneliness. Pot gave peace to my soul. Heroin shut out the guilt feelings and by the time I used coke, my life was messed up. In order to fund my habit, I lost my butcher shop. I remember taking my ten-year-old daughter's piggy bank, 400 Shekels, money she had received on birthdays and holidays.

Tears well up in Uri's eye, he continues his story steadily:

At nights, I would leave my family, who tried to keep me safe. At 2 a.m. I would slip out, like a thief, knocking on the neighbors' doors for change. How did I dare to humiliate myself like that? Whenever I came back in the early morning hours, I would meet my wife and children on the balcony, worried and tearful. My autistic brother died when a car hit him. My parents died from sorrow and pain. I felt I was to blame for all that – my brother's death, my birth, my family's fate. I used in order to reinforce my illusions. I ignored everybody. I felt beautiful, smart, most successful, and strong. When the effects of crystal wore off, I would fall into the pit of depression, sadness and despair. Those pits were insufferable. I felt infinitely miserable with sadness and a desire to die. My life had no meaning.

Maya, my wife, tried talking to me, suggesting we go out, travel, go to the movies, get together with friends. She had no one to talk to. I simply wasn't there. I remember with great pain the sadness reflected in her brown eyes. I saw it but could not feel it. I continued stealing or blackmailing for money. I humiliated myself when I sold my body. I couldn't take that any longer. I dropped 20 kgs, I didn't have the strength to steal or even use anymore. I gave into despair, suffering, and futility. I came to seek help. Thank you for listening to me.

Neglect and hatred, as manifested by Uri's story, and the emotions he experienced as a child because of the significant people in his life, bear a highly important influence on shaping the child's nature in adulthood. Human experience develops in childhood and can be ruined in childhood. This platform can yield a happy individual or, alternatively, a hurt individual. Death is one of the most traumatic, painful events encountered in a lifetime. For every individual, not only children, a threat of death poses one of the most extreme emotional issues. Fear of a traumatic experience involving a near-death experience, or being present at such a scenario (which any individual might encounter in life), might demonstrate to the practitioner who treats trauma victims the extremity of psychological states associated with traumatic experiences (car accidents, sudden death, terrorist attack, losing one's job, etc.). Such situations can incur stress and trauma that victims carry with them for many years (Sharfstein, 1984).

Williams and Poijula (2002) started to write their book addressing trauma treatment just before the Twin Towers tragedy, and completed the book following the September 11 2001 events, namely, when public opinion worldwide was significantly more prepared and open to hear what civilian trauma is and to try to understand them. I would like to believe that my writing also contributes to the professional discourse regarding the suffering of millions of stress and trauma victims worldwide. I hope to contribute by providing additional information and knowledge, to be part of the "civilian trauma" treatment, and by providing tools for coping, to assist practitioners within the therapeutic forum, as a public service.

Another book offering treatment methods for PTSD victims suffering from drug abuse is *Seeking Safety* by Najavits (2002). I address this book in two ways: the trauma and post-trauma discourse; the discourse regarding therapeutic methods. In my eyes, Najavits is a writer and a researcher who greatly contributes to understanding the traumatic backgrounds to addiction, and develops innovative therapeutic techniques that address issues comprising addiction and post-trauma. Through personal revelation, which requires courage and openness, the author describes herself as a third generation trauma victim in her family. The author relates that her grandmother and mother were negatively affected by the Holocaust, while she was hurt by an attempted rape she underwent as a child. One line from her book deeply impressed me: "If only we could grant those individuals a future that will be brighter than their past." I found that line highly meaningful because I too feel that way, attempting to facilitate those who suffer trauma and substance addiction.

The dual diagnosis, comprising post-trauma and addiction is manifested by the following data:

Among male addicts, 12-34 percent are PTSD victims; among the female addicts, the rates are higher, reaching 30-50 percent. Individuals with dual diagnosis are more likely to experience recurrent traumas than substance addicts who do not suffer PTSD. Women in the dual group suffered both physical and sexual violence while men suffered war combat and violent events (Najavits, 2002). Our data somewhat differs at Rothschild 2 Center; we've found that, similar to the women, most men coming for treatment because of a dual disorder were also victims of violent events and sexual assault rather than by war combat and violence. Najavits portrays "a spiral deterioration," which I address in Chapter Nine, The Cycle of Suffering. In spiral deterioration, the drugs intensify the traumas, and the traumas, in turn, intensify the substance abuse.

Foa et al (2004) portray the symptoms characterizing PTSD in detail. Among PTSD victims, the recollection of a traumatic experience arouses feelings of helplessness, fear, or any other feeling experienced by the victim during the event. Those feelings do not wear off over the course of time. Those who recovered from a trauma, states Foa, replay it in their mind differently than those who experienced a trauma but did not recover. The cognitive fear pattern, which means to facilitate recognizing a dangerous situation, remains engraved in the trauma victim's experience. The traumatic experience's fear pattern includes actual representations associated with the stimulus (such as the sight of the aggressor or the vehicle he drove), response characteristics (intense panic, frantic heartbeat, freezing, and screaming), and the characteristics of discernment by the victim (such as interpreting the situation as dangerous). (See examples in Chapter Three.)

I could see Luba and Titiana repeatedly become somewhat paralyzed when a dark-skinned man raised his voice, ordering them to approach him. As a therapist serving as an observer, I could not understand how Luba went to Moshe, who had once assaulted her, as though hypnotized, as a deer caught in the headlights. "Go back to the group," I would tell her, while she was sitting in my room, "You owe Moshe nothing. He does not deserve you, and you believe this too." Yet Luba would immediately leave and go to Moshe when she heard him call her name, saying "I want to have a word with you; it'll only take a couple of minutes." My stomach was in knots with apprehension, since I anticipated what was going to happen next. I wanted to keep her in the shelter. My professional relationship with trauma victims prevents me from acting, and anyway it is impossible in the initial treatment stage for Luba. A week later, a police officer from the central district called me, questioning whether I knew a woman named Luba. He informed me she had been found dead in an abandoned apartment near the Tel Aviv Central Bus Station. In her pocket, he found a receipt from the Rothschild 2 Treatment Center.

Normal fear arises in a dangerous situation, and it diminishes when danger is gone. A pathological fear pattern is so intense that it disrupts functioning and withstands changes. The pathological fear pattern comprises the following characteristics:

1. An excessive number of response characteristics such as avoidance or physiological arousal (I avoid going to the night club)
2. Unrealistic elements that do not represent the world as it is (this is a dangerous situation and I am helpless)
3. Associating non-dangerous stimuli with avoidance and flight (e.g., a bald aggressor, a gun)
4. Associating response characteristics and a negative self-image (I have no coping ability)

In terms of PTSD, states Foa, "a pathological fear pattern develops, where stimuli, responses and meanings are unreasonably connected with erroneous associations and assessments." Under those circumstances, any information related to the trauma employs such a fear pattern. There is trouble regulating emotions, mainly angers, as further stated by Williams and Poijula, also addressing the trouble those individuals encounter while experiencing helplessness, trouble forgetting the traumatic experience, and thoughts of revenge they induce; the trouble they face maintaining healthy, positive relationships with others, suspicion responses, a feeling as though they are unable to save themselves, or that there is nothing that can save them. Trauma victims demonstrate an inability to find meaning to their lives. They have trouble maintaining trust in others, and seem to view their future as filled with despair and hopelessness (Williams & Poijula, 2002; see also ICD-10, 2002).

COMMON PTSD SYMPTOMS AMONG SUBSTANCE ADDICTS AS REVEALED AT INTAKE – STAGE TWO

Anxiety and Dissociation	Nightmares	Depression and Denial	Bursts of Rage
Intrusion	Avoidance	Flooding	Difficulty Concentrating
Over-irritability	Difficulty Sleeping	Substance Abuse	Damage to Interpersonal Relations

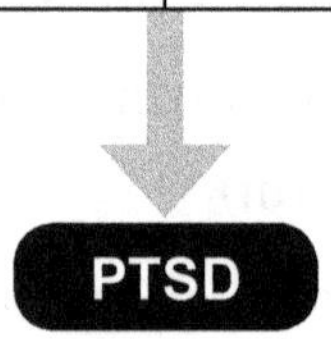

PTSD

Figure 3: PTSD symptoms commonly identified among addicts and stress and trauma victims.

When I encounter substance use disorder (SUD), I attempt to convey feelings different than those known to the victims in the first moment of treatment. I attempt to create a situation in which they feel that the therapeutic setting is safe and calm, and that we practitioners will do anything to shelter them, reinforcing that we will not hurt them once they have revealed their story. Furthermore, I often remind staff members not to use commanding tones or raise their voices. I am convinced that situations with raised voices or commanding attitudes could damage the calm work setting required to treat trauma victims. Many professionals who treat trauma victims agree to such rules.

The memory of trauma is not dangerous, but the feelings associated with it may be unbearable. I tell the patients they do not have to remember in detail everything that happened within the trauma's framework, though it is important they know how to share the flashback with me, since by addressing them, we may facilitate the therapeutic process.

Exposure to trauma may damage thinking patterns and beliefs individuals hold relating to five key psychological aspects: confidence, trust, sense of power, self-esteem, and ability to experience intimacy (Williams & Poijula, 2002).

The following are several impaired cognitive beliefs and thinking patterns, viewed by trauma victims differently than individuals unaffected by trauma:

- The ability to initiate events or influence them
- The ability to be sensitive to another individual, and imagine oneself in the other's shoes
- The ability to refuse to do things one finds unpleasant
- The feeling of having time to engage in various activities or enough money to obtain necessary items
- Honoring commitments to others and believing in commitment and its importance
- The ability to distinguish one's possessions from another's possessions
- Belief in one's strength to a significantly lesser extent, having trouble accepting one's weaknesses
- The feeling that one will let others down, as a self-fulfilling prediction

Williams and Poijula (2002) indicate the following statements expressing discomfort identified among trauma victims:

1. I feel tense although I am trying to calm myself down.
2. I feel scared, anxious, or tense.
3. I try to fall asleep, but feel preoccupied.
4. I must always be vigilant.

The study addressing post-traumatic experiences attempts to formulate commonly agreed, uniform parameters that serve the practitioner when assessing and treating post-trauma clients. There are several questionnaires aimed at examining PTSD among adults: Child Posttraumatic Stress Reaction Index (CPTS-RI) (Frederick, Pynoos, & Nader, 1992); Stanford Acute Stress Reaction Questionnaire (SASRQ) (in Friedman & Schnurr, 1995); Trauma Symptom Checklist - 40 (Briere & Runtz, 1989); a questionnaire by Foa and colleagues dated 2004; many others share several common statements:

From SASRQ:

- I had difficulty falling asleep
- I felt restless
- I tried to avoid feeling the stressful event
- I had recurrent nightmares of the stressful event
- I responded in panic to trivial stimuli
- I felt tense and jumpy
- I had a strange sense of myself
- I felt irritated and experienced bursts of anger
- I forgot major parts of the stressful event
- I tried to draw away from places that reminded me of the stressful event

From CPTS-RI (1992):

- I feel unsatisfied and am easily irritated
- I have difficulty concentrating or paying attention
- I have dreams of what happened, or other bad dreams
- I have trouble remembering important parts of what happened
- I try to draw way from people, places, or things that remind me of what happened

- I have difficulties falling asleep at night or I frequently awake in the middle of the night
- I argue or quarrel
- I fear bad things will happen again
- I have an intense physical sensation when somebody reminds me of what happened (rapid heartbeat, headache, etc.)
- I do not think I will live long
- From the questionnaire by Foa and colleagues (2005) (See full questionnaire in the reference list):
- Thoughts or images of the traumatic experiences came up when you did not want them to appear
- You have had bad dreams or nightmares of the traumatic experience
- You have experienced physical reactions when you were reminded by the traumatic experience (e. g. sweating, rapid heartbeats)
- You have failed to recall an important part of the traumatic experience
- You have felt drawn away or disconnected from those around you
- You have attempted to avoid activities, people, or places reminding you of the traumatic experience
- You have had difficulties falling asleep or sleeping
- You have been irritable or easily panicked
- You have been over-alert
- You have felt emotionally dull (for example, inability to cry or feel love toward others)

Have you, as practitioners treating substance abuse victims, encountered such a description of feelings among your patients? I have consistently encountered them. In Chapter Three, I indicated the three key symptoms apparent among post-trauma victims;

hyperarousal, intrusion, and constriction. In this chapter, I attempt to expand the discussion of those three as manifested in therapeutic processes among SUD.

Hyperarousal

Herman (1992) portrays constant alertness and readiness among trauma victims:

> Following the traumatic experience, the individual's self-protection system seems to have become permanently alert, as though danger may return any minute... Trauma victims easily panic, respond irritably to the slightest stimulation, and suffer sleep disorder (p. 53).

I begin group therapy with a discussion on the "psychological suffering caused to us by substance abuse" today. Lior responds to Moshe's words:

> *When you said you were going through a process of change, I could not understand what you were saying. I see you every night in rehab, where you are scamming and scheming.*

Moshe blushes, wrinkling his brow. He seems as though his eyes are about to pop out of his head and that he could strangle Lior. He screams:

> *Who are you anyway?! You've learned to suck up to the counselors here at Rothschild in the morning, and at night you kiss up to the private center staff...*

I ask Moshe and Lior to settle down:

> *Take a few deep breaths. What set you off, anyway? What was it that you wanted to tell each other? Both of you, like your fellow group members, came here to save your lives. You are both drowning in a stormy sea, so to speak, but instead of trying to hold on to the lifesaver, you're arguing. You are both going to drown. Both of you might die.*

The group grows silent. Moshe sits, contemplating. He has trouble envisioning himself sitting quietly, not acting out or reacting violently.

I am trying to figure out how I felt when Lior pointed out my behavior. I felt she was criticizing me, making fun of me and ridiculing me.

Lior sheds a tear:

I was so hurt by your answer to what I said. I can't stand myself when I'm pleasing others. I am always like that, though. I want everybody to love me.

I interject and share my view:

Lior and Moshe, you are here now, and this group follows a code of conduct. Both the group and I want to protect you. For many years, you didn't know any better than to give aggressive reactions or attempt to please when you felt threatened or hurt. Now you are here, in a group who loves you and protects you. Try to recall a past event when you felt similar to what you feel within the group's framework now...

Jacob raises his hand and asks to speak.

I can relate to the times when Dad came home, after Mom had already told him that the school called, complaining about my behavior. Dad, that nasty man, would point a finger toward my room. I knew the ceremony that followed. I knew I had to wait for him there, with my pants and underpants off. I had to wait in bed until he came to beat me with his whip. I remember that part more vividly than the actual whipping; I dreaded waiting for him to come. Waiting two hours was more painful for me than the whipping itself.

Moshe responds to Jacob's words:

You literally spoke from my own soul... because I also experienced those threatening moments as a child, and now I can no longer stand threats. I explode and would rather attack than be the helpless child again who has to bear a belt whipping.

121

Lior:

> Yeah. I remember the fear that flooded me when my brother gestured to me with his head to come upstairs. I was paralyzed by the fear and the desire to please. More than anything else, I didn't want him to hurt me while raping me. I tried to be as kind to him as I could.

The group grows silent. Kamma's sudden bark causes some of the members to startle.

Intrusion

The traumatic moment is coded as an abnormal memory that bursts out on its own accord into the conscious mind, as flashbacks, and, in sleep, as traumatic nightmares (Herman, 1992, p. 54). Even years of therapy do not always facilitate the client in coping with the feelings of intrusion, the memories of abuse and of being betrayed. I realized that it is typical of many of the clients I treat.

Sometimes, I am very frustrated. I have known Aaron for two years within the framework of the groups, have had coffee with him during breaks, and was at his wedding, with some of other the staff. When the work conditions changed and I re-scheduled group sessions, Aaron felt it was all about him: "This is your way of telling me I've been in therapy too long. You just feel uncomfortable kicking me out, so this is the way you choose to do it."

In these moments, it doesn't matter that the decision to re-schedule applies to all group members. As an individual wounded inside, Aaron felt the decision was aimed at him. Aaron's response may have been insulting, frustrating, and discouraging had I not understood the motives underlying his feelings. All his life, Aaron encountered individuals who abused him. His father broke off relations with him when he went into a relationship with a woman. Aaron perceives any adult as sexually abusive. It is sad and difficult to even fathom, but when Aaron was a child, he felt he was receiving praise from adults because he fulfilled their perverted instructions, while in practice those individuals were sexually abusing him. Even during his military service, a commander took advantage of his trust and slept with him. Aaron's memories of his past wounds, especially by those who were supposed to care for him, induced in him a feeling of threat and risk, undermining his trust in others. So, it is no wonder he responds the way he does.

"Even the regular, safe environment, then, may thus be perceived as dangerous, since the victims may never be absolutely certain they would not encounter any reminder of the trauma" (Herman, 1992). Aaron asks:

> "Everybody tried to take advantage. Everyone; Now, I know you are like that, too," Aaron tells me during group session. At night, Aaron awakens from nightmares of the older man who assaulted him at school. "I can see him coming, wearing a black shirt, watching me play basketball, offering to walk me home. Just like back then, when I was seven years old. When he touches me, I awake startled, muffling my scream. Even now, I would rather sleep alone, get it?

I tell him that I understand his feelings and his behavior.

Constriction

> Changes in states of consciousness constitute the core of constriction, or indifference, the third key symptom of post-traumatic stress disorder. Not only horror and rage develop from situations where one feels there is no way out. Sometimes, paradoxically, it induces distant serenity, where horror, rage, and pain dissolve (Herman, 1992, p. 61).

Many years of work with substance addicts who are also sexual abuse victims has introduced me to extreme phenomena of emotional dissociations and statements such as, "I feel nothing for the dozens

of guys I have slept with. I have no emotional baggage from them";
"Sex means nothing to me. It's just a technical act. It is done and
that's it. I feel nothing for the man I sleep with. Kissing is far more
embarrassing"; "I am embarrassed when I am questioned, or when
somebody expresses interest in how I am feeling. I am used to voicing
myself in bed. By having sex, I speak. This is my language." Following
the rough sexual assault they suffered, I have heard many women
who constrict their scope of feelings.

Indeed, as stated by Herman (1992), "Traumatic experiences serve
as powerful triggers of the ability to become engrossed in trance."
The intensity of an assault is so difficult for both females and males
to bear that dissociative reactions, detachment, and even repression
are well known to SUD professionals.

I join the group discussing childhood memories. Nitzan, Adi, Marlene,
Aaron, and others participate. Many patients in the initial treatment
stages remember little of their pasts, but they might recall them as
the treatment progresses. The long-term drug abuse among most
patients at Rothschild 2 Center is misleading. A practitioner who is
familiar with the characteristics of a trauma victim will probably be
less biased as for the types of memories borne by those individuals
from their pasts. One may notice that sometimes, even the memory
has been damaged because of the decline in cognitive abilities, which
is a consequence of prolonged substance abuse. Quite often, the
patient tries to avoid recollection in the stages when he or she still
does not feel safe, and sometimes, the memory imagery and the
ability to experience become detached. Macom (www.macom.org.
il) assembles dozens of articles from various countries, addressing
the components of sexual assault and the traumas stemming from
them, thereby raising the many ways in which sexual assault and
trauma connect to addiction issues.

Shame and the guilt often sustain the trauma victim's feelings. According to Herman (1992) shame and guilt are the feelings guiding most sexual assault victims. "Almost all victims feel guilt and inferiority when they look back at their behavior during the traumatic experience, judging it," (Herman p. 74). Guilt might be encountered by the victim while addressing his responses to the event, prior to it, and even witnessing an event where he did not interfere, or was unable to help. "Guilt is experienced particularly harshly by victims who witnessed others' suffering or death," (Herman p. 74). Occasionally, I meet post-trauma victims that later become aggressors themselves, hurting others. Many of the clients were severely wounded in childhood by physical or sexual assault experiences. Many of them have also hurt others physically or sexually, throughout a life of suffering, delinquency, and crime, lasting many years. Rothschild 2 clients have more trouble describing themselves as aggressors than as victims (these topics are further discussed in Chapter Six).

The damage to interpersonal relationships and the risk of consequently suffering post-traumatic stress disorder are great when the victim remained not only a passive but also an active party involved in a violent death or an act of horror (Herman, 1992). At the beginning of the therapeutic process at Rothschild 2 Center, most patients feel guilty for what they have gone through and whatever had happened to them. Most patients who were sexually abused as children, with consistent physical violence within the family, on the street, or at school, suffer feelings of guilt hanging over them for many years. "I was the black sheep of my family"; "I brought all that suffering on myself"; "I chose to use drugs. I could have chosen otherwise." All these are common statements among users. How was this guilt rooted in those individuals?

In his first month of treatment at the Outpatient Care Center, Shir shared the feeling that all the troubles faced by his family were his own doing:

I asked my brother to drive me to the party. He was killed in the car accident. Because of that, my mother has high blood pressure and my father lost his job. All my siblings are educated and have families. I was the only one who didn't get around to that. I've always been the "black sheep" of the family. As a matter of fact, I was the only one sent to a Kibbutz at ten.

Further into Shir's treatment, a different picture revealed itself. Shir was sexually assaulted as a child, when he had visited his neighbors with his father. His father didn't know the assault happened every time they went over to the neighbors while his mother didn't notice the sharp decline in his mood and the eating disorders that arose. His parents didn't stop his brother from driving without a license, they'd always neglected their health, never going to routine medical exams, smoking and getting drunk almost daily... all this long before the brother's tragic death. Shir blamed himself.

Shame is a feeling of embarrassment and regret for acts perceived as being improper, feeling sorrow for negative thoughts and attitudes, and a sense of loss for things one has not done or prevented from happening. Often, the abusive individuals induce those feelings in their victims, as implied by the Macom website (www.macom.org. il). The aggressor causes the victim to feel that if he does not fulfill his or her request, he will suffer. They induce a feeling of shame and guilt for his cooperation and responsiveness to the acts done to him. They instill negative views in the victim regarding his strength and ability, even resorting to threats that they are still capable of hurting him. These threats result in the victim's feeling that any response on his part may result in his imprisonment, hospitalization, divorce, or even the aggressor's death. It is no wonder, then, that many victims feel guilty.

Aaron tells us, "I agreed to go with the old man who offered me money for sex. I did not have to go with him. I did not have to wait for him where he told me to."

Lior felt embarrassed that she had agreed that Caryn's friend join them during sex. "Now, I feel extremely embarrassed when I recall how Caryn's friend was watching us. It was not pleasurable for me. I did it because she treated me well and showed me warmth. I am so embarrassed by that."

Treating substance use disorder has taught me that many users were isolated from their families in the final stages of their addiction. They withdrew from or were rejected by their loved ones because of broken trust or ostracism.

Tiran's story demonstrates an extreme condition in SUD treatment. Tiran told me of a life replete with traumatic experiences, which he has trouble recalling and even accepting. When Tiran didn't show on the day when the terrible Dizengoff Center bombing occurred, I recalled his ethnic origin. Previously, during the long months of treatment, Tiran's ethnicity had not played a significant role, and I repressed any thought related to this matter. When Tiran finally showed up at Rothschild 2, he was full of cuts and ripped clothing. A large bandage covered his ear, and, a few days later when it was removed, I saw his ear had been chopped off during the kidnapping attempt he had undergone. His right arm was in a cast to the elbow, and its remaining part was covered in a white bandage, spotted with iodine and a yellow paste. A large knife had ripped the bandaged part—his flesh cut to the bone. I assessed by the bandage's colors that dry puss mixed with congealed blood.

Tiran told me he used to collaborate with the Israeli Defense Forces (IDF), so Palestinian secret forces commanders in the Jenin area marked him as a target. Tiran trembles as he speaks:

They will persecute me for a lifetime. I was forced to give up a great deal of information and secrets under the pressure the Israeli security services put on me. The harsh detox symptoms I went through allowed your defense services to get almost any information out of me. I desperately needed a hit and was willing to do anything to get it. Once, following some information I had provided, your defense forces arrested one of the PLO officers. That officer was a major drug dealer and used to play a part in my trafficking network. On arrest, the officer went through harsh interrogation and died. To this day, I do not know the exact cause of his death. Perhaps he committed suicide because he couldn't withstand the humiliating interrogations, and also because he desperately needed drugs in order to detox properly. The Palestinians would rather say he died from the torture. The Palestinian officer's death and the arrest of many villagers from the Jenin area were an outcome of my collaboration with your defense forces. All these factors marked me as a traitor to be wiped out. From that moment on, my life has been pointless and hopeless.

One day while walking on a street corner in southern Tel Aviv in the late evening, a blue Subaru with yellow license plates pulled up by me, here, in the middle of the city, in central Israel. I knew that if I were kidnapped, I would be executed that very evening, and I fought for my life. I remember all the adrenalin in my body just exploded. The butcher knife cut into my arm. Another knife tore off my ear, but I managed to escape from their car.

Back in those days, when Tiran heard on the radio of the terrorist bombing in one of the Israeli towns, he preferred to stay at home. "Harsh criticism and a heated climate make it dangerous for an Arab guy like me to walk on the streets of Tel Aviv," he stated, adding that "in times of peace, I'm persecuted by Arabs and when there are bombings, I am persecuted by Jews, all because of my drug habit."

In my sessions with Tiran, I tried to bridge the huge cultural, educational, and religious gaps. I could easily relate to Tiran's stories of the village where he was raised, to the agricultural roots so similar to mine. His stories of removing stones at the foot of the tall mountain reminded me of my youth in the fields of the kibbutz at the foot of Mt. Gilboa, when we worked alongside one of the kibbutz elders. We plowed one stone after another from the red-brown earth. I was on one side of the mountain; Tiran, as it turned out, was on the other side.

When the trust grew deeper, he dared to relate stories that demonstrated the huge educational and cultural gap between us:

> *You know, Amir, when I first went to a brothel, after rehab, I was very embarrassed. Because of the drugs, there is no erection, and long months passed with no interest in sex. After rehab, I had days when even if I felt a sexual impulse, I would lose my erection, just like that. Under such conditions, I wanted to avoid embarrassing a girl... A friend offered me to join him when he went to a brothel. I didn't know what to do or how to choose a girl. When I walked in, I was so ashamed I wanted to run away. I blushed beet-red. It seemed to me that the girls were laughing at me; I was being ridiculed by the whole world. My friend set me up with a girl and paid for the first time. The room was a bit dark and Tanya asked me to wash up. She helped me unwind. Thereafter, I returned to Tanya many times. She treated me so well. I think she is in love with me.*

There are further components to post-trauma. Again, most clients treated for addiction issues at Rothschild 2 suffered prolonged exploitation, violence, abuse, and deeply stressful events. At this point, I address acute stress disorder (ASD). Even if this data appears as random, empirically speaking, at Rothschild 2, the practitioners' main working premise is that many of the trauma victims treated for drug addiction experienced ASD events in their pasts. Several initial reactions to trauma affecting the development of ASD:

- An experience during which an individual feels his life or physical being is in danger
- An individual's response to an event where he felt tremendous fear, terror, and helplessness
- A feeling of emotional detachment (dissociation)
- Constricted awareness of others; the individual feels his close environment is unfamiliar or detached
- Split perception, the individual feels as though he is in two different places at the same time
- Forgetting the event and then an intrusive experience where the individual constantly, or at least a significant part of his day, relives the traumatic feelings – in dreams, thoughts, and flashback images related to the event
- Extreme alertness, startling, or hyperarousal
- Declined performance in life tasks and daily functions
- The phenomena last two days to four weeks following the traumatic experience

In " personal trauma" situations, which are mostly associated with situations of prolonged abuse in a domestic or any other familiar setting, it is more likely to encounter "complex trauma syndrome" Herman (1992).

The likelihood of developing complex PTSD, state Williams and Poijula (2002) is greater if it concerns prolonged, interpersonal childhood abuse.

In a post-trauma condition, the individual responds unusually long after the traumatic experience occurred. As I portray later on, the common diagnosis among professionals is that quoted in the ICD-10 psychiatric categorization (2002) and the psychiatric categorization by

DSM-IV dated 1994. When there is prolonged exposure to trauma, as I witness in most of my patients, it is no wonder the victim develops complex post-trauma.

According to Williams and Poijula (2002), the following demographics are less prone to complex PTSD: children, because of their personality's flexibility, particularly those benefiting from their parents' support and help; women who experience a sexual assault respond by developing PTSD in lower rates than sexually assaulted men, a gap accounted for by gender differences in coping behaviors.

Perhaps those who possess a high self-esteem, who benefit from broad human support develop complex trauma syndrome to a lesser degree.

Most clients seeking treatment from a public service for prolonged drug abuse are those who have experienced ongoing, interpersonal childhood trauma; here are the seven main characteristics identifying complex post-trauma syndrome's clinical picture, as cited by Herman (1992); Williams and Poijula (2002):

1. **Change in the ability to regulate emotions and urges** (such as difficulty regulating angers, self-destruction, taking risks)

2. **Change in attention abilities** (such as sleep-related difficulties, dissociation from the self and from reality)

3. **Somatic reactions** (chronic pain, digestion problems, difficulties related to breathing and heart)

4. **Changes in self-perception** (such as a prolonged feeling of guilt, self-blaming, greater sense of vulnerability, shame, and feeling that nobody will understand)

5. **Change in perceiving the abusing individual** (idealization, attributing super-human powers to the aggressor, and feelings of attempting to please the aggressor)

6. **Changing attitude toward others** (constant suspicion, constant failure to defend oneself, and disruption to intimate relationships and difficulties arousing within such relationships)

7. **Changes in the meaning and faith system** (e.g., loss of faith and feeling of hopelessness and despair)

I quote several more passages from the journal Adi gave me. In the first passage, she portrays the intense physical and psychological pain she experiences while searching for a hit:

> *It is morning now, maybe six thirty. I had the shakes when I awoke, because of the cold. I still sleep and live in that tin ruin, between the fruit trees in Halissa Quarter, Haifa. I'm holding. I have no problem getting it. I always make sure to leave a dose for the morning. As long as I my legs are strong, I'll always have it. If I get out to the streets every night, then getting it is no problem. I sniff it a bit to calm down, but it no longer affects me. I need a hit right into the vein. I am going out to the fruit trees. There are always people out there, waiting for somebody to pity them and give them some. I don't know how to inject it to myself, so I watch them. They're dirty, they smell like me. I am cold, and so are they. I feel sorry for us all. I can help only one of them so he can inject me in return. I choose the best one. I have gotten to know "Dr. Sergei," as I call him. "You have tools?" I ask him. Yes, and we head to near the kindergarten. Nobody is there at this time of the day. I feel dope sick. I am trembling, my nose is runny, I have chills all over my body. I spill the drugs into the lid, half for me and half for him. He heats up the drug. That bitter smell makes me nauseous time and time again. I vomit a yellow, bitter fluid. I forgot when I last ate. Sergei has trouble finding my vein. My veins are all inflamed because of the injections. He pricks me ten times until he finds a vein. It hurts. I don't want to feel pain anymore. I want to die. That's it. He found my vein. I slowly collapse, until the next hit.*

In the second passage, Adi portrays the harsh humiliations she goes through in order to obtain drug money for her and for her addict boyfriend: I thought he loved me. Every day, my money goes for his games and gambling. I spend ten hours a day at the brothel, meeting disgusting guys; something else, out of this world. I depend on those perverts' graces. I am disgusted with them, with myself, with the world. I never thought there were such people in the world, who pay to buy the most beautiful, intimate thing in this world. It never occurred to me that I would sell what's most precious to me, my own self. Every day, ten hours at the brothel, subject to the owner's whims. But never mind. The more I do, the better. At the end of the night, he'll come pick me up. He persuades me with hugs and kisses to go gaming: "It is not much money. After that, we will go get the stuff you like."

"First we get our stuff, and then we go gambling," I say, but am not heard. One hour, two, three, four hours go by and he loses it all. He is now blaming me, saying it is all my fault, because I nagged him to go home. At home he curses, screams, and hits me. I promise him to work harder at the brothel tomorrow and we'll have extra money for a good score. It is worth it, I thought. Who will love a junkie whore? He is actually doing me a favor by being with me. I am worthless. I thought he loved me.

In the third passage from her journal, Adi writes:

I wrote down words from a song by Sarit Hadad [a popular female Israeli singer], I hope I can get them right:

To face pain directly

To hold tightly on to life;

Never give up, believe wholeheartedly that it will all get better, and we will overcome the obstacles despite of it all.

And from a song by Shlomo Artzi [a popular male Israeli singer], I recall the following words:

Those who have not been able to withstand this pace of life

Have gone crazy; committed suicide; their lives became a living hell.

I am crazy. There's no other option. I am suicidal, in living hell. The horrible drugs control life. My body betrays me. I want to be normal like everybody else. Why can't I be like everybody else?... I remember Dad telling me I am the Queen of the Road. Maybe I wanted to prove him right. After all, he was always right. He used to be God-like to me. Now I'd be better off subjected to the Angel of Death. I hate everybody, absolutely everyone. It is because of them that I am standing here now.

They all love me and wait for me to come. If I wished it, my worst enemy could be my friend. True, it's only because I score. So what? After all, it has always been that way. I have always been loved for what I can give. Even back then, as a small girl, so small I couldn't say no, I don't want to. He loved me for what I've got, and it's been like that ever since. Even at school, I was the beautiful, big-boobed one. Many older guys loved spending time with me. After my military service, I became a whore. Why not take advantage of that, and better yet, for money. Now this money pays for the temporary peace drugs can give me.

Monday—staff-meeting day—ends. The life stories of Adi, Tiran, Shir, and others I met today go with me into the evening hours. When we hear news reports of parents abusing their children, many people, my friends among them, talk about them for hours in disgust. As for us, the hundreds of professionals who treat SUD, the stories sound quite usual.

In the afternoon, I give a course addressing drug addiction at the Haifa University campus. There, too, I hear students' incredulous responses while hearing the abuse stories reported on the news. I attempt to present my students with the facts known to me, namely, the relationships we therapists witness. There is a great deal of injustice and pain in our world. The news reporting is unusual, rather than the events in themselves.

When another day of work at Rothschild ends, I go for another round in the building, assuring all the pets have food and water, that Kamma's kennel is organized, and that the linens are starched and fresh, turning off the lights, locking the doors. "Bye, Kammush," I tell her. "I will see you in the morning." Kamma casts her glance down. I feel she doesn't like to say behind, alone.

Psychological trauma has yielded the development of the post-traumatic syndrome, arousing anxiety, depressive affects, tantrums, sleeping difficulties, and other psychological sensations portrayed in this chapter. Without therapeutic, psychological assistance available, some PTSD victims turn to drug use as self-medication. The following chapter portrays psychoactive drug addiction as one of the developmental continuum's components of stress and trauma events.

CHAPTER FIVE

Addiction

<hr>

The therapeutic group is in crisis. Apparently, the secrets overcome the group's ability to engage in discourse. I ask the group to stand in a circle. A roaring pigeon flies above, landing in the middle of the group circle.

"What have you come to tell us?" I ask the pigeon. The pigeon stands in the middle, circling itself, shitting, flying, and then – it's gone. What have you come to say, brown pigeon?

A considerable number of books addressing drug addiction exist in Israel. The most significant include *Drug-Head* (Aviad & Rosenman, 1988); *Living in Another World* (Teichman, 1989); *Drugs: Facts, Questions, and Issues* (Green, 1995); From God's Nectar to the Poison Cup (Teichman, 2001); *Substance Abuse Victims in Israel: Treatment and Rehabilitation* (Hovav, 2002), and *Addiction and Recovery* (Michael, 2007).

Substance addiction is an interesting, fascinating, and intriguing human phenomenon. Emotional sensations, an outcome of the substance addiction process, raise the human emotion to climaxes, low points, and extreme experiences. Substance addiction strikes many individuals, damaging families and human settings, employment, military service, and schoolwork. Addiction damages many addicts directly and indirectly.

Drug addiction drives millions to the edge of human experience, bliss, or bliss-like states, pain, illusion, fantasy, absentmindedness, and emotional dullness. I can understand why addiction is a special issue for discussion, and an intriguing research topic, and why thousands of researchers and therapy professionals worldwide engage in treating it.

Tuesday mornings begin with a brief meeting with Maya and Effy. We consider whom, of all the clients, to include in the group therapeutic work today. Mischievous Choco sits with us, jumping for joy upon seeing my colleagues. Choco loves receiving food from people. So she has good memories of the employees.

Some clients have already engaged in work this week, and we have managed to assess them. Others, who are quieter, convey the pain of their soul through nods alone, unaware that we perceive the feelings as identification with their fellow group members. Midweek is a good time for assessment, and we begin with Effy's group. One of the clients requests to be included in the therapeutic work.

Later on that day, the clients will meet Zehava and Maya in the Mirroring Group, where they learn to mirror one another's behavior, verbal abuse, insults, deceptions, and unfairness. In the Mirroring Group, there is also room for compliments and expressions of gratitude toward those group members who have assisted their mates. The clients learn a different way of speaking. A group member who mirrors fellow group members remains speaking, and the fellow member whom he has mirrored remains quiet. Practicing tolerance among the group members is required, as well as mutual respect, and hearing quite difficult messages from one another. How many of them would welcome such an opportunity in their daily lives? I think only a few. Fortunately, sometimes I get to share moments of those morning updates, the invigorating smell rising from the macchinetta. Maya or Effy must have prepared the coffee on arrival.

Four characteristics that define a drug:

1. The drug has an immediate effect on emotions
2. The psychoactive effects influence areas of emotion in the brain
3. Using the drug induces tolerance over time
4. Stopping use of the drug induces withdrawal

These four aspects distinguish—in terms of professional and psychiatric-medical assessment—between negative abuse of substances and use of a substance as prescribed and medically monitored by a physician. I address this again later.

It is common to identify several approaches attempting to account for the substance abuse problem. I treat the main approaches.

Social Learning Theory

In the initial assessment stages, many clients report on how their peers influenced them in relation to the first using experience. The feeling that an adolescent often imitates actions common among his peers is the basis of the social learning theory. Adolescents do not wish to seem different, or bizarre, relative to their peers. He wishes to be like them and identify with their experience. We assume that many of the initial experiences with drugs occur within the contemporaries' social, recreational settings. The social learning theory also accounts for drug abuse by attributing it to cultural experience and its social and sociological settings. Thus, the adolescent could perceive his initial drug use as promoting the determination of his nature, personality, and his social association (Michael, 2007). Furthermore, this approach views substance use as a learned response to environmental pressure, an acquired behavior stemming from a deficient socialization (Teichman, 1989). Many clients attribute their first experiences with substances to be the influence of their friends and contemporaries, all of which may occur under the influence of various life stresses and by force of deficient modes of connecting to society.

Medical Approach

Approximately fifty percent of the clients treated for substance abuse issues in Tel Aviv receive substance substitutes such as methadone, naloxone and subutex. The remaining fifty percent receive treatment in five ambulatory treatment centers, where the requirement is full detoxification from any drug, as a condition for continuing the therapeutic and rehabilitative processes. The medical approach emphasizes the Disease Model of Illness associated with drug addiction. This model allows no room for any moral component, or such components associated with the addict's willpower (Michael, 2007), thereby yielding the immense difference between the way substance substitute distribution clinics perceive the addict's issues and the common professional view in the ambulatory treatment centers, operated by the Welfare Ministry and the Addiction Treatment Division.

Medical theory perceives addiction as an illness rather than a consequence of circumstances or conditions. Thus, this approach contrasts other approaches that view addiction as a symptom of crises, conflicts, emotions and other psychopathological conditions. The medical approach refers to the biological-genetic and hereditary-physiological components of addiction, perceiving it as a chronic illness. It is difficult to cure chronic illness, but can be treated moderately by means of intervention through medications and various therapies (Michael, 2007).

Situational Factors

Studies by Israel's Anti-Drug and Alcohol Authority indicate extremely high percentages of experimentation with substances among young adults who travel to the Far East, India and Thailand. The studies reveal that approximately sixty percent of Israelis who tour the Far East experiment with substances. This data is not sufficient to argue that sixty percent of these young adults will be addicted to substances, and we assume that most will stop using substances when they return to Israel and enter academic studies and employment structures. In my opinion, many families in Israel agree with this assumption.

Indeed, researchers are familiar with situation-dependent substance abuse from studies conducted among American soldiers who fought in Vietnam in the 1960s and 70s. Even then, it was commonly known that approximately sixty percent of soldiers experimented with substances while serving in the Vietnam War, with only about twenty to thirty percent who continued to use substances upon returning home (Kulka et al., 1990).

Other cultural factors are known to be situation-dependent factors which influence substance use. Researchers from countries where unique substance use is common and acceptable—such as chewing coca leaves in South American, or gat leaves by Yemenites and other ethnic groups in Canada, or using opium in the Netherlands or Iran— witness that continued use does not necessarily result in entering the increasingly escalating addiction cycles, but rather, use that seems to be associated with each country's cultural and social characteristics.

The Family Systems Theory and Social Approach

This approach perceives substance use by one family member as a "family pattern," or a "system symptom," which manifests the family's struggles. The social approach views physical and socioeconomic distress as a significant cause of substance use, while emphasizing the influence of social alienation and ethnic discrimination on social phenomena. I have often raised the voice that repeatedly echoes during sessions with my clients who feel they have caused suffering to their families, being the so-called black sheep, and believe that their actions are what ruined everything. I am convinced that most clients realize through the therapeutic process that their addiction is merely a symptom of a broader family issue.

Quite often, through therapy, these clients turn out to be the most sensitive figures in their family structure, individuals who could no longer withstand the pain of the injustice going on in their family. According to the system approach, there is a belief that not only does the family contribute to its children's addiction, but the family even preserves it, so as not to cope with pain, a secret or any other threatening difficulty. Other than the family system theory, which is represented by the addiction of one family member, family approach supporters maintain that some families view substance abuse, substance trafficking and involvement in crime as a channel toward social mobility and a way to enhance their socioeconomic status. Those are tough assumptions for any individual concerned with the wholeness of the social structure. I have met many addicts whose involvement with substances, and even the abuse in which they engaged, were supported by their families. They are encouraged because of their ability to accumulate capital and money from their crime, as well as hidden encouragement of their ability to enhance their social status. This phenomenon is common among populations who subjectively feel discriminated against within Israel's socioeconomic structure. I think the policy makers in Israel should consider the voice of protest rising from these more vulnerable sectors, and be attentive to the semi-legitimization of their sons' engagement in substance trafficking and crime. This information receives attention mostly from sociologists, criminologists and those who engage in social and cultural research in Israel. Moreover, this information is supported by many studies conducted by the State's law enforcement branches (Shoham, Rahav, & Arad, 1987).

The Legal Approach

An assumption marginally raised by the family systems theory about drug addiction and crime, is that the legal approach views addiction as a legal issue and the substance abuser as an individual who has broken the law. Those who follow this approach argue that the law is supposed to provide rules and regulations as to how an addict, a criminal, should be treated (Michael, 2007).

This approach affects the cycle of suffering, addressed in Chapter Ten, because law enforcement affects sanctions and penalties enacted by judiciary authorities. This has a ripple-effect on the immense suffering caused to the addicted criminal, resulting from the involvement of police officers and law enforcement personnel.

In discussing this approach, due to lack of knowledge, I cannot address all the professional clauses under judiciary and civil rights protection authorities in Israel. However, throughout this book, my attempt to voice the human suffering experienced by my clients is quite prominent. Thus, my call for constructing a different model for professional views and new coping modes with the substance addiction issue in Israel is perfectly clear. Many clients tell me about humiliations they've faced because of recurrent arrests, street raids, audits, and frequent imprisonments.

To me, it is obvious that the legal approach is soundly in favor of the outlook of the judiciary and law enforcement authorities, whose role is to protect the rights of a civilian damaged by delinquency and law-breaking by substance addicts.

The legal approach is insufficient for curbing the scope of drug addiction and crime, and the suffering that follows. Other branches, namely, therapeutic ones, should support the legal approach's branches. It is commonly known that even in countries where drug dealers are subject to capital or physical punishment, the issue of drug addiction has not been terminated, let alone the issue of trafficking. Thus, this approach is not sufficient. I address this issue more broadly later.

The Moral Approach

This approach views drug use as a voluntary return to a hedonist lifestyle. This approach may apply to a small number of individuals only, who are supposedly capable of controlling the drug's addictive effect; many who use substances, or "do drugs," as they colloquially refer to it, without losing control over their lives, mood, behavior, or the morals and values guiding their lives.

These individuals, parents and adult family members, who support the moral approach and use drugs in the privacy of their own homes should bear in mind that this parental model is very likely to pass on to a younger family member, and even damage their family in the future. As a chaperoning parent on my daughters' school trips, I have met parents who use drugs even during the trip.

In the lectures I give at schools, I have met young children who burst into tears when they realize the prospective dangers that could strike their addicted family member. Think about these conditions prior to using drugs in the presence of a younger family member. In my work as a therapist, I encounter these same clients who have lost control of their drug use. Thus, the moral approach is ineffective for them coping with their issues.

The Psychological/Psychopathological Approach

This approach perceives addiction as a solution to the individual's personal issues, relying on the self-medication hypothesis (Stewart, Rioux, Connolly, Dunphy, & Teehan, 1996; Brown & Wolfe, 1994; Khantzian, 1985). According to this approach, the substance abusing individual seeks an effective way to ease their emotional pain, and moderate their depression and anxiety.

The Hereditary, Biological, and Physiological Causes Approach

Research into the hereditary and biological aspect of addictions investigates a multitude of various directions. One research direction is associated with exploring the genetic-hereditary aspect to the addiction phenomena (Teichman, 2001). Another research direction addresses the brain's activity, attempting to identify neurotransmitters or brain areas whose nature of activity may indicate a future disposition to addiction or alcohol dependency. Thus far, the research findings only partially support heredity's influence on alcoholism. Studies do not support other hereditary related assumptions associated with addictions. Studies investigating the interaction of twins, non-twins, and addictions also partially support the prospect of a hereditary and genetic relationship, and support to a lesser extent the prospect that substance addiction stems from genetic circumstances. Biologically, the addiction perception "refers to the poisoning element... poisons and potions fulfill a significant role... in inducing a spiritual atmosphere and ecstasy," (Michael, 2007). The biological effects of various substances modify the body's functions and even induce a decline in bodily functions as drug dependency escalates. A study from the biological viewpoint regarding a substance's effect on our physiological function can be found in Kalat's (1984) body of work from that year.

The Cognitive Theory

Various studies have investigated the way in which cognitive factors affect the outset and duration of an addiction (Teichman, 2001). Cognition often distorts under the influence of various substances. The addict's thoughts may become compulsive, paranoid, involving anxiety, depression, and weakness, sleeping difficulties, and damaged motivation. "The addict's emotional world constricts and alters. At times, the addict may lose various emotions, while other emotions become extreme and detached from their normal, ordinary context,"

(Michael, 2007). Additional material on the subject matter may be found in the literature I recommend at the beginning of this chapter.

The Interpersonal Factors Theory

Some studies attempt to investigate the way views, values, and behaviors affect substance and alcohol abuse (Teichman, 2001). Many studies have even investigated the way peers' expectations affect substance and alcohol experimentation, as well as society's influence and the way both interact. Some studies investigate the way that social learning, modeling, and other mediating parties influence an adolescent who begins experimenting with drugs. The substance user, or addict, gradually loses their social and intimate relationships, claims Michael (2007). The addict loses interest in others and his social skills become blunted. The substance becomes a friend, a source of interest and pleasure, "to me, it is the essence of life itself," as I have been told by many addicts.

Simultaneous to the continuous dissociation from his normative relatives and friends, the addict often forms connections with other addicts, with whom he survives long months of drug addiction. Those new connections bear no social or emotional nature. Friendships among addicts while abusing substances is based on the interest they share.

Summing up the various approaches accounting for drug addiction, I believe they are to be integrated. This integration will enhance the ability to account for the drug abuse issue. It is for good reason that many professionals believe that there is no sole, crucial cause of substance addiction, but a combination of biological, psychological, and social causes. In other words, there is causality to the addiction issue, consisting of many causes, which includes a genetic/biological predisposition, which overlaps other psychological, social, and cultural aspects with which it interacts.

The sequence-like way in which the book unwinds is what inspired its core idea, raised in the introduction. This is to address an issue rarely discussed in the professional literature available in Israel, namely, the way in which past stress events, abuse, and trauma are associated with future addiction to drugs.

As Najavits (2002) states, among substance addicted males, the rate of those suffering PTSD ranges from 12-34 percent, while among substance addicted females, the rate ranges from 30-54 percent. Drug rehabilitation will not solve their PTSD issue, but will aggravate the problem even further if there is no involvement of professional therapy as well. The downward spiral, where apparently substances escalate trauma, and trauma, in turn, intensifies substance abuse, as argued by Najavits, is well-known to many addicts and therapists, most of whom are undoubtedly familiar with this field of discussion.

Another point to be discussed in this chapter and the following chapter indicates a harsh item of data in terms of outcomes: In 39-50 percent of violent assaults, the aggressor is under the influence of a substance (Najavits, 2002).

Hence, it is important that we posit questions associating drug addiction and violence within Israeli society in this book as well, since this area of discussions cannot be ignored:

1. Do substance addiction patterns relate to acts of violence in Israeli society?

2. Simultaneous to reducing the rate of drug addicts in Israel, would it be possible to lower the level of human suffering in Israeli society?

3. Could immediate treatment of stress and trauma events reduce the future addiction rate in Israel?

4. Compared to the current situation (where professional intervention programs addressing trauma and drug addiction issues are

scarcely known), would we be able to plan future interventions consistently?

In a leading Israeli newspape, in the edition dated February 22, 2008, pp 2, 4-5, we find the following articles:

- A Nightmare at School: Two Student Cases - Videotaped Peer-Molestations Revealed

- The Ministry of Education: A 24 percent increase in the number of children complaining of sexual assault; 602 complaints concerning sexual assaults, from sexual harassment to severe sexual crimes such as rape and sodomy were filed in the previous academic year. The article presents the breakdown of the sexual harassment report; 602 complaints filed regarding sexual abuse; 166 complaints filed regarding adults' abuse of minors; 404 complaints filed regarding minors abusing other minors; 367 complaints filed regarding abuse in elementary schools.

- Neglect in Boarding Schools: Three Children Cruelly Raped at Boarding Schools they Attended have been admitted to Poriya Hospital

In the first week of April 2008, many articles addressing parental abuse appeared. The whole country was up in arms. These are common newspaper headlines, the tip of the iceberg in terms of the stress, trauma, and abuse that occur in Israel throughout the year.

I assume that the harassment and trauma cases that came to the attention of professionals and parents were handled professionally, preventing the child from seeking self-medication, and even from abusing substances in the future. Unfortunately, therapists and family are not informed of the trauma and stress victims early enough. They probably do not receive treatment right after the abus occurred, thus, I am quite likely to meet them in the future, while working in the public services offered to substance addicts.

As previously mentioned, physiological, physical, psychological, cultural, and philosophical causes underlie drug addiction, manifested by the various approaches attempting to account for the drug abuse issue. I know literary figures, directors, singers, poets, athletes, soldiers, doctors, workers, male and female executives, adolescents, and children who experiment with drugs. In this chapter, I quote only a small part of the existing knowledge on the subject matter. I continue by further portraying various approaches to the drug addiction issue, particularly emphasizing the apparent relationship of events preceding a trauma and future substance addiction. The life stories written or orally related by SUDs, who are in varying stages of their treatment at the Rothschild 2 Therapeutic Center, have facilitated a change in my feelings and understanding in terms of the intensity of psychological pain experienced by a trauma victim who is a substance addict.

What is drug addiction and what are the key terms in professional definitions associated with addiction?

ICD-10 (2002) refers to the dependency syndrome as "a set of behavioral and cognitive phenomena where the individual highly prioritizes using the psychoactive chemical or several psychoactive chemicals. Dependency Syndrome's key characteristic is the intense urge (often so highly intense that it is uncontrollable) to consume a drug (whether or not medically prescribed), alcohol or tobacco." According to ICD-10 guidelines, "Dependency diagnosis should be unequivocally determined only when three or more of the following parameters have been demonstrated or experienced throughout the past year," (p. 88):

- Intense or compulsory urge to consume the chemical
- Difficulty in controlling the chemical consumption related behavior, in terms of beginning and ceasing use, and the consumed quantity

- A state of physiological withdrawal when ceasing or reducing chemical consumption, as manifested by the withdrawal syndrome typical of that particular psychoactive chemical, or relief or prevention of withdrawal symptoms when using an identical or similar chemical

- Evidence of tolerance development that results in the need for a larger dose of the psychoactive chemical, in order to attain outcomes initially attained by smaller doses

- Progressive neglect of pleasures and other interests due to psychoactive chemical consumption and/or the length of time required to recover its effects

- Consistent use despite the clarity of its damages. It should be assured or expected that the user has indeed realized the nature and depth of the damage

In his book, Green (1995) writes: "Addiction is a physiological or psychological dependency developed by chronic consumers of psychoactive chemicals," and Nadler (2002) states that addiction is a physical and psychological dependency for functioning purposes.

Substance Tolerance is "a state of reduced reactivity to a certain type of substance resulting from recurrent exposure to that substance. When tolerance develops, ever-growing doses are necessary in order to attain the effects which would have previously be attained by consuming smaller doses," (River, 1992).

My book discusses the individuals who became addicts because of past traumatic experiences, but I cannot ignore drug addiction phenomena stemming from a search for excitement, social pressure, self-confidence, extrovert abilities, or any other cause. We find other references to these issues in the professional literature recommended earlier in this chapter.

Substance Abuse as a Means of Coping with PTSD

Some respond to traumatic memories by avoidance. PTSD victims often avoid intrusive memories and thoughts, suffering declined performance in various functional aspects of life (Zomer & Bleich, 2005). Does avoidance facilitate the victim's continued active life in the long term? In my opinion, it does not. Does substance abuse facilitate a victim's long-term performance? Of course not!

Some PTSD victims resort to self-medicating while others do not. I cannot avoid the question of which individuals who suffer various psychological difficulties will resort to substance abuse, and which will not. Who are the typical clients who abuse drugs, and which drugs do they use? What psychological condition lead a client to abuse, and what psychological condition would lead them to stop? These questions indicate complex courses of thinking and discussion.

I am involved with a group of professionals who have identified the strong causal relationship between previous stress and trauma events and later drug abuse. I have indicated in previous articles the relationship of a client's past, as an individual physically or psychologically abused, and their addiction to drugs (Pirani, 2004, 2005, 2007; Pirani & Teichman, 1999; Pirani, Fishelson, & Zacks, 2001; Pirani & Shani, 2003).

Green (1995) outlines studies assessing the factors affecting the initial experimentation with drugs. According to Green, drug and alcohol abusers are individuals who treat themselves by means of substances. He argues that addicts cope with life's challenges through chemical means:

> Alcoholics address feelings of anxiety and depression, while those using opiates use them to attempt to moderate psychological pain and suffering. Tranquilizers and sedatives supposedly ease stress, while hashish and marijuana, cocaine or crack cocaine, are used to elevate the spirit.

Other assumptions support the view according to which addiction is often a consequence of a preceding psychological state. These conditions call for substance abuse in order to ease some psychological distress. These assumptions support the view I present in this book, the deductive by-product of which is as follows: Addicts who seek treatment from public services use a substance as part of self-medication for harsh psychological condition which they have suffered for many years.

Michael (2007) further questions, "What is addiction?" His response is: "Addiction is an attempt to ease the pain yielded by an insufferable reality. The drug or alcohol addict attempts to treat his vulnerability and emotional-psychological difficulties through the substance..." The attempt to treat the wound supposedly succeeds, but only temporarily; thus the problem and solution form a kind of vicious cycle, addressed in the theoretical model I have established, The Cycle of Suffering, as appears in Chapter Ten.

Briere (1988) also reports victims of childhood abuse as demonstrating the tendency to abuse substances and alcohol to a greater extent than other patients. For those individuals, the substance constitutes a refuge from anxiety, depression and psychological stress. Many articles I present in this book portray the damage to the components of an addict's personality, as triggers of his drug addiction. I also cite research literature indicating that there are many factors affecting drug addiction. However, the endless, vicious cycle of psychological suffering, addiction, and further psychological suffering may not be attributed to a sole factor. One interpretation associated with the psychoanalytical theories perceives substance abuse as an action indicating a transference action that, for the addict, represents an unconscious fantasy of adopting an "ideal object," and assimilating the benefits within himself and his body (Amali, 1995). According to Amali's view, this is one of the more common reasons for substance abuse conditions. My view is different, and I cite other studies to demonstrate it:

Eighty-five percent of those suffering PTSD develop psychoactive chemical addiction issues (Ouimette & Brown, 2003). For me, this extreme data is vexing. So many individuals wounded by stress events have resorted to substance abuse, having had no other option for a cure. Hence, by writing these lines, I am calling for a new direction in the discussion regarding treating prolonged substance addiction victims, which is different to that which is outlined in professional literature available in Israel. I seek another account for the wide prevalence of addicts who are also post-trauma victims, whom I encounter at the Rothschild 2 Treatment Center.

As opposed to the social consensus, which enjoys an open dialogue on the prolonged psychological abuse resulting from terror and war events (Zomer & Bleich, 2005; Herman, 1992; Kulka et al., 1990; Hendin & Haas, 1984, 1991), personal, subjective post-traumatic stress response, which leads to substance abuse, rarely features on the public agenda. Sometimes, drug addiction directly or indirectly resulting from sexual abuse and physical and verbal violence in childhood, encounters an amazing lack of public interest. It seems to me that the issue has been repressed beneath superficial public polemic, even though the issue's scope is rather broad, and the victims' suffering is immense.

In my work with drug addicts, I hear that their choice to turn to substances is due to the emotion-blocking and stunning effect that the drugs afford. This item of data is sufficient to understand many psychological proceedings that drive individuals toward substance abuse. Even if for some percentage of users, the substance provides an emotional response in searching for feelings of warmth and love, more prevalent are situations where the substance functions as a blocker against the addict's emotions and psychological pain.

Other researchers indicate the approach that assumes that substance abuse induces a so-called "intermediate phase," the point where the physical and psychological aspects meet, with the role of the substance being to bridge or even detach these aspects one from the other as a psychological survival mechanism. These approaches constitute a significant support for my own hypotheses (Amali, 1995).

Those who support this approach state when a substance is used, it manifests as an illusion. The substance's sly influence yields a deceiving intermediate area, which instills a false feeling of confidence and protection.

From what is mentioned above, it may only be assumed that clients suffering from PTSD who have lost their ability to feel and draw pleasure over the years, and have avoided situations which may have reminded them of the traumatic experiences, rely on substance use for a certain time stretch in order to dull the pain.

The apparent relationship between addiction's influence and the substance's qualities implies that the substance possesses qualities affecting one's senses. It is no wonder then, that substances usually serve the addict's need for dulling the sensations associated with the trauma. To them, substance and its influence signify a "transference action" (Amali, 1995); the substance serves as a temporary defensive-regressive mechanism, fulfilling their needs and protecting them from their feelings. Those who support these approaches assume that substance abuse demonstrates a circular process of desperately clinging on to the illusion it induces, as well as the difficulty giving up the illusion. The drug yields an "illusionary intermediate area," where the addict distorts the painful reality through which he lives.

Drug use constitutes a so-called container, as argued by those supporting these approaches: a tool allowing an emotional flooding on the one hand, which the addict may afford, and a tool filtering rough, insufferable emotions, processing them, on the other hand.

Paradoxically, Amali states that substance use is a behavior that, in fact, is intended to preserve life and seek meaning, but its outcome may sometimes bear the risk of self-harming, harming others, and even death.

Throughout my years of work, I have met more than three thousand clients who are victims of drug abuse, and my knowledge has expanded a great deal. But the theoretical knowledge I acquired during my professional training in social work and psychology has not yielded any significant professional discourse as to the nature and characteristics of the relationship between psychological trauma and substance addiction. I cannot understand why.

As I said, I have repeatedly noticed an item of data I find rather upsetting: The thousands of individuals who come to Rothschild 2 seeking treatment for their substance addiction issue have undergone brutal psychological abuse by another person. These individuals have approached me in order to treat their substance addiction issue, but in fact seek treatment for the outcome of a core psychological distress that preceded their addiction, namely, the suffering they experienced due to trauma.

It is hard to accept that many of the substance abuse victims treated by the public treatment services in Israel have never been diagnosed with PTSD, and most of them have never even been questioned in that regard. We find an identical argument regarding this condition worldwide in work by Najavits (2002).

Addicted individuals spend long years living with indescribable psychological pain. As trauma victims, they suffer immensely, but their needs remain unattended. As drug addicts, they are blamed for freely choosing to use substances. Though they live among us, their inner world is "dark, mysterious, and painful" (Warshaw et al., 1993). The ordinary defense mechanisms employed by humans do not ease their psychological pain. Professionals have not heard their cry due to the shame, guilt, and misery they conceal throughout their lives. For a while, the substance managed to ease their psychological pain, and enhanced their ability to survive. Some of those with SUD raise families; many of them integrate into the workforce and manage daily lives. Others realize that total repression of their traumatic past has allowed them to lead a functional life, for a while.

Many others, due to tremendous psychological difficulty, live similarly to the way PTSD victims live, mainly those who were deliberately harmed by another (Tiano, 1998; Herman, 1992), and turn to drug abuse, and cannot stop on their own. These individuals rely on substances to detach their emotions from their daily thoughts, allowing them to bridge their overwhelming emotions and their daily thoughts and functioning. They manage to ride the wave of their traumatic experiences for a while. They wish to protect their souls from pain, but when the wave has abated, they have to resume coping with life on the shore. Most of them cannot cope without professional intervention.

Unfortunately, I realize time and time again that many stress and trauma victims have not dared emerge and see if the threatening wave has gone, thus they continue engaging in the destructive abuse of drugs.

Those who become addicted to psychoactive chemicals have ceased suffering PTSD-related symptoms thanks to the substance, but only on the surface. Those who have repressed their harsh psychological feelings have relied on the substance to replace the dissociative mechanism detaching the painful experience from their reality. They continue escaping the memories of the horrific events they experienced, on a daily basis. These individuals failed to cope with these memories in a more adaptive mode.

Presumably, most of these individuals could have eased their pain through professional guidance and adequate psychological treatment. Yet for many reasons, only a few do so.

Why do professional assumptions, known to many therapists worldwide, rarely appear in the therapeutic discourse related to addiction victims in Israel? After all, substance abuse is common among PTSD victims. Many PTSD survivors rely on substances and alcohol in order to heal themselves and moderate the psychological pain associated with trauma. Many of them suffer depression or major depression, as stated by Foa and Rothman (1998).

It is no wonder then, that at one point or another in the life of a SUD substance abuse will be perceived as an issue; a life issue (an issue manifested by a shortage of money, encounters with the law, health issues, and issues related to employment and family functioning). At this very moment, I can identify the clients whose coping through substances has ceased to be effective, since they constantly feel as though they have failed to develop personally, lack resilience, and are incapable of positively integrating into the circles of life. Unfortunately, it is only at that point that they approach me, seeking treatment.

For a while, Frida had put off sharing the other tragedy of her life with me. Instead, she left me the following message on my answering machine: "This week I can't make it to the urinalysis or to sessions with you. I will be at my sister's." Since I'm normally alarmed by such messages, I immediately started to wonder whether or not she had gone back to using. Perhaps her financial situation had forced her out of her rented apartment. Or perhaps her father's condition, who was slowly dying at the retirement center, had deteriorated? Was she hiding information from me? Why didn't she leave a more detailed voice message?

I recalled my first session with Frida. She looked extremely thin, weighing about forty kilograms, her dry skin burned from the days she spent in the sun. Her clothes were weathered and torn. She walked slowly and with great difficulty. The attempts to find another vein for the needle were apparent on her arms. A few of her teeth were missing. Her sad smile disclosed embarrassment. Frida's hair was long and well-groomed, the last remnant of her days of glamour. Her body and soul knew many years of suffering, pain, and loneliness.

When she came for treatment following a few months of rehabilitation in the therapeutic community, I noticed the change in her, which is common among many clients who return from rehab; her speech was faster and she smiled often. I could feel the emotion seeping out of her wounded soul. I sat with her for an assessment, in order to see where else we could assist her. She told me of her father who had been lying for months in a geriatric home for the mentally frail, devoid of any memory or speech ability; an individual who had experienced nothing but pain and sorrow throughout his life.

I have not yet told him of the death of my older brother, Judah. My sister and I only told him he was not calling because he went overseas. What could we tell him? But Father, thanks to his fatherly instincts, and despite his vague, deteriorating memory, felt that something bad had happened. "Why is he not calling?" he keeps questioning me. "Judah'leh, Judah'leh," he mumbles at night.

Frida's only daughter was taken from her by social services. The law requires the protection of the physical and psychological well-being of a child under the custody of an irresponsible, dysfunctional, or substance abusing parent.

When Eileen was a year old, they took her from me, to a foster home. I was given one chance before they took her her away for adoption. Do you know what that did to me? I am 40 years old. In my physical condition, I will no longer be able to have children. Without my daughter Eileen, my life is nothing.

I feel the motherly, animalistic instinct inherent in any mother; it has manifested itself in Frida. She wants to fight for her daughter's life, to keep her in her custody. I am interested in channeling those psychological strengths toward her therapeutic process.

I feel as though I am sinking in choppy waters, holding on to a log. This is my instinct of life, my essence. Unconsciously, I wish to keep and protect my family's last set of genes. My oldest sister is single, my older brother OD'd, and my younger brother is a drug addict. My daughter and I are the only remaining genes.

I lost my mother when I was four. I vaguely remember her. My older brother, Judah, remembered her, but he OD'd about three years ago. Poor Judah shot up mice poison the dealers had cut into the heroin he bought in Lod. My oldest sister was six when Mom died of a heart attack. The trauma and sadness wounded her soul, and to this day, she is painfully lonely, working as a domestic helper to support herself. She lets every man pass by, take advantage of her, and move on. My younger brother was a year old when Mom passed away. Our home remained in mourning and deserted. I remember my father crying at night and have seen his heartbreak every day ever since. Dad was a Holocaust survivor. He experienced destitution, pain, and hunger in his life. The intense pain due to Dad's condition, his longing for Mom, and our tremendous deprivation from love, burned our souls and was the cause of my brothers and me turning to drugs. It gave us oblivion.

I recalled Frida's efforts from the year before to bring her brother to therapy at Rothschild 2:

I must save his life. I have only one brother left. What will I do if he dies too? Help me help my brother.

That conversation with Frida was harsh. I felt the burden of despair threatening to crush her soul, her futile cry, her intense desire to avoid further mourning of her brother who had become a victim. Frida spoke to me on returning to community rehab, when we continued the intake process:

Look at the pictures I carry with me. When my father was taken to the retirement home, the movers threw away all our pictures and belongings. Nobody kept the memories. This picture is my mother's, she holds me in her loving arms, these are the only memories I will carry with me for life. This photograph has been through all the horrors with me, that's why it's especially dear to my heart. I always get emotional looking at it, a photograph that has given me strength over the years, because it bears a powerful memory from a moment of true, genuine love. These are the photographs that survived my private Holocaust. I have nothing else to remind me of my mother. Her other photographs are gone.

Her hands trembling, Frida drew another photograph out of the tattered nylon bag, where she stands in a colorful bikini, her hair long and smooth. Many of the Rothschild 2 patients who grew up with Frida in the neighborhood, remember her as one of the neighborhood's prettiest girls. In those days, she had many suitors.

The third photograph which she presented me showed the whole family in a moment of smiles and joy.

Nobody reminds me of my Mother and the way she looked. Look what an adversity death brought about, just like a snowball rolling down the slope, ruining every flower and plant on its way. Death ruined my family and broke it apart.

On Sunday, I call her sister's home. Her incessant cries imply that another tragedy has occurred in her life. Her other brother was found dead, also from an overdose. The needle was still stuck in his arm.

How can I tell my father that Moshe, too, has passed away? My brother is gone. Will you come to the funeral? It would mean a lot to me if you could. I do not know if anyone but my sister and I will attend, to see my brother off before his burial. I want to pay my brother my last respects. I want his funeral to be attended by more people than were part of his life.

I believe that prolonged substance addiction is an extreme response to coping with psychological hardship and pain, a manifestation of an individual's attempt to protect the ego from threatening powers, repressed anxiety and depression.

From Adi's journal:

It is night; perhaps the sun will rise soon. I am standing on the road. I have become accustomed to the dark. The one standing next to me gestures to me that she has finished working. I will soon be done, too, I have made my killing for today. I just need one more client to be able to score; one more client to cover the cigarettes and maybe some orange juice. Cars pass by. Some question and drive away; others just stop to make fun of us and laugh a little; some cruise and even spit at me, and others stop for sex. There are some regular clients who leave tips, but all in all, they are all the same shit. Again, I lift my shirt up, showing what there is to show. Someone please come. This night is too long for me. I can't wait for it to end. By now, my legs hurt from standing, and I smell of the bodies that have lain over me. I even remember faces. Silence; no car passes. No, I am not afraid at all.

A young man passes by. "How much," he quickly questions. I do not usually go unless they're driving a car, but this time, I told myself, never mind, he'll be the last one.

"Regular price," I told him. "Oh, alright," he said and was gone into the dark. I followed him. He paid, did what he did. I dressed and suddenly felt chills, shock, and pain on my left side. I felt as though something warm was oozing from me. I began to feel the pain before I knew what had happened. He had taken off with my wallet. He had stabbed me. I didn't know what he had used to do it. I was in pain. The fact that I had no money for my hit tonight was even more painful. I had to get cleaned up and get back to the streets.

No, I am not afraid. I wish him only well. Poor thing; it's my fault that he is in prison. He said that had I not escaped from him that night, the gun would have not been found, the necessary gun. Then, he wouldn't have got caught and wouldn't have had to sit in jail. Poor him. He had nobody to care for him but me. It was all my fault. I went to my dealer and bought a lot of dope.

I arrived home, packed most of it for him, and left some for me in order to relax and seem normal.

No, I am not afraid. I have done it so many times. I arrive at the prison. The drugs are safely hidden, deep inside my body. Nobody will ever find them. I made a point to dress comfortably so I can easily retrieve them. No, I am not afraid. I have grown accustomed to it by now.

That's it. It's time now. I hand over my ID Card.

I have a name and a number. I am standing in line. I brought no thing with me, but a calling card. Cigarettes are sold inside. I enter the search room. The procedure is humiliating time and time again. The guards know I am a drug addict. The procedure is always the same, with the white rubber gloves. To top it all off, they openly express their disgust.

I am already familiar with the procedure. I completely unwind, "bend over and spread your legs apart." They search my clothes, my hair, even my hair band. But I have no fear. They will never find what it is they are searching for. When the search is over, they dispose of the gloves, as if I am contagious. Then comes visit time. He asks me if I have brought it for him. I hand it to him under the table. He swallows, and only then calms down.

That's it; another routine visit to prison. It's my fault.

I begin the Letters to Significant Ones group. It is important to address the various types of loss experienced by an individual with SUD. The instructions are clear:

You have come a long way in your lives. I suppose most of you have been hurt; some of you have hurt others as well. Each one of you carries a highly significant message that need not be a burden anymore. In today's group session, Effy and I will ask you to move to the hall where we are sitting. We will supply you with pens and papers. Think to whom you wish to write a letter. The figure to whom you will address the letter should be a significant one for you—mother, father, siblings, children, friend, boyfriend, or girlfriend. We want you to spread out and work alone. We'll meet again in about thirty minutes.

The instructions are associated with a complex, emotionally loaded issue, often arousing feelings of guilt, anger, shame, and rage. As facilitators, we know a great deal of emotion rises to the surface through this writing session. And so it does.

Marlene writes to her mother. Her mother lives in Romania; an impoverished family. Her father is ill, and was unconscious most of her childhood years:

Mother, I want to tell you I miss you so much. I have not seen you in a decade, in other words, as long as I have used, and must have caused you a great deal of sorrow... I am no longer angry with you now. Through therapy, I have learned to come to terms with your actions, which deeply hurt me. Now I know you are ill, and so is Dad. I am afraid I will not manage to see you anytime soon. I don't have money and are you are unable to make it here. I remember with great pain the beatings I received from you and from the guy who spent a few years with us, at home. I am sure you didn't know he was abusing me, sexually assaulting me while you were working nights at the factory. I want to believe you didn't know. I must believe you didn't know. It's because of that crazy man I escaped to Israel. The suffering I had to endure led me to drug abuse; my fault or yours, it no longer matters. I miss you so and want to see you and hug you.

Eran has chosen to write to the girlfriend he loved. Both of his parents died in a car accident approximately twenty years ago. Following the tragedy, Eran fell into a tough psychological crisis and was soon an addict. His girlfriend loved him, but was not willing to serve as the mistress in his marriage to the substance.

The letter I am writing to you, dear Hanna, has been with me for many years. I knew why you chose to break up with me. I did, but was too weak. I was devastated. I did know, but would not accept your breaking away. I would not accept your accusations towards me. I have cried a great deal over my love for you. I still love you dearly. I have not seen you in eight years. I heard you married and have two girls. I never wanted to know who your husband is. I never want to run into you in the neighborhood. There were years when I wandered only at night, searching for prey in the dark, a victim to rob. So, we were not likely to run into one another. Nowadays, I am sober from the stuff that blew my brains out. I can see your beautiful green eyes before mine; they are the world's wisest, most beautiful eyes. I can feel the smiling lips and see the most beautiful and perfect smile I have ever seen; your white teeth, the smile that radiates kindness and love. You were so wise, so talented, so comfortable socially. You had everything I never had.

The anger turned into longing a long time ago; crying was replaced by dreams of passion. Sometimes, I so want to come back to tell you how much I love you. I so want to look into your kind eyes again, gaze at them, and immerse myself in that green ocean inside.

Gadi writes to his mother. He is a single, lonely man. He used to be in a relationship, but never married. Years ago, he lost twins who died at birth. Now he lives with his elderly mother and feels the immense need to mend his relationship with her, severely damaged during the long years of substance abuse.

Dear Mother, I am writing to you words of apology and love, which I am unable to say to you out loud. You know little of my rough childhood. I experienced a great deal of suffering, which I never told anybody. It is only because of the therapy I have received in the past few years that I've been set free of the stress. I assume you didn't know that our single neighbor sexually abused me when I was eight years old. I was paralyzed by fear and terror, and I told nobody, as he had ordered me to do.

I am not judging your behavior. I suppose you truly didn't see my suffering. The difficulties relating to the family's livelihood, your life with my drunken father dulled your senses. I have learned not to blame you for that. Now, I am able to feel the pain of the days when anger drove me to hurt you, tearing golden necklaces from your neck, coercing you to come with me to the bank, to hand me your pension money so I could get high. On the 28th of each month, I would show up, acting like a monster. You feared me. Your expression radiated terror. If you refused, I would hit you as if hitting a stranger. I was angry with you for not protecting me as a child, for not showing affection.

Nowadays, I am trying so hard to have you forgive me. Spoken words are unnecessary. Now that I realize where I dragged you to, and how low, I feel so ashamed. For years, I abused drugs because of that shame. Using made me forget my past.

Mother, I ask for your forgiveness. I want to tell you how much I love you. I want you to know that I am ashamed of my behavior toward you, I can't ask, though I so badly want to.

The group members return to sitting in a circle, reading their personal letters aloud. In these moments, a great deal of empathy emerges among the group members. They encourage each other and do not criticize. "I wish," says Silvia, as though summing the session up, "there would come a day when I could write a letter to myself; a letter of apology for damaging my own image."

Moshe writes of his mother's first visit in prison:

Approximately eight months after I was locked up, I contacted my mother and told her I had been sentenced to four years in prison.

165

She came for a visit. I remember the intensity of my anticipation for her visit. I missed her terribly. I had a feeling she might be the saving force that could take me out of that place. I so badly needed kind words, warmth, somebody to tell me how much they cared about me and loved me. Our reunion was moving and harsh. When we saw each other, we cried at what had become of me, with helplessness and pain, of the suffering I had experienced and what was still to come. The feeling of loss and longing toward Mom strongly affected me. I longed for home, for the food she cooked, the confidence she instilled in me, her care and love for me. I wished she would tell me to eat or dress warmly. I felt that I wanted home—my Mother. I did not want to be in prison. I dreaded prison, as I did its people and atmosphere. I was filled with regret for my actions... I wanted to vow it would never happen again and ask forgiveness.

Mom said she was very disappointed in me, that she was not feeling well and suffering heart problems because of the stress. I felt so bad. I was so sorry for what I had caused her. I felt sorry for her, that she had a son like me, about whom she always worried without receiving any pleasure in return. I felt as though I failed and had an intense desire to improve and compensate. Her visit made me very happy. I felt that in spite of it all, she loved me, cared about me, and that I meant something to her in some way. I was greatly encouraged by that visit, and I maintained contact with her. I would call her whenever I could. On her visits, she brought me clothes, cigarettes, toiletries, shoes, anything I needed. I had missed that part so much. When she came for a visit, I would be excited and cry because of her very presence, her attitude toward me, her care, and unconditional love.

Even now, I know, remember, and feel that I have room at my mom's and that her door is open any time, unlike my father.

Mom, oh, mommy, I love you and miss you so much, miss hearing your voice and feeling your love and care for me. Things are different when you are overseas. The inner feeling is intense. I worry about you, and fear lest anything happen to you, God forbid. I still need you, I want you by my side with your support and love, your visits, and your care.

"What about your father?" I question Moshe, "you have not mentioned him at all."

I wanted to prove to him that I was capable and doing well, but he never even noticed me, and never supported me. He was constantly angry and disappointed in me. I felt very frustrated and angry. I remember envying my friends. Their fathers would play with them, support them, and express their love. There was nobody to tell me that. I was always frustrated that my father ignored me, that he felt mistrust towards me. I was sure there was something wrong with me, that I was dumb, a failure. I always tried to prove to him that I was worthy, so I put effort into athletics and made some progress. I played football in the Beitar Jerusalem youth league. I even made Israel's top youth team. I remember my mom being proud of me at the time and that felt wonderful.

Marlene, Gadi, Eran, and others were able to share the painful, repressed parts of their pasts. No matter how thoroughly we plan, the intensity of emotion is never fully exposed, nor is the psychological pain or the horrors they experienced. As a professional team of therapists, we feel it is important to prevent the clients from leaving the treatment center at day's end, unprotected in their pain. No matter how much longer it takes, we continue discussing the pain while empowering the clients, allowing them to share with us, and open the road toward healing their future and their lives.

Some clients are asked to stay longer, for another meeting with a staff member, because we feel an individual session is more appropriate. Since the Rothschild 2 clients come to the center from four municipal social services units associated with the town's administration, it is important to consistently and regularly convey daily updates to all teams of the various treatment units regarding their patients, while maintaining confidentiality.

Substance addiction is rather costly. Eventually, many of the addicts are drawn deeply into drugs, crime and delinquent behavior to make the money they need to use. The following chapter addresses the various aspects of delinquency.

Chapter Six

Addiction-Induced Suffering and Delinquency

One must not touch the newborn rabbits. The smell of a human hand draws the mother away from its offspring. When we returned a pink, day-old, newborn rabbit to his cage, his mother refused to take it back. We witnessed how she did not respond to his twitching and begging. He died after two days of agony and pain.

The following subject matter comprises this chapter's discussion. The first part addresses the victim and the aggressor. The last part addresses the psychological pain arising from leading a life of delinquency, including this pain within the therapeutic processes.

The notion that neither addiction nor crime is congenial runs like a red river through the whole book. I often share this ancient philosophical dilemma with clients. I cannot accept the nativist assumptions identified by Plato, the Greek philosopher, according to which one's way of thinking and behavior are basically innate. This assumption is too fatalistic, too extreme, not allowing for the educational influence of external intervention, nor does it allow unique, divergent thinking. Consequent to this reasoning, one may assume that an individual is born complete and unalterable.

I suppose my professional path corresponds more to Aristotle's philosophical approach. Man is a rational being, absorbing stimuli from his environment which he processes intellectually and experientially. An individual has acquired a given behavior consequent to life events and development. There is room for change. The inclination of the human heart is not evil from youth. Through education, assistance, and treatment, delinquent behavior may be tempered.

Through my years of work, I have encountered dilemmas stated by laypeople: "Nobody forced the addict into substance abuse"; "He carved out that path for himself, he should suffer and face the consequences"; "I will not donate to those who have chosen to abuse substances. I'd rather donate to victims of disease, or disabled individuals. People who have been hit hard by fate"; "How many more years are you willing to work with these people?", and many more.

> Many criminals have hurt and damaged others while being addicted, claims Najavits (2002) in her studies. This is a harsh item of data. Approximately fifty percent of harassing individuals and 39% of rapists are under the influence of drugs at the time of assault. Thirty percent of males who have been sexually abused as children keep on abusing their children or wives, a rate nearly four times higher than the statewide domestic violence rate (Brothers, 2004).

She further states that children raised in violent homes often bear mixed feelings toward the victim.

Children raised in violent homes approach their surroundings ambivalently. Some children will scorn the parent who was unable to protect them and himself from the harassing spouse. Those children may feel that their mother was too weak to protect them.

Other children pity the victim parent, empathizing with his pain and sacrifice (Brothers, 2004).

Some might claim this data disserves my attempts to prove that often the aggressor previously fulfilled the role of a victim. I do not believe so, and broadly address these arguments in this chapter. After all, addressing the terminology concerning the victim and the aggressor is not simple, and is even challenging, with crimes not being "crimes" in the true sense of the word.

> Reporting is even more challenging when crimes are not committed to a victim in the term's ordinary sense are concerned. In the case of abusing highly toxic substances, the victim is no other than the abuser himself (Shoham, Rahav, & Adar, 1987).

Chapter Two presented for the first time the various epidemiological data on which some of my professional arguments rely. It is important that this chapter, too, present the studies addressing the victim-turned-aggressor:

- A study investigating which criminal group typifies the most violent criminal group, found that most violent criminals were physically or sexually abused as children (Groth, 1979; Seghom, et al., 1987).
- A study exploring female delinquents and abuse narratives found that more than seventy five percent of delinquent women had undergone sexual abuse. Furthermore, these females could be very likely candidates for sexual and physical abuse in prison as well (Smith et al., 1998).
- A study investigating the gender of criminals who sexually abused children found that the significant majority are male. More than ninety-five percent assaulted girls, and more than eighty percent

assaulted boys. Most of them were assaulted themselves as children (Fergusson & Mullen, 1999).

- Qualitative research investigating abusive characteristics in criminals sentenced to capital punishment for murder in the United States, found that of 14 criminals sentenced to death in 1987, 12 had undergone brutal physical abuse. Five of them had been sodomized as children (Lewis, 1992).

- Another study investigating convicted murderers, similar to the study by Lewis et al. (1988), found that 83.3 percent of the subjects had undergone physical and emotional abuse as children, and 32.2 percent were subjected to sexual violence as children (Blake et al., 1995).

- A study investigating the prospect that women sexually assaulted as young girls would become abusive and/or violent reveals an intriguing finding: Eighty percent of the women abused as children would assault or abuse their children as adults, as part of an assault and abuse cycle (Kaufman & Roux, 1987).

- For several years, Van der Kolk (1987) investigated abuse and addiction cases. He indicates that children who were victims of abuse will demonstrate experiences of guilt, flashbacks, nightmares, phobias, depression, alcohol and substance abuse, humiliation, lack of vitality, feelings of ugliness and harshly violence. He, too, identifies abuse as the traumatic process' outset, since, with no adequate professional treatment, what follows are harsh feelings associated with post-traumatic stress syndrome, and in many cases, drug addiction.

The studies mentioned indicate a widespread phenomenon of abuse during childhood, victimhood, delinquency, substance abuse, aggressiveness and hurting of others. All share a common history, needing clarification.

Various approaches are common among delinquency researchers. Some perceive delinquency as a consequence of biogenetic factors. Others view crime and social deviation as phenomena associated with personality disorders, while further others realize that delinquent behavior is, by essence, a consequence of a learned process based on social, cultural, and economic influences. The process, that begins with the child or the adult's first few steps leading to crime and ends when the first crime is committed, stand as key issues in criminology, as stated by Shoham and colleagues (1987).

Among my patients, those were the first steps of psychological pain, stress and traumas that led to drug abuse, which they then had to fund by means of delinquent actions. This is a different insight related to a different type of delinquency.

This process, too, is part of the publicly discussed issue of perceiving the concept of victimhood and public attitude toward the victim of assault. This is a philosophical, perplexing issue, complicated both ethically and legally. The views yielded from this concept are one of the largest obstacles to altering public opinion toward SUD. As a professional treating SUD, I would certainly be very interested in facilitating the alteration of the general public's viewpoint in terms of perceiving the concept of a criminal, understanding them as an individual, and the attitude toward them and their past as a victim. It is only through the process, beginning with alteration of our view, that we can secure additional SUD treatment structures in the future. Only that way could we put an end to the cycle of human suffering where hurt individuals hurt others who, in turn, may hurt others in due course. Even if one understands the reasoning behind the public's emotional and intellectual difficulties in accepting SUD history and the foundations of a user's pain, a major change is still in order. Thus, there is no doubt that changing thought patterns is difficult, let alone the required change of heart toward understanding SUD.

Those unfamiliar with the research, regarding the rate of aggressors who used to be victims, feed on reports and inquiries regarding crime and hurting others, which arouse fear and terror. They find it hard to understand that most addicts seeking treatment from social services used to be victims of stress, abuse, and trauma events. I previously presented the personal stories of Marlene, Adi, Aaron, and others to introduce the reader to the every-day reality I encounter with individuals abused by others, now hurting others in return.

Barsade (2008) documents her work with adolescent and adult sexual assault victims. Her article conveys the human voice rising from sexual assault victims' traumatic experiences. These voices are familiar to me because of my work with SUD.

Now I set my structured, objective writing aside to address the wounded individual's soul, rather than relying on logical thinking patterns, research, and epidemiological findings and theories.

A client who seeks treatment at Rothschild 2 has frequently experienced apprehension and doubt. He often lives with the pain and feeling that he will never be safe on this earth. Hopefully throughout the treatment he will be able to take another path, where he gains trust in me, in us, the professionals unknown to him.

Even while writing the therapeutic plan for the addict, who still lives the memories of the abuse he experienced from those in his closest circles, he will still come across as constantly tense and alert. SUD creates sensitivity to social and intimate situations, even to the extent of fearing them. He will encounter similar situations in the therapeutic process as well, because they bring the psychological states to where we reconstruct intimate and interpersonal closeness situations.

The addict's need for a stable, constant therapeutic figure is intense; a figure conveying empathy, acceptance, order, and even the sense of boundaries; a figure who was not present in his inner world as a child. However, dependency on such a positive figure, who cares, works at making amends, as a therapist, may arouse much fear in him, causing resistance toward the intervention and treatment processes.

As aforementioned in previous chapters, most clients with SUD who seek our treatment, were wounded by stress and trauma, incest, sexual abuse, and even violent assaults in their own homes. Their parents and families were absent at the moment they were severely wounded, and frequently, they were the perpetrators. Thus, intimate closeness may arouse a sense of threat and danger for the addict, since he projects the specific assault case onto the daily, generalized experience of interpersonal, close encounters. With SUD, no protection was received from relatives (the specific case), and there's fear of being hurt by other figures who offer assistance and treatment (the general case).

I notice Adi's recurrent attempts to induce distress situations: "Why is that?" I question her, "Why do you keep hurting yourself, time and time again?"

"I don't know," she replies.

It is Adi's way of demanding attention while testing our sensitivity to her distress. Adi follows the same behavioral patterns she used with her parents. It is a deceiving feeling. Adi may come across as a functional, strong woman, who may even assist her fellow group members. Yet deep down, Adi remains the little girl whose vulnerability goes unnoticed by those interacting with her. Adi lives a complex psychological condition. One part of her, the rational, mature part, realizes she needs help, so she approaches treatment. Another part of her, the wounded, younger part still holds on to anger toward adult figures who offer their help, those who betrayed her trust and failed to protect her in an earlier stage of her life.

In those situations, I wonder how, in fact, Adi would ever be able to trust a therapeutic figure, no matter how empathic and mature, having learned from her rough life experience that she may want repeatedly to test her trust in such a figure. After all, in her life thus far, Adi has cried for help at three levels, but her cry remained unheard by those figures who should have assisted her.

At the first level, during her abusive sexual assault, nobody offered a helping hand; nobody noticed her distress or protected her. Perhaps even those closest to her noticed her distress, but chose to ignore it.

In the second instance, when Adi demonstrated boundless sexual behavior - reckless, provocative, and lacking any intimate component or emotional expression - again her cry went unnoticed.

In the third event, when Adi started abusing drugs to detach herself from her emotions, her entry into prostitution, crime, and personal survival facilitated this. Her disconnection from her emotions, feelings of suffering, and psychological distress allowed her to shield herself from the moments of suffering within the traumatic experience, encountered at the first level.

Even her cry on that level went unnoticed by adult figures who were supposed to assist her. Layer by layer, the pain accumulated, and nobody noticed Adi's suffering. When Adi sought treatment as a drug addict, I wondered how she would be able to trust the therapeutic network we would establish for her benefit. After all, to that day, her experience had shown her that adult figures would not come to her assistance, but rather would attempt to harm her, and most adults she knew had hurt her.

Another crucial point I have noticed in my encounters with SUD throughout my therapeutic work is the dissociation from emotions and the fact that addicts develop dissociative abilities, which they employ whenever they experience a threat or psychological distress.

> When the victim encounters the aggressor's rigidity and persistent determination to hurt, he has no choice but to employ rigid defenses to his aid, such as dissociation, denial, and repression, which facilitate him in surviving the trauma (Barsade, 2008).

It is a question, therefore, of what event preceded the addict's becoming a criminal: were those the ways in which he was brought up, the choices he faced? Perhaps a destructive parental model? Psychological trauma or stress events? The general public questions how rough issues of delinquency, inefficient deterrence mechanisms and means of punishment are addressed. The same public, rather justifiably, strives to draw the aggressor away, and often fails to grasp the motives from which delinquency stems.

> Many researchers have suggested that the broken family constitutes the cause for delinquency. It has been recurrently found that the rate of prisoners coming from families that were destroyed due to a parent's death, divorce, or breakup is much higher than the rate in the general population (Shoham et al., 1987).

"A broken family" is an issue separated into various research factors. What is a broken family? Is a functional family where the child is sexually abused then a broken family? What happens in all those families where a behavioral or functional deterioration on the child's part has gone unnoticed because of the abuse? Are those families functional or destroyed?

There are families who prefer, by force of cultural and social norms, to keep secrets regarding sexual abuse within the family. I have presented examples for such situations in the Ultra-Orthodox and Arab communities in Chapter Two. Do we consider these broken families? Many children, by fear's paralyzing force, and by the force of family, cultural, or social norms do not dare share with their parents the assault they have experienced. What kind of families do they come from? What about families who don't believe in psychological treatment and don't refer their children to therapy following a family adversity, divorce, or other stress event – what kind of families are those? These questions may not be answered through a dichotomous continuum, ranging from "normal" to "broken," since they are far more complex. It is no coincidence that Shoham and colleagues (1987), and a study by Rahav (1976) indicate: "The structure of families of youth arrested in 1961 was not found to be related to the number of offenses they had committed."

I believe that families fulfill a large role in identifying instances where the child has been wounded by stress events, abuse, or trauma, and finding an adequate response to treatment. I also accept family's importance as an initial interventional party in situations identified as such. Yet the thousands of SUD cases I have encountered have proven differently.

Shoham and colleagues (1987) cite: "An extensive employment of physical punishment is often associated with an approximately ten percent increase of delinquency rate among those victims." A study by Hanita Zimrin (in Shoham et al., 1987) reveals that "In Israel, children who have been referred to treatment as battered children, were, several years later, more delinquent relative to other children of the same social setting." When I encounter these victims of the past, even now, after 20 years of work in the field, I still wonder who is going to piece together all those pieces of information to form a conceptual tapestry, and which theoretical and therapeutic structure will more properly address such issues. At this point, I cannot answer these questions.

This book addresses a specific demographic, namely, individuals resorting to substance abuse and delinquency following stress, trauma, and abuse. I do not think this sector reflects on the addicts or criminal population as a whole. Yet it does exist, and needs highlighting and isolation in order to assist those thousands of suffering individuals I have encountered in the past 20 years.

Obviously, there should be a "professional umbrella" to identify situations where a child is wounded by stress and trauma, understand them, explore them, and guide the professionals in the field to take action. Feelings of compassion, concern, and love expressed by an abused child's parents are not enough to prevent the lapsing of his psychological condition. Professional school committees are not sufficient, though they usually act professionally and with care. Rather, a theoretical, therapeutic, and even a practical follow up is required where a boy or a girl has experienced a great deal of psychological pain, if, in retrospect, we realize that an untreated trauma has resulted in substance abuse as self-medication.

As far as I know, in my 20 years of engaging in therapy, no professional discussion regarding adolescents or families with a substance abuse issue has been conducted in Israel. My attempts to seek an explanation as to why such a discussion has not been conducted have been in vain.

Currently, most local authorities in Israel hire addiction experts. They hire education, welfare, psychology, and medical experts. Some authorities also develop expertise in the fields of trauma and post-trauma. In this book, I call for uniting forces toward establishing a "professional umbrella" to cope with issues resulting from stress, trauma, abuse, and early delinquency, at their initial stages. Taking preventive steps would be wise.

Is there a misconception in the way in which drug addiction is perceived in Israel? Isn't a transformation necessary?

> The innovative individual is often a rebel almost by definition. Since he views things differently and presents them in a way that is unique, his creative work is almost automatically placed in conflict with the contemporary cliques, which supposedly possess the right to maintain the status quo (Shoham and colleagues, 1987).

SUBSTANCE - DELINQUENCY - FURTHER SUFFERING – STAGE 4

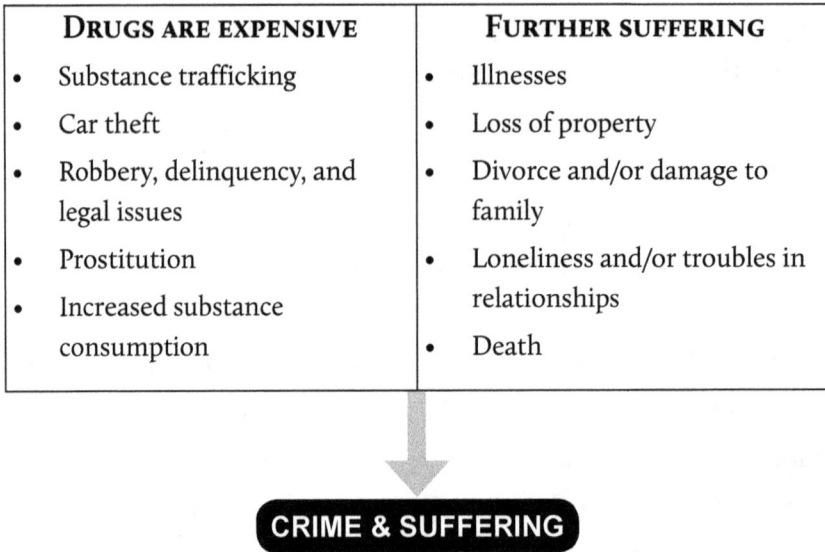

DRUGS ARE EXPENSIVE	FURTHER SUFFERING
• Substance trafficking	• Illnesses
• Car theft	• Loss of property
• Robbery, delinquency, and legal issues	• Divorce and/or damage to family
• Prostitution	• Loneliness and/or troubles in relationships
• Increased substance consumption	• Death

CRIME & SUFFERING

Figure 4: Engagement in Delinquency as Prompting Further Psychological Suffering

The second main idea of this chapter addresses the following situations:

a) Situations of violence where victims continued suffering and being wounded by violent episodes even in their delinquency life

b) Would the individuals who physically or sexually abused others be willing to address the issue through therapy?

The issue addressed in the second point, even if well known to many other therapists treating delinquency and addiction, is rarely raised during therapeutic sessions. I assume the client finds it easier to relate the abuse and wounds he suffered, rather than to relate the pain he caused others, since, as assumed by other authors, the public mind is capable of pitying the victim, expressing compassion toward him, and listening to him, but has trouble hearing an aggressor. Any individual will find it emotionally, intellectually, and behaviorally difficult to develop feelings of empathy toward an individual who assaults others. Reasonably, the general public often has trouble encouraging the provision of treatment to an aggressor.

The following is a citation of Marlene's narrative of being a victim who became an aggressor, in order to demonstrate and more thoroughly explain the ideas presented in this chapter:

Two months ago, in therapy, I spoke of the abuse I experienced, my loss of confidence in Bucharest following the fall of Ceausescu. Until I came to therapy, I had not even been able to connect to my feelings of guilt as an aggressor, as though I made myself forget my own behavior. I would not remember how cruel I was and how badly I had hurt others.

The past few nights, two months after I started therapy at Rothschild, I have not been able to fall asleep; brutal images from the past keep flashing back at me. I remember that while I was using, I joined a group of young addict punks like myself. We had no values or compassion. We totally ignored everybody and everything. We had been hurt so many times. We learned first-hand that there was nobody to assist or save us. We learned to survive in the big city, where all government supervision and law enforcement had collapsed. I had nobody to look up to – certainly not the police officers who raped me after finding me, as a victim of rape, wounded and bleeding; not my mother, who was so drunk that she allowed her boyfriend to rape me, not my guy-friends who gang raped me... I remember one evening when I stayed back at a dance club with a friend of mine. We were the last ones left, and five men raped us. Nobody came to our aid. A few days later, I recruited a few of my friends and we returned to that club. We found three of the men, accompanied by two friends who had not been involved in the gang rape. We dragged them into a dark corner outside the club. I remember their terrified expression, when they realized they were trapped. We dragged them, beating them mercilessly. We literally trashed them. I remember how my friends and I kicked them and their friends. I remember how I kicked them in the face with my shoes. I kicked and hit them with wooden planks until their bones were broken. I wake up at night, hearing the sound of their bones breaking. Only someone who knows the sound of breaking bones would know what I mean.

I also remember the old lady I attacked, with the gang under my leadership. I am afraid we took her life. Dozens of elderly people suffered our violence.

Marlene sounds agitated, and we do not interrupt her.

I was so deeply into substance abuse. I had no conscience or values. I needed money—a lot of money. We would follow old women walking alone, waiting for them to go into stairwells. We would push them and grab their handbags. If any tried to scream or resist, we would kick them, punch them in the face, and beat the hell out of them. How could I have been such a brute? I can't stand myself. My nightmares and feelings of guilt wake me up each night. I am a monster who was hurt by other monsters.

It takes a while before professionals speak out as cited by Najavits (2002): "I drew away from them until I realized how traumatized they were and how substances facilitated in turning off their feelings."

I know it takes a long time, months of therapy. This is the basis of the first point. Instinctively, we reject the aggressor and feel compassion toward the victim. This is human nature. This applies to many medical professionals as well. The establishment, organization, and administration personnel, and many other professionals I encounter, not only laypeople, view substance addiction victims as individuals who need no compassion, a somewhat judgmental outlook, which is a consequence of public opinion because of those individuals' actions and damage to society. Within every one of us, a dissonance emerges, resulting from an encounter with an aggressor, because of the aggressiveness lying within us; we have trouble facing this feeling of dissonance. Professionals are familiar with this complex data, that most addicts, perceived as causing damage to society, have experienced a preceding severe stress, abuse, and trauma.

I question, therefore, what is to be done to bridge the gap between research data and gut feelings, which influence decision makers, considerations regarding budget allocations, and modes of establishing therapeutic policies. It is clear that eventually, an absurd situation forms, perpetuating the rates of abuse and future victims. The questions raised here aim at addressing the cause and effect of violence and delinquency events. We should ensure not to miss our target.

One day, I went with Ofer, a former participant of the Rothschild 2 therapeutic program, to get a copy of his criminal record from the police station in his neighborhood. Ofer was applying for a taxi-driver training course, and he had to present the legal authorities with a document certifying he had had no criminal offenses against him in the last seven years. The data shown in Ofer's criminal record helps me to justify the point I develop in this chapter. The list contained approximately thirty various clauses, specifying further offenses. Most records had been closed due to lack of evidence, and for some, Ofer had been arrested for long stretches of time, up to 30 days at a time. The following are examples from the list:

1. Record closed August 25, 1971, due to lack of evidence. Charged with possession of a dangerous substance; Clause 7 (I) of the Dangerous Substance Order, 1936

2. Record closed November 6, 1972, due to lack of evidence. Accused of a hold up; Clause 228 (I) of the Criminal Law Order, 1936

3. Record closed March 3, 1976, due to lack of evidence. Accused of possessing suspected stolen property; Clause 311 of the Criminal Law Order, 1936

Ofer sought treatment at our clinic at age 56, after 30 years of substance abuse. We know he has hurt dozens of people throughout his life, mainly by damaging property and breaking into homes. Apparently, nobody knows that at six years old, Ofer was sexually assaulted by his stepfather for approximately three years. At nine, he ran away from home and wandered the streets, stealing and robbing to survive. He started using so as not to feel the trauma and abuse he experienced.

Nir is a young man in his early 20s, who looks different to most patients who come for treatment at Rothschild 2. Nir's body is fit. His eyes sparkle and his father, who radiates the impression of a successful businessperson, escorts him.

Initially, I assumed Nir was one of the young individuals who fell victim to substances following raves held in the Carmel Forests on summer nights. Then again, I think he must have got in trouble with the law, and had to seek professional help. Nir requests to speak to me without his father's presence. His father waits in the corridor, sitting at the waiting area. Nir's eyes seem terrified to me. When he starts speaking, he radiates deep anxiety:

> I went on a backpacking trip in India with a few friends when I got out of the army. We wanted to go to Goa, because we heard we could get stoned there. You have to understand: That was my first time with drugs. I never used to experience any unusual psychological experiences. Now I know I am the Messiah's messenger. I am his medium. I have come to convey a message. I know you look at me funny. This is how everybody looks at me. I want to tell you, and only you, a secret: The Messiah will come during Hanukkah.

I felt a mixture of fear and sadness. Only a therapist who is sitting in a clinic with a psychotic individual, caught off-guard, can understand what this feeling is like. I was facing an individual whose responses I could not anticipate, and who was staring at me, without blinking for a second. There was no doubt in my mind as to how Nir and his family were suffering due to his psychological and mental deterioration. In this case, psychiatric intervention was necessary. I continued sitting, facing him. There were moments during which I realized that he was attentive to the voices rising from his odd inner world. I hoped there would be a moment when Nir would pay attention to our connection. There were very few such moments throughout the session.

I wonder if, in his distorted thinking, I could be perceived as somebody who is plotting against him. I feel threatened and scared. For a moment, I regret not informing any of the staff members about going into that session. I break out into a cold sweat.

Intuitively I realize that at this moment, there is no room to hint at any embarrassment or distress, and such a behavior might only intensify Nir's psychotic thoughts. Nir's gaze is frozen. *Hell*, I say to myself, *he's not blinking at all.* I am saved by a knock on my office door that sets me free from his gripping, psychotic gaze.

In my sessions with Nir, after he returned to us from a three-month psychiatric hospitalization stay, I learned that during the Second Lebanon War, a few of his friends had died in battle. Nir started using substances in an attempt to ward off the images of death and loss. The drugs cost a great deal of money. Nir would steal to get his hands on it, hurting old ladies while grabbing their handbags. The trip to India came only later on. Again, I was encountering a victim who had become an aggressor. His initial psychological pain was undoubtedly traumatizing.

Most therapists in the addiction and trauma fields do not treat both disorders, trauma and addiction, simultaneously, even if they are aware of the importance of treating each problem and disorder separately. As maintained by Najavits (2002) and Ouimette and Brown (2003), this yields an absurd state, in which patients do prefer an integrated treatment that addresses both trauma and addiction, but most of them are not given the chance to benefit from such a treatment. Furthermore, most addicts do not undergo a well-structured assessment to identify PTSD in their past, and are not aware of the prospects available for treating PTSD (see the Questionnaire Appendix at the end of the book).

Every week, I meet professionals who come to Rothschild 2 for visits and introductions. I also supervise juniors at the Haifa University Social Work program, and give lectures to visitors and those who express interest. Repeatedly I hear questions such as, "Does the patient agree to address the painful traumatic experiences he experienced?"; "Isn't a longer cleanliness period required in order to begin addressing the traumatic memories?"; "How should we approach a patient who shares his memories of past traumas?"; "Is it even possible to treat past trauma? Wouldn't they rather leave it beehind in the past? How can we one convey these matters to co-ed therapy groups?"

I remember many encounters with psychiatrists who treat drug addicts with conservative approaches regarding their work with SUD. They maintain that treating traumatic memories among addicts would not be right, since "the traumas will throw them back into substance abuse," they tell me.

In her journal, Adi writes about additional experiences of psychological suffering, associated with her substance addiction:

> *He is drunk again. I returned home in the early morning hours from the brothel. He sat facing me, and started to cry.* "Why? What do we need that for?" *He told me. He forgot that he was the one who had said to me,* "Let's go away, move to another town, where you'll work, so that we can save some money. Why do you let other men touch you that way? You are mine, you are mine, mine, mine." *He is drunk, and like every other time, it ends badly. Extremely badly. I try to comfort him, hug him, make him feel good, and snap out of his depression before he explodes.* "Whore," *he screams, and the first slap is quick to follow.* "You're a whore, aren't you? I'll show you a whore." *The punch hurts; my nose bleeds. I'm bleeding. He turns*

me over and cruelly rapes me. I smear the blood off my face, on the wall, so as not to forget. I am fed up.

When everything is over, he cries again, begging for forgiveness, promising it will never happen again. I ask to go downtown for dinner, and in my head, I plot my escape. He agrees to go out for dinner. I shower and cry. I wash off the filth of those before him, and his filth. I wash my face from the dried tears, I dress, and we leave.

At the restaurant, he tells me he's going to buy cigarettes. I offer to go myself. Once I leave, I start running. I escape. I take a cab and go to the owner of the brothel. I tell him I am fed up. I know he has the power and can protect me. After all, would he want to lose his best employee? The next day, I show up for work at the brothel again. My boyfriend arrives, drunk and armed. He is kept out. He threatens that if I don't come out to see him, he would shoot everybody. The owner tells me: "Get out, and I'll send the police to follow you."

I leave, and he takes me to the beach, to talk. He assures me he isn't armed. We walk towards the beach, and I realized we're being followed. We arrive at the beach. I go to take a pee, and then he comes with a gun; a drunkard playing with the gun, touching my body with it, asking how I could leave him and run away. The gun goes off, and fortunately, I am not hurt. I am afraid to die. He says he will kill me and run away. I promise him I will stay with him: "Please don't shoot me. Please, I'm scared. I'm so sorry I ran away from you. I'll do anything for you; I love you, please." *Since he is drunk, he believes me and says he loves me, cries, and asks for forgiveness. We start walking toward the main road and then the police show up, thank God."*

I find it a great pity that to this day, many professionals in Israel who engage in treating drug addicts, are not trained to provide an integrated treatment, addressing both problems, namely, trauma and addiction.

See, at least I have some possessions. Look how many substance addicts end up in great poverty. I own a small house, which is mine; a sweet boy; I managed to keep my beauty. I walked along a dangerous path; I was wounded by tragedy. I have come to seek your help.

So Dalit, a beautiful young woman in her 30s, a single mother to one child, started her conversation with me. Dalit is a young woman of exotic Middle Eastern beauty, her black hair going down to her waist and her eyes brown, sparkling, but so sad.

When you read my life story, you will not want to treat me anymore. I can tell you about myself, but I have such a hard time talking about myself. Between us, anonymous addicts, everybody is on her or his own in terms of writing life stories. I would rather have you read it when I am not in the room. By means of pen and paper, I have managed to write down things I have not told anybody. Read them. Perhaps you will gain a deeper understanding of the individuals you have been treating in the past six months.

I accepted Dalit's request, and, looking back, I understood why she had such trouble relating her life story to me. I was thinking to myself, *what have I actually managed to find out about Dalit to this day? What was I able to draw from the mold of the assessment questionnaire, which I filled on her behalf during our first few sessions?*

In June, I went on a house call to her place. I found a spotless, clean house, filled with up-to-date appliances. Her ten-year-old son had a new computer in his room. We were sitting in the living room, furnished with antiques, drinking the coffee she had made me. I was impressed with her good taste, apparent in every corner of her home.

Have a look at the beautiful photograph that hangs in my bedroom.

I felt embarrassed. A house call by a professional at a patient's home is a sensitive, complex issue. A patient feels as though their privacy has been invaded; the professional peeks into the small kitchen, into the living room, the other rooms, the bedrooms, noticing how clean the house is, or alternately, how dirty it is. It is a rather intimate, embarrassing occasion.

For a moment, the instructions which I provide the social workers who go on house calls come to mind, regarding the caution and safety measures required on these calls. We need to imagine how we would feel if we were offered to drink from a glass in this particular home; how the patient would feel if we refuse the refreshment or drink they have offered us; would asking to have a look in the fridge be an appropriate act, or should we skip that? Should we ask the patient to show us all the rooms, or rather, only a few of them? And here I was, in a complex situation. On the one hand, if I don't go and have a look at Dalit's special photograph that hangs in her bedroom, she might be offended. On the other hand, if I do enter her bedroom, in a house where we are alone, she might misinterpret the moment. These are only a few of the dilemmas encountered by professionals who go on house calls required by their work.

As soon as I stepped onto the threshold, I noticed Dalit's giant photograph, featuring her as she looked in her days of glamour. In a photograph one by one meter in size, Dalit's beauty looks radiant. Her teeth are white and shining; her gaze radiates energy and joy. I understood how Dalit could put on a mask, and how she could charm the world of men. The mask concealed her tremendous suffering. I was thinking how much psychological strength and behavioral effort Dalit needed in order to pose for a picture implying such great pretense. Then again, perhaps my thinking is too far-fetched? Perhaps Dalit simply wished to present me with a beautiful part of her life, a unique photograph implying joy, pride, satisfaction, which she chose to enlarge, frame, and hang in her bedroom... Later, while reading her life story, I was able to better understand her appeal.

I recall myself running away at six; running into the open fields surrounding our settlement. For years, I tried to understand what was behind my escape, but I couldn't.

Thus Dalit chose to present her life story.

I was hiding the whole night, shivering from the cold, scared to death, in a field of dry, prickly thorns. I slept underneath a giant mulberry tree. My mother was not home that night. I remember she had gone to Haifa to visit her sister. My father was a city janitor. I would tell everybody he worked for the mayor, to avoid the shame. In the morning after he left for work, I would sneak home and sleep until my mother returned. From that day on, I have recalled nothing but fear; 30 years of fear. I was scared to be alone, I was scared of the future, and I was scared of the world. The future seemed empty and meaningless. Most of all, I was afraid to say "no."

At 16, I was invited by a guy I knew from the neighborhood to go cruising. In those days, I was still naïve, extremely gullible. Soon the ride became an act of kidnapping, gang rape, and abuse that lasted several days. At home, nobody was concerned about me, nobody looked for me. They knew I could disappear for days, ever since I was a small child. Nobody ever asked me why I was running away.

In that gang, Isaac was the one I feared most. He would threaten me with an x-acto knife, saying, "If you even dare refuse our wishes, I will make you ugly." That was enough to shut me up and make me fully subservient to them and the humiliation, and to the perversion his sick brain would devise. I am not sure you can understand; the paralyzing fear that only people like me can understand. When they released me, or finished satisfying their urges, I would walk, broken and hurt to my parents' home; followed by endless nightmares, crying, a desire to end my life, and showers. Countless showers. I stopped eating. I wanted to die.

Now, I am certain that such an event would make the headlines for a full week. The headlines alone would rip those maniacs to pieces. Back then, who even dared complain? It did not occur to me that there was somebody to approach, that the police and professionals could assist me. It hurts me to think of my inevitable lapse into substance abuse, delinquency and prostitution.

Do you remember how I once told you that using made me a prostitute, and prostitution made me use? That was the vicious cycle of my life, as a call girl and as a substance addict whore. There were years when I counted the money by heads of people who had taken advantage of my distress. I would see men and immediately calculate how much money I could make out of them. There were days when 20 and even 30 men would pass through me.

Twenty men a day, can you imagine? Some were fat, some were ugly and hairy, and others were old. I could not have sex with them without drugs.

Are you sure call girls are sexually abused? Those days, I was certain I knew how to take advantage of others. I especially liked taking advantage of the UN guys. I knew the pub where I could find them. They were so horny, being so far away from home, from their girlfriend, or wife. They came from northern countries and were turned on by a dark girl like me.

Now I have trouble thinking of prostitution. It seems so humiliating. Each man had his demands, perversions, and ways of humiliation. There were men who would pay double for anal and oral sex. I recall with disgust a religious guy who would regularly come to me, to fulfill all the sexual fantasies his wife would not even allow him to talk about. The UN guys were, in fact, polite, courteous, and even behaved like lovers sometimes. They were burly, tall, and blond. Back in those strange days, I thought I was having fun. I was getting laid by the world's greatest hunks, and making money on top of it.

Suddenly, Dalit's face grows gloomy, and her gaze becomes contemplative and sad.

Why am I scared? What has been haunting me all these years? Yesterday, I dreamed that I...

Her speech ceases abruptly; her eyes well with tears. I assume the dream was connecting her to some repressed pain.

I dreamed of visiting the zoo. It was dark and all the visitors had left. I remember stopping by the bear cage. I saw a huge, black bear, hairy, without a face, who was raping a rag doll. I started to run away, screaming while I ran. As I ran, and I was out of breath, I saw my father standing naked and hairy, just like then, when I was six years old, when he caught me. Then, I woke up.

In this story, Dalit is the victim. As a victim, she committed so many offenses in so many episodes of crime and prostitution, that her former history of victimhood is hard to remember. Is Dalit a victim, a criminal, a victim who commits offenses? I hereby draw a situational picture of the therapeutic group, through which I connect delinquency episodes in therapy to risk situations. These situations are common in the SUD world, and assist me in clarifying and demonstrating the idea presented in this chapter.

Every few months, I feel a rift forming between me and the group. This feeling is harsh for me and the other therapists. At the Urban Daily Care Center, we meet the patients, get acquainted, monitor their minds, and work with them approximately eight hours a day, 40 hours a week. The professional staff learns to identify what underlies each patient's smile, indications of sadness, moments of relief, joy, and gloom, as well as the initial relief a patient experiences when they manage to reveal a secret that was hidden until then. We see long years of burden released the moment they sets free the memories associated with repressed stress episodes. When a rift is formed among the group members, as well as between the group members and the treatment staff, our ability to identify client behavior is disrupted. So it is today. My gut feeling as a therapist tells me that the group is hiding a secret. The group members sit there, demonstrating boredom and indifference; not responding to each other; inattentive, not expressing any suffering or pain. My experience indicates that group members do keep additional secrets.

There are several types of secrets among trauma victim addicts, for example:

1. A secret within the group may sometimes imply criminal activity by one of its members. The accomplice patients, the interested parties, might share the secret, or cover up for and defend each other.

2. Sometimes, the secret relates to an intimate relationship between two of the group members. In this instance, the group members defend their fellow members by hiding the secret, since they know we advise group members to avoid intimate relationships throughout the initial stages of recovery. During the initial stages of treatment, a patient still does not know how to regulate and balance their responses and feelings (Najavits, 2002). Hence, intimate relations in these stages yield risky emotional conditions, when patients could relapse.

3. A third condition characterizing a group rift could indicate various benefits obtained by one group member from another. For instance, when one group member offers a fellow member to pick him up in his car in the morning on the way to Rothschild 2, both members will no longer be able to mirror situations to one another, comment, or criticize each other within the group's framework.

4. Substance abuse group members are hiding from each other or from the staff

Seldom, once or twice a year, we choose to conduct a professional intervention, to which we refer as The Shady Business Group. The Shady Business Group grants immunity to all its members. It's granted to any member to open a discussion regarding a group secret, relating to a broken group rule. Even if a client admits to using while in treatment, he will not be expelled from the group, although his behavior contradicts the rules.

In that type of group intervention, delinquency patterns still rooted in the clients' lives usually emerge.

In this activity, each group member is instructed to find a spot on his or her own and think of their recent behavior within the group. Then, he or she writes their secret or any dishonest behavior toward the group on a white board. This is quite a complicated proceeding of exposure to the group members, the treatment staff, and the patient's own self-perception, which he or she is attempting to modify.

I remember the Shady Business Group where the group members revealed the following secrets:

- a month ago he sat down with a friend for a glass of wine
- in the past week, she has been dating one of the group members
- a week ago, he saw group member D selling stolen property
- while preparing the center cleanup duty chart, he purposefully assigned another patient a crappy job
- he drives to the center in his own vehicle, but parks far from the center so nobody will know he gives a ride to another group member every morning
- during the recent holiday when the center was closed, he relapsed twice

The group continues its therapeutic work processes, cleansing itself of the secrets, lies, dishonesty and other processes that can destroy the recovery process. Sometimes, the group activity lasts many hours, until a decision is made, or until the secrets sabotaging the group's work are revealed. Some situations pose a dilemma to the professional staff:

"If we grant the group members immunity, we will not be able to cease their treatment, even if it contradicts the treatment rules and our professional point of view."

In another type of intervention, the group seemed to be stuck in its therapeutic processes. We investigated the relations among its members by means of a sociometric questionnaire. As a team, we felt the group was stuck, making no progress toward its recovery. We felt that fear had overcome its members: The clients weren't prepared to honestly mirror their fellow members, and certainly not to make any comments, or criticize each other. The staff felt s a group climate where the members were sabotaging each other.

I instructed the group members to spread out around the hall, each in a separate area. Each member was provided with a piece of paper and a pencil, on which they were to write discreetly, without signing their name, the name of two group members who were distracting the orderly proceeding of the group, or were damaging the group process. Simultaneously, on the same piece of paper, each group member was to write the name of another group member on whom they could count or rely for help. The clients dropped the note into a cardboard box, in a sort of voting proceeding. All clients had to participate in the activity. Those who were not interested in doing so, literally drew themselves out of the group. The staff took all the notes and calculated the results. One list contained the votes for each group member who had been voted in as a "distracting figure." The second list contained the votes for each group member who had been voted in as a "positive, supportive figure." On the third list, the staff recorded group members who had not been mentioned at all, or other comments that seeedm important for the discussion to be held at the assignment summary stage.

I presented the group members with the results:

1. L. received five votes from his fellow members as a distracting member within the group.

2. N. received four votes as a distracting member within the group.

3. D. and R. received: three votes each as distracting members within the group

4. Y. received four votes as a supportive, encouraging force within the group

5. R. received three votes as a supportive force within the group

6. H. and T. did not receive any votes from their fellow group members, neither as distracting members nor as supportive members. We suppose those individuals do not fulfill a significant role in the group, for better or for worse.

How do we implement the results? We didn't want to sabotage the therapeutic process for those group members who had been described as distracting by their fellow members, but rather enhance the group's condition, in terms of therapeutic work, openness toward one another and trust; eradicate delinquency patterns from the root; and grant strength to the clients for later courses of treatment.

Following a discussion with the group members on the intervention results, we ask those who had been described as distracting to leave the group for a few days, return to their individual therapists, in order to work on the consequences of the message conveyed to them by the group. When the group remained without the distracting or threatening figures, I immediately felt the change, as though a heavy burden had left the other group members' shoulders. The intimacy, sharing, criticizing, and therapeutic climate returned.

The questionnaire indicated the group's positive leaders and the members who still employed delinquent patterns. This is a highly important message for clients who are still in the midst of a therapeutic process, inducing change. Group members mentioned individuals whom they perceived as insignificant. We addressed this point as well.

It is seven in the morning. While still absorbed in documenting those episodes, I receive a text message from one of the center's female patients: "Alex's mother called me. He was found dead on the street. Call me when you can." I feel intense pain flowing through my body. Here we go again.

At this point, I note that our professional layout, as well as the group's regulations, is a consequence of a stinging memory – members who passed away due to relapse. The group's regulations serve as a STOP sign for each and every group member: "Caution: Substances Can Kill!"

I am sad and restless. We had tried to help Alex for many years. We grew to love him. He relapsed many times and left the group but would always return. Alex could not look into our eyes. We could not tell whether he was shy or guarding a traumatic secret that drew him down into a black hole, as is written by Eshel (1997):

> The black hole is some kind of endless pit, with no limit or bottom, an insignificance, nothingness, chaos, and terror that could not be named. Where the mother was torn away too early, leaving behind intense terror and the danger of falling inside.

Had Alex been experiencing a similar feeling of pain in the past few days? For many months, we sat with Alex and spoke to him. Sometimes, he seemed relieved. We also spoke to his aunt. The family had experienced previous tragedy. Both Alex's brother and uncle had committed suicide. Alex had had a spouse who had left him when she was only a few months pregnant. Alex had never seen his son. In the final few months of his life, we had thought we could no longer assist him, as though we had given up. "Perhaps your pain is greater than our capability to assist you," we had told him. Alex had agreed to see a psychiatrist, who had recommended anti-anxiety and antidepressant medications. Following the diagnosis, Alex started the medication. Thanks to his cooperation, we allowed Alex to stay in treatment as long as he took his medication. Alex's condition improved. He was in a good mood and he seemed livelier than ever. I, too, was feeling better. Perhaps we had succeeded in helping him. The staff had planned to include Alex in a new therapeutic group that we were opening, and then, on Sunday, Alex's mother informed us that he was gone. The next day, the employee's text message informed us of his death.

I decide to go for a walk. Perhaps a 20-minute walk will help me relieve the uneasy feeling weighing me down, heavy on my chest. Somebody who was alive the day before is no longer with us. I feel that my feelings are weighing me down. I am sad. I feel sorry for Alex and his family. I am trying to sort my thoughts out. The employee who informed me of the news is a new employee, and I assume that her defense mechanisms are now operating in full force. Perhaps she is blaming herself for Alex's death. I am concerned for her as well. I call her, asking her to come to the center. For her, this is not a workday, but I am willing to assist her, along with the professional staff. We all need an initial process to sort out our feelings and thoughts. Sitting together will help us, too. During our years of work at the center, since 1992, we have lost numerous patients. "Our friends who could not bear the pain," I wrote on the commemoration board I dedicated to those patients, in the area designated for commemoration at Rothschild 2.

What will I tell the group? At eight thirty a.m., I facilitate a sequence group for yesterday's Shady Business Group; how will the group undergoing a crisis to begin with, deal with the death of one of their partners who had walked alongside them on the path? I assume some of them will have difficulty receiving the news. I fear the emotional response of those clients who are in the early days of sobriety. I am concerned for their prospective connection to harsh feelings of loss and death.

One of the staff members repeats the line, "He wouldn't quit," as a mantra. She intends to say that Alex did not want to quit using substances. I respond to her with a typical resolution. "What do you mean he wouldn't quit, for heaven's sake? How can you say that of an individual who has just passed away? I feel Alex just couldn't go on suffering. I can't accept that mantra," I tell her. "You have the right to think it, but you have to learn to say it differently. I have trouble hearing such a statement at this painful moment."

I enter the group session. The group members have not heard the news yet. I can tell by their behavior.

Good morning… since yesterday, we, too, have had trouble with our decision to grant you immunity. I must be honest with you. You raised much shady business and many secrets in this group, which call into question your attitude toward the therapeutic process. However, as a staff, we will keep our promise. There is one more thing I need to tell you: About an hour ago, I received the very difficult news that Alex has died from an overdose.

The group members respond with shock. Their faces mirror profound sadness. Two of the female group members burst into tears.

I want to tell you that we had a rough day yesterday. I felt that your lives meant less to you than other behavioral processes. I think Alex, in his death, gave us one last message: Watch your actions, guard your lives. Substances can kill you, a painful secret which remains hidden can kill you; suffering could kill you. In a heartbeat, Alex shifted from group membership and presence in our lives to the memorial board, honoring our friends who have passed away.

I disagree with the approach stating that some people are natural-born criminals. This is also the message I convey to my patients:

> *I believe that each and every one of you was born into a pure, clean world, where no pain and delinquency exist. None of you summoned the experience of cruel events, which hurt and wounded you. Deep inside, you are not to blame.*

My thoughts lead me back to Marlene, Yoni, Ofer, and many others. Had I been familiar with their delinquent, aggressive side only, the abusive part of their behavior, I would not have been able to assist them, because I too, as a therapist, feel rage and anger toward any individual who assaults another individual without provocation. However, I know very well that nearly none of my patients lapsed into delinquency because of money, or because they were interested in hurting others, or because of the desire to do so. In most cases, delinquency is a consequence of a preceding wound – stress, trauma, and abuse. Delinquency emerges on the grounds of severe, past emotional and physical wounds, an abnormal environment, where there is no conscious treatment, and no law enforcement or order. As therapists, we are to establish the "therapeutic umbrella" I discussed in Chapter Two.

Daniel's story portrays the victim-aggressor relations as well:

> *There were four of us in my parents' home; my brother, my parents, and me. Father would come home every six months. He was in the Navy. I saw little of him. He would come home after a long time at sea to rest, and he would drink. That's how the fighting started. My drunken father thought that when he came for a visit every six months, he would be able to discipline my brother and me, which irritated me very much. In the six months I didn't see him, I missed him terribly, but when he would arrive, everybody would fight. He would beat me terribly with a leather belt and put out cigarettes on my bare skin, and he was violent with my mother. At night, I would*

cry in pain and rage, frustration and sorrow, over the father figure I could not love.

When I discovered heroin, I felt relieved. I wasn't as fearful, and I was far less sad, less anxious and less sensitive. Drugs detached me from my emotions. I could no longer feel pain and sorrow. I loved it for that. When I ran out of money, I started asking for small loans from every person I knew. Soon, though, even that wasn't enough. I humiliated myself, doing anything to get money. I remember wandering around a Haifa hospital one day. I knew wounded individuals with handbags and wallets were hospitalized there and were sometimes all alone. I saw an old man lying on a stretcher in the waiting room. I assumed he was waiting for X-rays. I felt no rage, compassion, or any other emotion toward him. I yanked a valuable gold bracelet off the dying man's forearm. I remember seeing a number on his forearm, tattooed by Nazis at the death camps. Back then, I felt no compassion, pity, or shame. Now I can't even look myself in the mirror. How could I hurt an individual my grandfather's age? How could I behave like such a monster? Thanks for listening to me. I know that only here I can relate that period of my life. I am so, so ashamed of my acts. I am in great pain because of my aggression.

In my 20 years of work at the Rothschild 2 Treatment Center, we have experienced several cases of loss and death. Unfortunately, these patients who had come to us in order to try and save their lives, had chosen to end the stressful and traumatizing memories which were damaging their lives. Choosing death is not a decision viewed as autonomous in contemporary western society. The so-called choice of death issue is a complex philosophical and ethical question, even for us professionals.

Such was the story of Luba, recounted earlier on. Luba came to register at the treatment center with a man who was 20 years her senior. Those chaperones appalled me. There was an air of greediness, exploitation, humiliation, and fear about them; an unbearable possessiveness toward ill-fated women like Luba. My experience has shown me that an intimate relationship is a pathological one, and a dangerous one at that, in Luba's case. I knew Luba would not dare act without her spouse's permission. It was clear to me that Luba would please the professional staff, and avoid criticizing her life as her spouse's hostage.

I asked Luba to show me her identity card, a routine procedure for anybody registering at the center. Her captor held on to the ID, holding it hostage. I asked Luba several questions of information verification and her substance abuse history. I asked the so-called friend to leave the clinic. I wanted to speak to Luba in person, to draw her attention to her condition. We openly discussed the nature of her relationship. In other words, I tried to present her with the risks of a relationship where somebody who describes himself as a friend holds her identity card. All the while, the supposed friend was sitting outside the room, and he might have managed to hear some of our conversation. It was clear to me that he would not allow his captive bird to fly away.

Luba's eyes were sparkling, with a mischievous smile spread across her face, radiating false strength:

I know what you're implying. Don't worry about my condition. Without that friend, I would have nowhere to sleep. You know that. You, the establishment, have no solution to offer me. Where would I wash up? Where would I eat regular meals? I spent six months at a brothel; you know what I'm talking about. There, I lived in rougher conditions. Fifteen gross men passed through me every day. They hurt and humiliated me. They didn't know I understand Hebrew. None of them thought I was suffering, nobody pitied me, thought I was in pain, miserable, troubled.

I contemplated for a moment, "Who was I to criticize Luba? This was her life of survival. Luba knew better than anybody to what extent she was willing to live in suffering, disgust, and filth. "Any door I enter leads to the exit. I'm not worried," she told me, giving me her mischievous, deceiving gaze. She reminded me:

> At the brothel, I worked in order to use and used so I could work. Has it ever occurred to you what a woman like me can do when she is in a room with one of those men? Don't worry. There are two sides to each door – entrance and exit.

The next day, at the state conference for substance addiction professionals, I received a phone call from the Tel Aviv District police: "We would like to check with you if you know a woman named Luba. She was found dead, perhaps from an overdose, at an abandoned house last night. In the pocket of her pants, we found the Rothschild 2 receipt."

Gil was one of the most humane patients I had ever known throughout my years of work. He looked rough, a muscular man, in his mid-40's. Every handshake of his was like an iron pincer, radiating strength and power. I remember that, among the staff, not once did we speak of the way his crushing handshake could be interpreted. We tried to devise a way to tell him to be a bit gentler, as his handshake was painful and unpleasant. How could we tell him, without hurting his feelings? Many years later, I still wondered how I was supposed to interpret Gil's intimidating handshake.

At the time, I did not know his handshake was a sort of mask concealing his depleted mental strength. He was a family man. His boys attended high school and an advanced elementary school class. Iris, his wife, would not leave him for a moment, though she had experienced many years of suffering because of her husband's substance addiction. She said there had been good days, day trips and recreation, but all that was a long time ago. Gil was a violent man, who hit his wife and children when he was in withdrawal and needed another hit.

As many wives of addicted men, Iris, too, was dependent on her husband, supposedly addicted to him. On the one hand, she would take his beatings and humiliations. On the other hand, in Gil's moments of crisis, being needy and submissive, Iris would transform from a battered woman to devoted caregiver, a savior, a woman who finds meaning to her life of suffering. I know many women who live in a cycle of days when their husband is enraged, beats them and hurts them, followed by days when their husband apologizes, becomes ingratiating, and morphes back into a needy husband.

After a year of psychological treatment, when she had gathered strength, she started to speak about getting a divorce. Suddenly, Gil became a desperate husband, a child holding on to his mother's apron. The tables turned. He stopped showing up for treatment at Rothschild 2, and relapsed into substance abuse. We no longer saw him, as if he fell off the face of the earth.

In time, Iris told me that even while he was not attending, he was very interested to know what I thought of him. I was saddened and touched to hear those words. She further related that all his life, Gil had carried profound sorrow due to the loss of his older brother, who had hung himself at their parents' home. Gil was a child when he found his brother dead. His intense longing for his older brother repeatedly called to question why he had committed suicide, leaving him a bereaved brother. "Those were Gil's breaking points," Iris related, "He didn't share that with you in therapy. That was a secret he kept only to himself." The loss of his brother, his desperate wish to see him again, the longing, and the troublesome memories were a heavy burden on him.

His desperate outburst of rage, inability to come to terms with his wife's wishes for divorce, as well as his desperate fear of another awful goodbye, devastated him. He hung himself at home, in the room where his older brother had done the same, 30 years earlier.

Baruch was the third client we lost at Rothschild. At the time, he attempted to put an end to his suffering through psychological treatment, but the collapse of the mask that the drugs gave him resulted in his own collapse. For a long time, I doubted Baruch's capability to live without drugs. Repeatedly, I attempted to advise him to turn to therapy through which he could receive medication to treat his depression and the anxiety attacks he suffered, but he refused, as do many patients. Most fear an addiction to the pills, as well as the stigma associated with "seeing a shrink." He was 30 years old the last time he came for treatment. Female patients thought he was incredibly handsome, but he had never felt that way. He had a magnetic gaze, a combination of beauty and mysterious silence. Women immediately fell for him. None of them knew how mentally shattered he was. Baruch had never shared his sad life events with us. His mother had died of lung cancer when he was seven years old. From then on, he had not had a single day of happiness, only days of tears, pain, and intense longing for her. He found an escape from his agony through heavy drugs; only they managed to ease his longing. His brother had failed to cope with the loss of their mother and had committed suicide two years earlier by overdose.

No professional had ever intervened to treat Baruch and his ill-fated family. Baruch had never mourned the harsh deaths in his family, and the drugs blocked his emotions each time he would start to feel psychological pain. Baruch knew how to do so, and he decided to live. He was not a natural criminal. He was a sensitive, vulnerable individual, who never hurt anyone. As Baruch detoxed, the nightmares began to recur. In his dreams, he would see his mother leaving their home holding a brown handbag, a white scarf embroidered with red roses on her head. Baruch repeatedly pleaded to her to glance back at him just one more time, to wave goodbye, but even in his dream, his mother would not turn around, and would continue walking farther away. Baruch had not had the chance to bid his goodbyes to her before her death. At night, he would wake up covered in sweat, trembling, screaming aloud and in tears. Sometimes, he would rise and chase his mother's imaginary figure. Baruch's wife tried to protect him, to dry the flow of tears from his eyes, to snap him back to reality, to the love and desire they shared to one day become parents.

One Friday night, all of her attempts were in vain. On the 20th anniversary of his mother's death, after he awakened from one of his nightmares, he ran to the abandoned storeroom at the commercial center near his home, and hung himself with a strong nylon thread. Baruch had joined his mother and brother.

Chapters Seven through Nine lead the reader into a discussion on various intervention methods for treating SUD. Clients wounded by stress and trauma episodes developed PTSD, abused substances, and engaged in crime and delinquency in order to get money to buy drugs and reached rock bottom. When such individuals come seeking therapy, it is our duty to provide them with the best professional assistance available.

CHAPTER SEVEN

Treating Substance-Addicted Trauma Victims

One day, five chicks hatched from the eggs. Their mother hen signaled to them with a special tweet whenever she came across some food. We saw the sadness in her eyes when no more chicks remained. They had all been devoured by the black cat.

It is Wednesday at the Rothschild 2 Treatment Center. Eli joins us; he's an experienced counselor from the treatment unit of Kfar Shalem, Neve Eliezer in Tel Aviv. On Wednesdays, we test for drugs. The urinalysis examination is conducted immediately by means of a kit-tester, resembling a pregnancy test. The kit tester examination yields extremely accurate results, even more so than the toxicology laboratory test administered at Tel Hashomer hospital.

Not only does this examination require abundant professional experience, but also great alertness and sensitivity to the client on the staff member's part. Sometimes, a staff member's intuition can identify a client who has relapsed into substance abuse prior to the test. Professionalism and experience fulfill a significant role in the decision making: What kind of substance could we attempt to detect in some of the clients, and who is in an advanced enough stage of their therapeutic process to be exempt from the test?

Wednesdays are also the day we have three therapeutic groups; the first is an open discussion with Eli; the second group discusses processes associated with shame and is facilitated by Maya, and the third group sums up the day with Zehava, referring to the weekly summary to be held the next day.

SUD treatment integrates several elements, and requires several skills:

1. An understanding of and familiarity with the skills essential for treating individuals suffering from stress and trauma

2. An understanding of and familiarity with drug addiction issues, as well as relevant treatment techniques

3. The ability to integrate both disciplines

This chapter discusses SUD treatment through the dual diagnoses of PTSD and SUD (Najavits, 2002).

Since this therapeutic intervention requires professional skills integrating both stress and trauma victim treatment techniques and substance abuse treatment techniques, therapists are to master these intervention techniques. I meet many SUD therapists who feel embarrassed to treat trauma memories among addicts, and who pose questions such as:

- Will the patient relate painful traumatic memories during the substance addiction treatment, and throughout the rehabilitation process?

- Are we, as therapists, to demand the addict be clean before working on the PTSD?

- As a therapist, am I required to cease the PTSD treatment of a relapsed patient?

- Which interventions do I apply with a clean patient demonstrating PTSD symptoms?
- Is psychotherapy appropriate for the SUD population?
- Am I to demand the patient attend NA or AA support groups?

I attempt to respond to these questions in the following chapters. Throughout my years of work, I have encountered questions addressing similar matters, and have received the impression that most clinicians in Israel, even if they are aware of the importance of therapeutic work with SUD, do not employ interventions integrating treatment techniques unique to both issues. The question is, "Why?" How were the foundations of professional intervention with addicts laid in Israel? Why are professionals who treat addiction not trained on the subjects of trauma and post-trauma? My experience has shown that most patients would prefer to receive treatment that addresses both their substance addiction issue and the trauma episodes they experienced, and it is desirable and even necessary in many other senses. Hence, why is it that most treatment centers in Israel do not provide their patients with integrated treatment? In Israel, a broad discussion is required regarding the nature of SUD staff training in all certified institutions.

The issue addressing SUD treatment techniques raises two questions. The former relates to staff training, and the latter relates to PTSD assessment. Most drug-addict clients do not undergo such an assessment, and are not even aware of the prospect of receiving integrated treatment. I am certain we must establish a different professional intervention.

The Rothschild 2 Treatment Center implements various interventions in treating SUD, on several levels:

1. The center assesses a client while raising initial diagnostic assumptions as to their traumatic past, which is typical of most clients seeking our treatment.

2. The center explores treatment methods that are suitable for a client.

3. The center trains its employees to work with traumatized patients.

For many years, I have been aware that survivors of trauma have trouble seeking help due to avoidance, mistrust, symptoms perceived as normal by the survivor, or fear of the prospective outcomes of counseling, as written by Shalev and colleagues (2002). I argue that this difficulty among SUD is great (Also see Najavits, 2002; Williams & Poijula, 2002). It is important that the trauma victim receive treatment as early as possible, when the victim remembers all the details of the trauma, and no repression and amnesia processes have yet occurred (Munitz, 2003). However, working with SUD usually introduces therapists to prolonged trauma that usually occurred long before, with a first traumatic incident, mostly in childhood, through trauma of exploitation, assault, and long-lasting abuse, to recently experienced trauma. My clients have used drugs for many years to avoid traumatic memories. Indeed, I notice that early in the SUD treatment, there are prominent elements of repression and amnesia, without which the clients would not have survived the psychological suffering they were experiencing.

Munitz (2003) indicates that treatment of a trauma victim "requires putting forth therapeutic efforts toward overcoming amnesia through recurrent conversations, where the trauma victim is required to recall in detail all the particulars of the traumatic experience and effectively recall the experience through catharsis." We attempt to follow a similar line of intervention with SUD. The abundant experience I have accumulated throughout my years of treating substance addicts has indeed convinced me of the effectiveness of interventions similar to that catharsis, yet at a time when the client is ready for and interested in that catharsis.

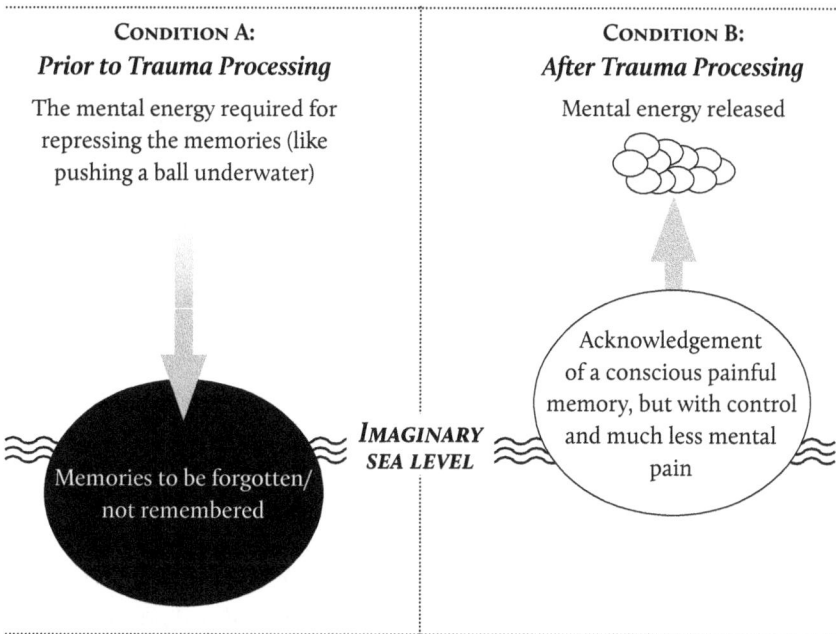

CONDITION A:	CONDITION B:
Prior to Trauma Processing	*After Trauma Processing*
The mental energy required for repressing the memories (like pushing a ball underwater)	Mental energy released

IMAGINARY SEA LEVEL

Memories to be forgotten/ not remembered

Acknowledgement of a conscious painful memory, but with control and much less mental pain

Figure 5. Channeling mental energy toward repressing memories related to traumatic episodes

In my opinion, the main difficulty in employing therapeutic techniques designated for traumatic episodes among addicts stems from the fact that most therapists in Israel who work with addicts have not undergone any professional training based on working with stress and trauma (Zomer & Bleich, 2005; Seligman & Solomon, 2004). Even if many therapists in Israel do address the client's traumatic memories in their therapeutic work, a professional agenda consisting of a planned therapeutic system designated to treat stress and trauma memories among substance addicts is still difficult to find. An example of such a system is cognitive-behavior therapy through imaginary exposure to a past traumatic event, as well as gradual exposure to stimuli related to the trauma. These are unfamiliar to professionals training in the treatment of addictions in Israel (See Chapter Two).

Courtois (2004) states that "the therapist working with cases associated with abuse is responsible to develop specialized knowledge relating to abuse, trauma, memory, and post-trauma treatment, as well as to develop skills associated with that type of treatment." It is likely, she claims, that throughout a therapist's formal clinical training issues related to working with trauma are not addressed, since they are rarely included in the medical and mental health curricula. The fact that issues related to abuse and trauma are not included in professional training programs poses a great challenge for SUD therapists: They are required to learn through their work and actions. This is an erroneous professional structure. This item of data supports my argument that to this day, there is no adequately planned and professional therapeutic plan for SUD in Israel.

I have reviewed the intra-institutional publications I managed in 2008. These comprise the curricula in Israel's universities and colleges in the field of addictions, and the curricula and training programs of The Central Social Workers' Training School in Israel. The review implies that academic material related to SUD therapist training is lacking, and there no such material exists on an adequate professional level.

As the director of one of Israel's largest SUD treatment centers, I could not go on working under such conditions, and therefore felt committed to provide comprehensive training for the Rothschild 2 personnel on how to address their work with trauma victims, and enhance their professional skills. In 2007, the Rothschild 2 staff received a 42-hour workshop on addressing techniques of intervention and treatment of stress and trauma memories.

Most professionals worldwide who work with stress and trauma memories emphasize that gradual exposure to stimuli associated with the trauma will eradicate or reduce the trauma. Although the abundant professional experience in interventions with stress and trauma worldwide indicates that the gradual exposure technique reduces the level of anxiety associated with the trauma (Munitz, 2003; Foa et al., 2004), and as far as I know, may be of great assistance in reducing anxiety with SUD, this technique is hardly employed in the addictions field in Israel. There is no doubt in my mind that implementing this type of therapeutic technique with SUD may contribute greatly to constricting the scope of their recurrent relapses into drugs.

Traumatophobia is a condition in which a trauma victim is overwhelmed with fear and anxiety, resulting in an attempt to draw away from situations that remind them of their wound and avoid them as much as they can. Trauma victims and SUD victims encounter these situations while engaging in intercourse or meeting the relative who hurt them, in nightmares, dreams, or other recollections in their daily lives. How can these recollections be treated by addiction treatment professionals? Which variables should they consider during the assessment and treatment stages? How can they be of assistance if they have not been trained to provide this particular assistance? Additionally, behaviors resulting from high noise sensitivity and a low stimulation threshold may be identified. Drug abusers, like many trauma victims, immediately become irritated by even the smallest stimulus. Whatever was insignificant to them prior to the trauma now causes anger outbursts toward those around them, demanding peace and silence. They have trouble falling asleep, and thus consume increasingly larger doses of drugs. Often, a trauma victim asks those closest to them not to irritate them and be considerate of their great sensitivity, which, in turn, only poses greater difficulties in understanding their issues (Munitz, 2003).

Nevertheless, even if it is inferred that most people who seek treatment for addiction problems from social services have SUD, we must avoid generalizations. Most professionals treating addicts are social workers, hence they are not supposed to identify psychological conditions, but rather only to raise diagnostic assumptions and refer patients for assessment.

I support Courtois' (2004) statement, according to which with all the common signs identified among post-trauma victims, we are to adopt a neutral therapeutic position in relation to the prospect of previous stress and trauma episodes experienced by a client, even in relation to past abuse. Therapists should make a point to pose open-ended questions, without jumping to conclusions too early. A skilled therapist, not hanging on to unequivocal diagnostic assumptions, will eventually succeed in reaching out to any client who is interested in undergoing a therapeutic process in order to cope with their traumatizing memories.

WE HAVE ALL BEEN WOUNDED
SPEAKING UP IS NEITHER PRESSURED NOR INSTRUCTED

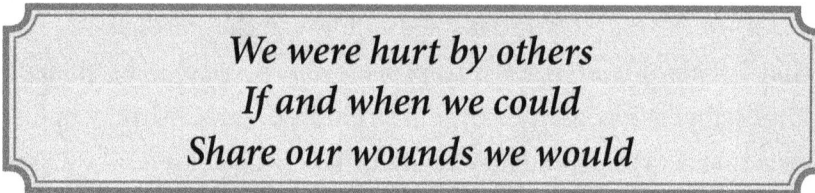

We were hurt by others
If and when we could
Share our wounds we would

Picture 1: A therapeutic message designed to calm clients

My clinical experience shows me that it is not necessarily correct to assume that those who do not remember most of their childhood memories are repressing or denying childhood abuse. In my opinion, several more elements and variables are involved in this context, of which the therapist is to be alert:

The therapist needs to be open to the likelihood of other traumatic occurrences in childhood. These may account for the post-traumatic symptoms apparent in a client (not only stress and trauma episodes involving violence and sexual assault).

The therapist is to notice a declined attention capability and limited motivation for work as well as the feeling that the individual may not withstand the recollection burden. While at home, a client is unable to draw pleasure from resting. They are nervous and edgy, tending to smoke extensively, and bug their family members. Often "because of their noise sensitivity, they avoid listening to music, watching television, going out to the movie theater or to social gatherings," (Munitz, 2003). These may be post-traumatic symptoms, with which we must be familiar while working with addicts. The trauma victim often complains of severe insomnia, as well as detailed dreams, nightmares, loss of sexual desire, and sometimes even weight loss or eating disorders.

Many people, including family of addicts, blame the addiction rather than other known syndromes apparent in the traumatized individual, which they have suffered prior to their substance addiction. Substance abuse is the so-called treatment instrument available to the user. We, as professionals, must provide them with other professional instruments that allow them high quality rehabilitative activity, to fulfill a greater adaptive role in life; instruments through which they can cope with the feelings associated with their daily recollection of the trauma.

There are many therapeutic approaches to working with stress and trauma victims. Each offers a different therapeutic intervention method, but their common core is the understanding of the soul. I outline in bold some of the therapeutic approaches I have adopted while working with SUD at the Rothschild 2 Treatment Center.

Psychoanalytic Theory - Freud brought a breakthrough in terms of understanding the soul's components and portraying human experience and behavior. His dynamic approach to psychological being constitutes a core component of my work with SUD as well. The justification: While treating psychological problems, Freud offered healing by catharsis, through a process of relief called abreaction. The essence of the treatment is to elicit repressed memories, perceived as signifying essential traumatic experiences, and bearing a powerful emotional load from the past, and release them. Freud assumed that a client represses traumatic experiences to the unconscious, since these pose an unbearable difficulty and threat to their psychological being. Freud connected the repressed psychological energies to a dynamic psychological process, which he viewed as full of active, dynamic psychological energy. He argued that painful, traumatizing experiences, repressed by psychological forces into the unconscious, wish, by their energetic, psychological force, to return to one's mind. In the one hundred years that have passed since Freud published his theory, human suffering stemming from a traumatizing episode has not changed, but the attempts to account for such a condition and the prospects of treating it have expanded. The unconscious in Freud's model is the human soul's core. It is the part that stores the repressed matter, which we attempt to avoid feeling and experiencing. In the dynamic model, where Freud portrays psychological being, the soul's forces of curbing and repression are influenced by an anxiety that signals danger to these individuals. These feelings of anxiety fulfill a key role in psychological processes. Hence, Freud concluded that one of anxiety's implications is an encounter of threatening feelings, repressed to the unconscious, and the attempt of these threatening feelings to burst out into consciousness. I encounter these types of feelings on a daily basis in my work with SUD. Initially aroused by the stress and trauma episodes, feelings are silenced by substance abuse. Later, when the so-called shield provided by the substances collapses, they rise again, threatening to burst out in the form of extreme anxiety, during which the individual is overwhelmed by feelings with which they cannot cope. These situations also include harsh psychological feelings aroused by severe stress and traumatic episodes. In my work, I very frequently meet individuals who have been affected by a traumatic episode, but who are repressing it with all their might. One of the ways in which my clients deny a traumatic memory is prolonged substance abuse. The latter is repression. According to Freud, some clients repress the severe traumatic experiences they underwent by using the soul's defense mechanism, namely repression. Zomer and colleagues (2005) refer to these situations as dissociation processes.

Otherwise, some clients repress stress- and trauma-related memories by abusing psychoactive drugs. In both situations, the so-called unconscious goal of the client is to disconnect their harsh feelings from their daily thoughts. I disagree with the statement made by many SUD therapists who argue that therapeutic work with these clients will not always be effective, and that for some it may even be risky. In my opinion, the repression and dissociation mechanisms applied to the stress-related memories have prevented them from processing the memories related to their traumatizing experiences and thereby have protected their soul. SUD therapeutic intervention involving "exposure" requires a high degree of caution. Exposure may overwhelm a client with tough feelings, with which they may not always be able to cope. We should bear in mind that the SUD client has abused substances for many years in order to form that feeling of dissociation and repression. Now that the other conscious states among trauma victims and SUD are familiar to us, we can assess them among clients whose traumatic experiences are located in the so-called "in between" recollection area, according to Freud. When we realize they are capable of processing them, we will be able to recommend their referral to a therapeutic process integrating cautious, moderate exposure and processing of the trauma. This process requires great skill and expertise in SUD treatment. Any encounter with anxiety-inducing memories associated with traumatic experiences among SUD may prompt their relapsing into substance abuse in order to blunt the psychological pain that has been aroused. Within the framework of therapeutic intervention, we have to progress carefully, one step at a time. On the one hand, we remove the defenses that the SUD has established for many years through substance abuse. On the other hand, we support them and guide them on how to cope with past memories.

Beck's Cognitive Therapy (Beck, in Munitz, 2003) portrays another important aspect to personality theories. Beck maintains that the soul consists of structures that assess the situation and process information regarding external and internal occurrences that the individual experiences. The cognitive process integrates affective and motivational variables. By means of such structures, human behavior is designated to serve a goal of survival. For the sake of this chapter's discussion, I address Beck's theoretical model, particularly the part portraying the human coping state under circumstances of threat and survival. When a threat emerges - for the purpose of this particular discussion, stress or trauma experiences - an individual employs four different psychological mechanisms, as follows:

1. An affective mechanism that responds by feelings of anxiety or aggression

2. A cognitive mechanism that processes the feelings of threat

3. A motivational mechanism that arouses the body for action

4. A monitoring and control mechanism that organizes the body's actions (similar structural terms are to be found in Foa et al., 1998, 2004)

In order to teach clients to identify clues that could arouse their fear and these clues' association with the stress and trauma they experienced, we at Rothschild 2 rely on elements from Beck's cognitive theory in various therapeutic interventions. Furthermore, we provide clients with other coping instruments for psychological situations where paralysis or fear emerge while recalling traumatic episodes or situations where various clues might remind them of their traumatic experience. Integrating these therapeutic instruments, that rely on understanding stress and trauma according to Beck's cognitive theory, enables us to facilitate the implementation of a greater variety of intervention and treatment techniques for SUD.

In their book, Zomer and Bleich (2005) address the importance of intervention within a brief, efficient time stretch when dealing with stress and trauma stemming from terror and war related events. I believe that many principles cited in their books are also effective in interventions addressing stress and trauma stemming from sexual or other types of abuse, even if these took place months or years before. I cite some of these principles, by demonstrating therapeutic intervention with a client named Anne.

> The intervention goals in the immediate stage, namely the acute reaction stage, are designated to moderate the level of distress, balance psychological condition, and restore functioning to as full as possible in those suffering an acute stress reaction (Zomer & Bleich, 2005).

The therapeutic encounter with Anne demonstrates the resemblance of the "acute response" stage intervention and the therapeutic intervention process in SUD:

Anne, a single, 24 year old, came for treatment at Rothschild 2. We knew Anne from her previous attempts to join the treatment program, all of which had failed. Anne related that two days prior to her entry into the treatment program she had shot a large dose of heroin, thereby "breaking" her six months of sobriety from drugs. She had sought death to put an end to her suffering. We knew she was under psychiatric supervision, receiving anti-depressants because of a complex episode she had experienced approximately six months before, when a friend of hers died in her arms while injecting heroin into a vein. We assumed that Anne's past was full of traumatic experiences, still unknown to us, but that would be revealed in due course. We also assumed that her level of anxiety was very high whenever she detoxed from drugs.

The memories of Anne's trauma flood her. She feels as though she is experiencing them here and now, sinks into depression and anxiety, and suicidal thoughts emerge. Even if the stress and trauma Anne experienced were very early in her life, they have not completely faded. Anne would be protected, so to speak, as long as she used. Using heroin blunted her psychological pain and supposedly froze her feelings. When she quit using, she was drawn again into her traumatic past. This is a dangerous condition. Removing the dissociation and repression defenses provided by the drug aroused extremely harsh emotions in her. We viewed Anne's condition as identical to that of a trauma victim who was not employing dissociation defenses. On Anne's tenth day at Rothschild 2, during the therapeutic group session, she suddenly rose from her seat, and ran outside, saying, "I need a hit right now. I have no air and no desire to live." In retrospect, we realized that, at that moment, Anne was experiencing traumatizing memories that had arisen, memories related to the sexual trauma she had experienced. The supposed defense, which heroin had provided her over the past decade, was not operating and she was in a dangerous psychological condition. Irresponsible use of heroin, at that stage, could have caused her death due to the changes her body had undergone on shifting to different doses of the drug. Under such circumstances, our professional intervention is similar to an intervention with a trauma victim, as described by Zomer and Bleich (2005) in their book. A staff member goes to speak to Anne, trying to calm her down with words and breathing exercises (calming the somatic system by breathing is routine at Rothschild 2. I address this concept further in Chapter 9). The staff member assists Anne in orienting to the situation, demonstrating to her the love that everybody, the group members and the staff, feel toward her:

The staff member attempts to normalize Anne's extreme reactions, clarifying that her condition makes her reactions reasonable, common even, and that they would pass.

The staff member encourages Anne to express her feelings aloud.

The staff member counts Anne's achievements, reminding her of the optimism she had shared in the previous day's session.

The staff member offers Anne a glass of tea.

The staff member repeats the specification of symptoms typical of Anne's condition at this stage of treatment.

At this point, the staff member informs Anne's mother of Anne's condition, asking her to come and pick up her daughter when the activity ends.

The staff member mentions Anne's great care for her mother over the past few days of treatment, and the mutual love expressed between them.

The staff member asks Anne about the therapy group members to whom she feels close, or whom she loves.

The staff member supervises Anne for the two hours that follow. The group members hug her, expressing their support of her choice to remain in the treatment center, rather than relapse into drugs.

At a later stage of the treatment, two months later, I saw Anne participating in several groups, deeply empathizing with her female friends' stories, particularly with rape episodes they had experienced, even if these had occurred years before. Without the shield of the substance to blunt her feelings, Anne experienced tremendous anxiety, which she would share with nobody. The feeling of anxiety threatened to overcome her, and she wished to return to a condition where she would not experience her psychological pain. She wanted to relapse to heroin use, which was her most familiar defense mechanism.

Various patients treated for trauma differ from each other. "Some spontaneously reveal a history of trauma and abuse at the very beginning of therapy, while others do not reveal that information even when directly questioned," (Courtois, 2004).

We do not to seek to know everything.

Expressing curiosity as for what tomorrow may bring. Sometimes the reason is unknown.

Sometimes the cause is hidden.

Some things are hidden, beyond our understanding and knowledge.

We may act apparently for no reason. Not everything is to be inquired and questioned.

It is fine not to know it all. We do not seek a reason for each step taken.

We do not seek to reveal every secret.

Sometimes the reason is unknown, but we do not despair, rather we continue further down the road.

Some things are hidden...

There must be actions we have taken, not just a few.

If we have not yet found their reason, perhaps someday we will.

(Lyrics: Tami Levi Music: Moshe Nagar)

In working with SUD, we are aware of the differences between various patients in terms of readiness to recall past stress and trauma experiences. Thus, in this therapeutic work we include only clients who are willing and interested in participating. Not surprisingly, most are interested. The clients differ by their degree of readiness to reveal traumatic memories, as well as by their ability to address and handle those memories. Thus, we assess each client individually, based on their development and growth through the course of treatment. At Rothschild 2, many sources of information are available to rely on for client assessment. The professional staff's work follows an integrated approach, as well as collaboration among all professionals within therapeutic intervention with a client. Abundant information is yielded at each professional discussion. A client's private therapist presents his professional viewpoint, his group therapy facilitators input the clinical information gathered within his group's framework, while the day center staff provide details about him, based on their acquaintance with him through daily encounters, over a six-month period. The teamwork facilitates data analysis, thereby benefitting the client. The common model of post-trauma treatment consists of stages, initially aimed at balancing and enhancing a patient's functioning. Courtois (2004) presents a three-stage model, employed in treating a client who is a victim of stress and trauma during the assessment conducted prior to therapy:

Stage One: Aims at acquiring self-confidence, balance, and functioning; immediate problem and crisis solving, enhancement of interpersonal functioning, and development of therapeutic alliance

Stage Two: Aims at addressing traumatic content and emotion, regulated in correspondence to patient's abilities

Stage Three: Aims at addressing unsolved issues after the trauma processing stage

One can identify similar lines of action in the stress and trauma intervention model mentioned by Zomer and Bleich (2005) and the model by Courtois (2004). Both highly emphasize a trauma victim's functional balancing in the first stage of intervention, as well as calming of emotions and some normalization of psychological pain. I am certain that many psychological trauma therapists are familiar with and follow these interventions. This is the way we practice our therapeutic interventions with SUD as well.

Williams & Poijule (2002) - A three-stage model: "Functional balancing, working on trauma-related contents, and conclusion of therapeutic processes." These researchers offer well-structured, detailed programs, consisting of a hundred exercises and assignments, all of which may serve the trauma victim's therapeutic process. Their book is recommended for reading, as it presents various intervention methods through well-structured, ready-to-use worksheets, all of which are therapeutic interventions with stress and trauma victims.

I adopted the "black hole" concept from researchers **Hertzano-Letty & Toder (2006)**, who were mentioned in Chapter Four. These researchers indicate that treating post-trauma victims involves sensitive, delicate treatment, since any step taken without caution toward addressing the traumatic memory may strongly draw the client into the pit of depression. This is a feeling with which most therapists supervising a therapeutic process with trauma victims, including SUD, are familiar. Hertzano-Letty & Toder (2006) refer to this dangerous retreating state as "the black hole," a concept adopted from the astrophysics field, coined by Bion (1970) in the psychological literature.

As far as I understand my work with SUD, and following Hertzano-Letty & Toder, the plunge into the black hole can be attributed to the feelings of sadness, depression, and despair experienced by the SUD in the initial stages of treatment, which could lead to substance abuse. The treatment, as stated by Hertzano-Letty & Toder, should involve "an entrance into the black hole as controlled, cautious, and conscious, without escape or exerting any external force." Furthermore, "entering the so-called black hole together with the therapist allows introspection, understanding of the past experience, and discovery of new personal meaning in the traumatic wound." In SUD treatment, the risk is not only the addicted patient's plunge into a black hole of depression, but their return to substance abuse to escape that feeling. This is the immediate risk, and therapists are to be on guard. If Anne, like other addicts, was to inject an overdose of heroin at a moment of crisis, she would very likely die.

Thus, I expect a skilled SUD therapist to investigate the coping mechanism and the patient's safety network prior to beginning trauma treatment. It is important that an SUD therapist know how to identify the adaptive, therapeutic, and human sources of support possessed by a client and be able to assist them in future moments of crisis. It is important to teach a sober addict how to avoid their familiar safety network, namely, substance abuse, and, turn to other therapeutic tools as an alternative. It is also important to investigate an addict's coping abilities when encountering negative emotions. It is vital that such an investigation be conducted prior to their beginning trauma treatment (also See Ouimette & Brown, 2003).

Toval-Mashiach and Friedman (2004) address trauma treatment through the narrative and cognitive mode of coping. They state: "Identity development is the process through which one's life story is constructed. Psychopathology is, in fact, a story that has been damaged, and psychotherapy is an attempt to mend it." They further maintain that "trauma severs the sense of continuity and regular flow of daily life." In practice, their statements are supported by my conversations with my patients who argue that they are not the individuals they were prior to the traumatic episode. Most of them view the episode as "an experience of a split between the life prior to the trauma and the life following it," an undoubtedly rough experience. We treat clients who have been addicted to drugs for many years, most of whom underwent a trauma and carry with them an unbearable life story. While constructing the SUD client's new narrative, throughout the therapeutic process I provide them with definitions and instructions regarding proper behavior and action patterns. I intend for a clean addict not only to portray their life story in a newly constructed cognitive light, but also to construct a new behavioral pattern, since their narrative recovery will begin by healing their present life through new actions.

Perry (2002), too, views the rehabilitation of stress and trauma victims as the healing of their narrative through the historical reconstruction of their trauma.

Normal memories bear a story-like, narrative nature, and are subject to willful retrieval and discarding. They have their own time and place, and the emotions they arouse when they emerge are regulated, more controlled, and less threatening. Traumatic memories, in contrast (author's comment) appear with no control or willful ability to stop their flow.

Many SUD patients are flooded by harsh memories. They suffer nightmares, difficulties in daily functioning, and sexual dysfunction. Furthermore, they suffer anxiety and depressive affects (see Anne's, Yoni's, Ofer's stories, and the stories of others).

I believe that psychologically treating a client's traumatic memories while integrating new life practices, promotes a link between the traumatic memory and their present life, thereby somewhat easing their psychological suffering. This integrated treatment can contribute to enhancing a client's "psychological defense network."

It is advisable to plan the treatment of stress and trauma victims on a time line: "It is important that the intervention occurs in the acute stage of the syndrome's development, in an attempt to prevent its rooting as a chronic syndrome, which is extremely difficult to treat," Perry (2002). (Such views may also be found in the works of Zomer & Bleich, 2005; Courtois, 2004.) However, for many addicts, seeking treatment only occurs after many years of psychological suffering. As mentioned in Chapters Nine and Ten, there are many similarities to the narrative therapeutic approach cited by Tuval-Mashiach and Friedman (2004), Perry's approach (2002), and the exposure in therapy cited by Foa et al (2004, 2007).

The resemblance between the treatment of victims of trauma caused by various events and SUD treatment, has opened my eyes to the need to establish professional tools of intervention for the wide SUD population. It is for good reason that I repeatedly lay out this proposal throughout my book. The conceptual, theoretical, and practical resemblance of the narrative approach and the "exposure in therapy" is clearly evident in the professional assumptions and trauma victim treatment methods. Hence, it should be investigated how these components can be integrated into therapeutic work bearing commonly known theoretical foundations and effective therapeutic instruments.

I offer the following instructions:

A patient should be provided with an explanation regarding the work methodology, including the chronological reconstruction of the stressful experience, and portrayal of therapeutic goals. There should be advance clarification that the process might be tough and sometimes even painful, but that it is of great importance and might be effective. As maintained by Perry (2002), "this time we will face the psychological pain without the use of a substance,"; "The therapist's role is to facilitate the patient by reducing their distress." This:

> ...[F]acilitate therapists in concluding that the temporary suffering experienced by the patient early in the treatment is justifiable. [...] It may be compared to the temporary suffering caused by a surgeon to his patients during heart surgery in order to improve their quality of life in the long term (Foa et al., 2004).

The therapeutic path loaded with past baggage is not supposed to be of surprise to a patient. After all, deep down they know what it is that they have been escaping and why they have abused substances for so many years. It is important to inform a patient that during the treatment period, the intensity of the sense of "intrusiveness" of stress and trauma memories could be aggravated, but would ease in the course of time, as stated by Perry (2002). Such is the case regarding SUD: On the one hand, it is important to explain the psychological difficulty they could encounter throughout the process of addressing their traumatizing memories. On the other hand, they should be provided with new tools for coping with crises not by means of substances (broadly addressed in Chapter Nine). SUD treatment should emphasize the danger of death lurking with any relapse to substance abuse. The relapse implies a moment or period of time during which they are experiencing a psychological crisis. Treating SUD requires the establishment of an additional support system; therapy groups, support of fellow patients, family support, staff support and messages from fellow NA members. Prior to beginning the trauma treatment, their psychological strengths must be assessed, so that we know how to assist his ability to cope without drug abuse in future crises.

Instructions for a patient:
We request that you relate everything that happened to you during the event; what you saw and heard, what you did, what you thought, and how you felt, minute by minute (Perry, 2002).

A patient is requested to recall the trauma in as great detail as possible while focusing on thoughts, emotions, and sensory components (Foa et al., 2004).

Every session begins with reviewing the reconstruction conducted in the preceding sessions (Perry, 2002).

If a patient concludes the story within less than forty-five minutes, they must relate the story from the beginning, and repeat until the end of the planned session, write Foa et al. (2004).

This repetition affords the opportunity for recurrent coping, through the memories that flood the client, arousing their anxiety toward a situation. As mentioned previously, these approaches call for touching on the traumatic memories and coping with the anxiety aroused by those memories. As a therapist, I believe in this type of therapeutic intervention for SUD as well, based on my awareness of the lurking risk they are to face, namely, to make use of moments of psychological distress. In her article, Perry cites the summary by Foa and Street regarding treatment through exposure of memories related to traumatic episodes:

There are three essential components to the therapeutic approaches which have proven to be effective in reducing the level of symptoms among patients:

The treatment should include an exposure element, which arouses the emotions associated with the experience (emotional engagement).

The treatment should organize the trauma narrative and construct it.

The treatment should address the patient's basic beliefs regarding themselves and the world (Perry, 2002).

Briefly: Exposure, construction, and faith.

Work with SUD at Rothschild 2 includes another factor, namely, practice. While recalling the trauma, the patient is exposed to emotions which to them imply a risk, and which used to lead them to relapsing to substance abuse (Ouimette & Brown, 2003). Throughout the treatment program, we demand practice from the patients, meaning that they attend regular, consistent sessions with their individual therapist, participate in the weekly therapy groups to which they have been assigned, and consistently show up for urine testing as a routine follow-up on their sobriety from drugs. Each stage of practice is examined based on a measurable behavioral parameter of the change and regression and change processes in the long term, on a consistent, regular basis. Just as the client's psychological pain aroused by the therapeutic content could cause a relapse into substance abuse, so too their practice can facilitate growth and even lead to a cessation of substance abuse.

In her therapeutic work with memories related to trauma among drug addicts, Najavits (2002) too emphasizes restoration of balanced daily functioning, engaging in therapeutic work, and regulating emotion arousal following trauma recall. All of these take place through a consecutive and consistent process, until therapy ends. There is a clearly visible common therapeutic denominator between the approaches calling for addressing trauma memories and the approaches calling for calming down a client, balancing their daily functioning, and regulating their extreme emotional responses (See Figure 1).

In one of the tasks she was assigned through narrative therapy at the Rothschild 2 Center, Nurit relates the following:

> Yesterday, when I left Rothschild, my feelings were weighing me down. All day I thought about what had happened. There were moments when I regretted sharing my story, but I am pretty happy that it happened to me at Rothschild. I have learned to address even those issues, my memories; my pain. True, I do have thoughts of using drugs occasionally, but I do not want them to guide my actions. For that reason, I came here, to treat myself, to ease my pain, so I no longer need drugs. The daily schedule drags me out of bed, so to speak, obliging me to show up for treatment, not to give up on myself. I find the treatment helpful, at the points where I failed to facilitate myself on my own. Although I am pretty ashamed of what happened to me, I do not regret sharing my traumatic story.

In that same group session, Louie relates the following:

> When I was at my parents' this past weekend, I leafed through my photo albums, which I had not seen in years. The photographs showed me as a six-year-old child, the age I was assaulted. I questioned myself, "Where did the child from the photographs go, that boy who used to be so happy?" Only after I dared share my story in therapy, I also dared to return to look at photographs taken at that time in my life that I have attempted to erase by doing drugs. I believed that if I didn't open the album, my photographs from the time when I was six years old would disappear from my memory. Approximately

*three months after I joined the group, my fellow-members allowed
me to relate my life story. I now feel so relieved, as if I have spat out a
terrible secret threatening to strangle me day and night. I thank you
for not blaming me, for understanding and empathizing with me.*

Saul relates the following:

*I served three years in prison, which was actually the pruice I paid for
the assault I experienced as a child. Deep inside, I felt I was totally
alone. I felt worthless. In prison, I didn't realize I was sticking to
terrible secrets, and continued employing pleasing behavior toward
those around me and toward myself... I didn't feel right hurting
others, but neither could I feel my own pain, so I couldn't feel theirs.
Deep inside, not only did I feel humiliated, but I also felt exploited.
This feeling wouldn't leave me. Most of all, I couldn't understand
why, to this very day, the moment I dared share my own story, I was
not angry with those who hurt me. I thought I was weak, that I was
afraid; that I would hold on to the secret in my heart all my life. In
treatment at Rothschild, I have no time to escape into my fears and
habits, to use. Tomorrow morning I must be here. The group will be
waiting for me. It means so much to you, my fellow group members,
that I continue to stay clean.*

The therapeutic interventions indicate the prospect of integrating
components of various theoretical approaches with future uniform
therapeutic work. The approaches portrayed thus far are only a portion
of the trauma-victim treatment methods presently known worldwide.
Additionally, in this chapter, I wish to extend the therapeutic domain
to include not only the treatment of trauma-induced wounds, but
also the treatment of complex wounds resulting from trauma and
addiction.

I am portraying the therapeutic, emotional, behavioral and
disciplinary system implemented at Rothschild 2, and the work
regulations and foundations on which the treatment is based.

Individuals come for treatment at the center after many years of psychological pain, living lives controlled by stress events, trauma, delinquency, crime, imprisonment, illness, and, of course, drug abuse - all while being far removed from the socially acceptable, normative rules of behavior.

The professional staff offers two main group-categories to clients who come to Rothschild 2:

1. The Ambulatory Group - A group of clients seeking ambulatory psychological treatment and rehabilitation. In this type of treatment, the client comes for a session with a social worker during the week. They are required to perform a urinalyses three days a week, on Sunday, Tuesday, and Thursday afternoons. They also join a therapeutic group which meets one evening a week, for a period of six months.

2. The Municipal Day Care Center is a "train station" group consisting of 15-20 clients. These clients come for six months of highly intensive treatment, Sunday through Thursday, from 8.00 a.m. - 2 p.m., aside from the requirement specified in category 1.

At the day center, three different therapeutic groups are offered every day: Life Stories, Psychodrama, Animal Assisted Therapy, Mirroring Group; a group working on shame; Daily Review, and others.

In the groups offered at the day center, patients about to complete their six months of treatment integrate with patients who have just started therapy. The group's senior members guide the new ones, assisting them in adjusting to the therapeutic structure offered at Rothschild 2. It is impossible not to be deeply touched when witnessing the mutual support demonstrated by those who have emerged from a common hell of stress and trauma experiences. As stated by Yalom and Leszcz (2006), "The senior group members often assume the role of messengers by providing the doubtful, unconfident new members with spontaneous testimonies."

In order to provide clients with a therapeutic setting that enables change and growth, at Rothschild 2 we are required to create a setting free of delinquency patterns and situations posing a physical or verbal threat. We adhere to rules such as strict maintenance of activity schedules and absolute abstinence, not only from substances but also from non-prescription medications and medication unapproved by a physician.

As a therapeutic structure, Rothschild 2 does not allow any emotionally intimate involvement among its members, preventing the possible ridicule amongst themselves. The therapeutic center offers psychological aid and support to clients in a psychological crisis. All these are present and equal in importance to the discipline and behavior rules required in both structures mentioned above (see Figure 6). The structured daily schedule allows clients to become acquainted with each day's activities; the urinalyses are a given, and are prepared in advance, facilitating the supervision of a clients' abstinence from substances. Additionally, urinalyses are performed at Rothschild 2 for clients about whom the staff is extremely concerned due to their fragile state. We are interested in readily identifying risk factors in our clients, therefore we attempt to identify any behavior that arouses questions or doubts as to their abstinence from substances, or that points at their suffering an unusual and extreme psychological crisis due to having been stripped of the defensive shield previously provided by the substance. Along with the harsh content raised in therapy, which arouses memories of trauma episodes, the therapeutic structure supervises clients by examining measurable behavioral parameters of action, as well as parameters pertaining to tracking attendance in treatment. The times of individual and group sessions are pre-determined. In addition, clients are instructed in attire that is appropriate for the therapeutic setting, and other behavioral rules.

Noticing and identifying any change that occurs in a new patient within a few days, in terms of their appearance and personal behavior is highly important in my eyes, because I strongly believe this change may demonstrate willingness on the client's part to obey the staff and its professional recommendations. As long as a client is in treatment, the treating staff will do its utmost to be attentive to their feelings and assist them. It is only under the following three extreme conditions that clients are withdrawn from the treatment program offered by Rothschild 2:

1. Demonstration of physical violence (this condition includes both threatening to enact physical violence, violence toward animals, and, of course, violence against a fellow group member or a staff member)

2. Accumulation of five negative stars, symbolizing five events when the client failed to meet the therapeutic structure's discipline and behavior rules. The five prospective instances could be substance abuse; recurrent failure to abide by schedules of therapeutic activities or urinalyses; failure to pay the small fee to the municipality; or consistent improper attire during treatment. For withdrawal, we create a therapeutic setting; we employ discipline and insist on boundaries because they are vital to the therapeutic process, which not only strives to instigate change but also to provide the patient with a so-called line of defense. Through setting boundaries, a client learns of the support available to them, and the risk of potential damage to themselves throughout the treatment and recovery process

3. Negative changes pertaining to the client's psychological condition occur, requiring a different type of professional intervention

Following the initial introduction period, we assess the client's psychological capability of withstanding the therapeutic structure's rules and their psychological readiness for the course of treatment. We establish a personal treatment plan together with the patient, assign the professional who will treat them, and the therapeutic group that they will be joining. The therapists at Rothschild 2 work as a team. We update one another as to the main treatment proceeding that has been chosen for each client, as well as any particular difficulties they have, and track their participation in treatment. All staff members know every client who is in treatment at Rothschild 2. We assist them throughout the course of their treatment and rehabilitation.

Guiding Principles as a Mandatory Condition for Establishing a Treatment Plan Modeled by Pirani (2006)

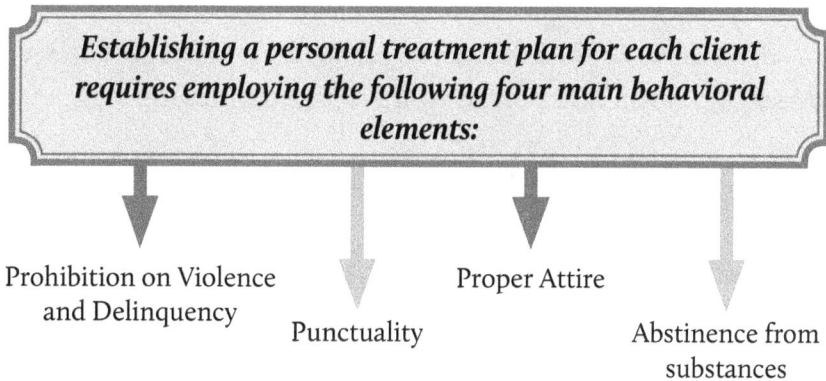

Establishing a personal treatment plan for each client requires employing the following four main behavioral elements:

Prohibition on Violence and Delinquency

Punctuality

Proper Attire

Abstinence from substances

Figure 6. Main Rules of Behavior to be followed at Rothschild 2

In order to establish a therapeutic system and an explanation of the treatment plan, we form a theoretical scheme of a "therapy table" to guide us throughout the entire therapeutic process with each client. Each of the four legs in the "therapy table" must be stable.

First leg – Prohibition of violence while the client is in treatment

Second leg – Punctuality: Adhere to activity schedule throughout the treatment period

Third leg – Full sobriety from any psychoactive drug on admission

Fourth leg - Display of respect for the treatment's setting, namely, the public service. This includes proper attire and politeness toward the other clients and staff in all therapeutic intervention settings

When one of the "table legs" is missing, either theoretically or practically, the stability of the "therapeutic table" is undermined. A patient whose "table legs" are unstable sabotages their own progress in treatment. Under such circumstances, the therapist faces difficulties addressing crucial therapeutic content such as stress and trauma memories.

Now that I have outlined the basic working rules and procedures at Rothschild 2, I will now portray its therapeutic structure:

This therapeutic structure guides clients through investigating measurable behavioral parameters of action and parameters related to tracking treatment attendance. We predetermine the individual session and therapeutic group schedules. In addition, we inform the clients of the structure's dress code, which should be proper for the therapeutic setting, as well as other behavior rules. To me, witnessing the change in a new client within a few days of treatment is important, in terms of appearance and personal behavior, since this change is sufficient to indicate the client's willingness to respect the staff and follow its professional recommendations. As long as a client is in treatment, the treatment staff will do its utmost to be attentive to their emotions and offer assistance.

The following are three situations in which a patient would be withdrawn from the Rothschild 2 treatment program:

1. A patient displays violence towards themselves, the people in their group, the staff, or animals

2. A patient accumulates 5 negative points by neglecting to take part in activities or urine testing, keep up their appearance or pay the nominal fee for the program to the Municipality of Tel-Aviv

3. A patient's state of health declines and demands another kind of medical intervention

After the introductory period, we assess an applicant's ability and motivation to work within the framework of the program. We then create a treatment plan, connect them with their main therapist and a group with whom they will experience group therapy and various activities. At Rothschild 2 we work as a team and every staff member knows each patient, through exchange of impressions and progress reports, as well as concerns, about patients. We are all dedicated to every patient's recovery.

The common characteristic of most post-traumatic neuroses is the sudden emergence of trauma (Munitz, 2003). Psychological stress and prolonged stress, trauma, and PTSD are characteristics of episodes threatening the human body or soul. This is common for all psychological stress victims (Zomer & Bleich, 2005; Najavits, 2002; Ouimette & Brown, 2003; Herman, 1992).

> The concept of psychological trauma indicates an episode resulting in psychological shock to a victim, which they interpret as risking a vital needs of theirs, such as security, self-esteem, social and economic status, or physical wholeness and being (Munitz, 2003).

It may be evident how complex the treatment of a trauma victim can be, when it occurs parallel to an issue of drug addiction.

Since 1992, approximately three thousand clients have approached Rothschild 2 Treatment Center. Most of them have survived for long periods of time in a severe mental and physical state and have experienced prolonged states of stress and trauma. Traumatic episodes undermine their psychological balance, leading them to develop a wide range of symptoms, which vary from one patient to another in form and intensity. Clients bear many years of psychological suffering, a life of trauma, humiliation, bullying, delinquency, addiction, social and familial rejection, and physical and nutritional neglect. Many have never been treated by a professional.

Most of my patients have experienced a prolonged, rather intense trauma, with extreme suffering arousing feelings of fear and helplessness in each and every one. Hence, I believe that very soon into the new client's engagement in the therapeutic process, the professional staff must integrate behavior and discipline rules, which are vital for addicts' rehabilitation, as well as empathy, warmth, understanding, and support, which are required in treating stress, trauma, and substance addicts. This is undoubtedly a complex professional combination.

I instruct the staff to employ the authority necessary to instill discipline, setting of boundaries, and proper behavior, as well as express sensitivity and empathy, warmth, understanding, and support.

After about twenty years of following these therapeutic principles, I still don't find it easy. The essence of the therapeutic process is not merely theoretical integration of boundary setting and empathy. Rather it is a process where the work demands of me to gather tremendous mental strength in practice, every day. Sometimes, I wish I could work in an organization where I would only need to express emotion and empathy. This wish is fulfilled through my reserve service as a mental health officer, and through my few clinical hours. Sometimes, I wish I could work for a "total" system where exertion of authority is particularly necessary, but it is not so at Rothschild 2.

SUD treatment is literally acrobatic-like. Throughout the entire therapeutic process, I am required to integrate varying boundaries of authority: On the one hand, protect the victim, while on the other hand, relay sensitivity and empathy toward the aggressor. This is a daily occurrence experienced by those choosing therapeutic work - it requires a deep sensitivity for clients' psychological suffering on the one hand, and the establishment of behavioral norms and discipline on the other hand. Integrated treatment isn't easy for clients or the staff.

I believe that order, boundaries, and discipline encourage a sense of organization and security in a client, precisely at the stage when they begin to reconstruct their life without drugs, and are more emotionally vulnerable than usual. In my opinion, a therapist who faces challenges throughout integrated treatment will also face challenges assisting SUD clients through their recovery and rehabilitation.

Lunch break. I set aside a few minutes to respond to e-mails and return telephone calls. Choco leaps outside, barking what I have grown to recognize as "the news." Lunch has been delivered. For Choco, this is one of the most exciting moments of the day, along with chasing cats and snapping at flies. While I sip my espresso, Choco makes a brief attempt to lick some water from one of the employee's Styrofoam cup. I feel pangs of conscience: *Where have I been the past few hours? Why had it not occurred to me that Choco's water bowl, at my feet, might be empty?*

I go for a walk in the yard. I head to the petting zoo. Kamma has managed to flee through the wooden doors that block her way out to the street. Just then, I see her returning from a walk, happily and proudly wiggling her tail, as if to say, "I've done my job. I'm no sucker." She is holding a fancy sandwich in her mouth. *Where did you get that?* I reproach her with a smile, as I usher her into the sheltered area of Rothschild 2.

The Rothschild 2 professional staff strictly follows the common stress-victim treatment principles, found in books by Foa et al. (2004), Zomer and Bleich (2005); Foa, et al. (1998), Ouimette & Brown (1995), Foa (2007), Foa et al.(2005), Brown (2003), Williams and Poijula (2002),

Najavits (2002), and others. We strictly follow the common principles for treating trauma victims, and integrate them with the expertise we have acquired through our many years of work:

Principle 1: Respecting a Client's Physical Needs

Generally, the therapist's basic position while facing any client must be one of caring, acceptance, honesty, and empathy (Yalom & Leszcz, 2006). At Rothschild 2, at our very first encounter with a client, we express our care for them, and identify with their pain and suffering. We make sleeping arrangements for them, supply basic products, and make sure they have access to a shower and toilets.

Aside from the wide range of welfare services provided by the Tel-Aviv social services, the administration operates a "Unit for Street Residents," assisting in both housing and sleeping solutions for homeless clients, and making sure to provide for their hygiene needs. There are many soup kitchens in Tel-Aviv, operated by various non-profit organizations, where we refer clients for a hot meal.

An SUD client who comes to treatment in great poverty must be referred to an assistance shelter. It is essential that they have a place where they can maintain some privacy and the prospect of getting a good night's sleep. SUD therapists must first respect a client's basic needs. Some clients come from a family structure of full support, have a place to lay their head and food to eat. Many others have no family relations.

These are the basic rules in working with SUD: Caring for their basic needs in correspondence to the rules derived from Maslow's hierarchy of needs (in River, 1992).

It is important to note that at a more advanced stage of the recovery process, many clients experience severe physical pains that emerge at the detoxification stage (toothaches, chills, joint aches, etc.). We make an effort to assist these clients with initial medical treatment as well. To this end, we obtain assistance from family physicians at the state health services and psychiatric services from the Ministry of Health.

In Israel, the entire framework set of social treatment for a drug addict is provided by the social services of the local authorities, government rehabilitation centers, and ambulatory treatment centers (Hovav, 2002).

Following a client's adjustment period at Rothschild 2, we strive to construct a therapeutic setting that serves as a safe place for them. This is another basic rule in working with trauma victims, which I have addressed earlier in this chapter. The therapeutic group members should feel comfortable within their group, that the group is safe and supportive, which allows them to openly express their secrets, the tensions they are facing, and the various challenges they are coping with.

I expect the professional staff to assist clients in maintaining a therapeutic setting clean of drugs and delinquent behavior patterns. Such a therapeutic setting allows no recurrence and reconstruction of exploitation, abuse, and trauma. The following episode best demonstrates this situation: Moshe, a 30-year-old single man, of muscular build, usually comes in sports attire. Moshe is new to the treatment center; Ada, a good-looking, 25-year-old single woman has been at the center for three months. Her behavior is provocative, drawing much attention.

They meet at the Early Stages Treatment Group, every Sunday at six p.m. This is their third encounter.

During group discussion, Ada indicates to Moshe that not all he has said up to then sounds credible. "I don't see any emotion on your face when you speak," she tells him. Moshe becomes embarrassed, and responds by bursting into a rage. It is evident that he has been flooded by emotions, but his ability to regulate and balance his responses and feelings is limited, as portrayed by Najavits (2002), thus he screams at her: "Who are you anyway?! I could beat the hell out of women like you, like that..." His eyes are flashing with rage and he is extremely agitated.

The facilitators need to respond immediately to calm the atmosphere, for if they don't, it could cause a past trauma to rise to the surface for Ada and other group members. Later, this event is processed and analyzed, as the facilitators investigate the messages or hints that had set Moshe off.

I agree with the argument made by Yalom & Leszcz (2006):

> Nobody should ever be punished for self-exposure. One of the most destructive events possible within a group is members using something against another member, when a conflict arises; sensitive, personal information exposed within the group is revealed on a trust basis. If such an event takes place, the therapist must resolutely intervene.

As stated, on attaining the basic conditions for a client's primary needs to be fulfilled, as well as a secure therapeutic setting, the professional staff is then required to assess a client's psychological strength, their feeling of security within the therapeutic setting, and their ability to work on their stress and trauma experiences. This is a delicate, sensitive investigation, requiring a high degree of professionalism. It should be kept in mind that at moments of psychological stress, SUD patients normally relapse into drugs, often as means of self-medication for psychological distress and stress responses (Williams & Poijula, 2002). It is evident that one of the complexities of therapeutic integration present in working with SUDs had surfaced between Ada and Moshe in this highly sensitive group session.

Principle 2: Informing the Client of the Situation

At this stage, which is still part of the complex situation associated with the pre-therapeutic stage, we inform the client of the feelings they may experience at various stages of treatment, namely, emotional and physiological responses. We outline for the client the guidance processes through which they will work with different staff members, and the situations they will be facing throughout therapy. We explain the nature of the treatment setting they have joined - "a structure treating addicts who wish to no longer experience psychological suffering." We verbally applaud a client for deciding to seek help and engaging in the therapeutic process. When a client stands before the admission committee, which every client who joins Rothschild 2 must do to register, we give over a similar message:

> We know you have suffered a great deal in your life. You have also suffered prolonged substance abuse. Individuals who wish to stop suffering are the ones who seek treatment. You will be required to gather much strength for the treatment... You are new here, new to therapy. Try to listen more and to speak less... In your first few days at the center, it is important that you first be attentive to your peers' course of therapeutic work. Observe your fellow group members. At this point, we do not expect you to discuss your suffering, past, pain, or secrets.

Principle 3: The Staff Enables Client Orientation and Learning at the New Therapeutic Setting of Rothschild 2

Entering a new treatment structure may arouse anxiety, tension, apprehension, and even shame. To facilitate the adjustment to the therapeutic setting, each client is paired with a "shadow." This shadow is a senior member of the therapeutic group, who facilitates the new member's adjustment, clarifying the rules of behavior required at Rothschild 2. It is important that each client understand the rules of discipline, modes of behavior at therapy, and treatment methods implemented in this setting. This shadow must convey the following message to the new member: *When I exposed my psychological pain, a*

*member who was my senior supported me, too. A supportive therapeutic
setting assisted me, too.*

The professional staff is attentive to a client's needs, searches for
information pertaining to them, and concludes various diagnoses
regarding their life as well. At the diagnostic information collection
stage with a professional, the client first reveals the stress events or
the psychological pain they have experienced through the course
of their life. At this point, they are asked to provide only details or
information of which they feel comfortable disclosing. The treatment
staff assesses, as early as this stage, if medicinal intervention should be
recommended as part of the psychotherapeutic process. We suggest
the client undergo a medical consultation with our psychiatrist. A
client who suffers a high level of anxiety or depression will not be
able to undergo the therapeutic processes involving the recall of
memories related to stress and trauma. For various psychological
conditions, and on our psychiatrist's recommendation, the client
can receive tranquilizers and antidepressants.

Caryn, a 22-year-old single woman with a troubling expression,
came to Rothschild 2 following a suicide attempt by ODing on a very
large dose of heroin and cocaine.

> *Yesterday, I celebrated my mother's birthday. It is for her that I wish
> to be clean of drugs. I ask you to admit me to the day center as soon
> as possible. I have heard this day center of yours has helped many.*

A few days later, we welcome Caryn to the day center, with her three
most recent urinalyses clean of substances. It seems that Caryn is
experiencing a psychological crisis, involving elements of depression
and anxiety. We are still not familiar with her life story, and I am
concerned with the apparent decline in her mental state, since she
only recently stopped using the drugs which afforded her apathy and
years of dissociation from her harsh memories. Her recent suicide
attempt implies difficult emotions. I assume she needs medicinal

treatment to initially balance the anxiety and depression. Caryn agrees to go for a medical consultation with a private psychiatrist to whom she has been referred, because unfortunately, it is impossible to schedule an immediate appointment with a psychiatrist from the public services, even in a sensitive situation like this, where there is a three-week waiting list.

Principle 4: Creating Boundaries: An Applicant Must Abide by the Rules at "Rothschild 2"

There are clearly defined rules of behavior and discipline at "Rothschild 2" which we fully enforce, as well as attention to a schedule of activities (described in this chapter, table number 6). I believe that the acclimation of the applicant, through therapy, will allow for the development of trust in the team and the ability to accept our advice and ideas as helpful to the healing process, with no intention to harm.

This is not a simple or clear procedure for individuals who have lost their trust in others. The treatment's disciplinary rules and boundaries also bear a protective force that manifests by defining the boundaries of the structure and the behavior acceptable within it. Any client who wishes to be actively involved in instigating a change in their life, should gradually adopt the new treatment tools, including the therapeutic setting's rules of behavior. Furthermore, they must trust messages of guidance, advice, mirroring and treatment, which they receive from their counselors, the professionals treating and assisting them, and their fellow group members. All these can serve as supportive anchors for the patient in their early treatment stages.

Many treatment structures construct their own therapeutic system, accepted and appreciated by the staff employed there. Some treatment structures strictly adhere to activity schedules while others prefer flexibility in establishing behavioral or disciplinary boundaries. I am convinced that working with SUD requires the setting of clear and strictly enforced boundaries, both by clients and by the treating staff, mostly to prevent the risk of relapsing to substance abuse.

Principle 5: Forming an Empathic Relationship

> The therapeutic group resembles a family in many senses; in both, there are two authoritative figures/parents, peers/siblings, profound personal revelations, intense emotions, and deep intimacy, as well as feelings of hostility and competition (Yalom & Leszcz, 2006).

We know that establishing a therapeutic group is a sensitive step towards forming the therapeutic relationship at Rothschild 2. This is the stage when we encourage clients through early acquaintance processes, to begin sharing their feelings and emotions, and begin to address the loss-related issue (if they have identify these in their past). We assume that at this stage, it is possible to begin discussing the loss that has been guiding their life and their years of addiction.

The professional staff at Rothschild 2 is highly sensitive to a client's difficulty in transitioning from the world of delinquency and addiction to treatment in a public, professional setting, which raises the banner of trust and sharing. The transition difficulties mainly stem from a client's lack of trust, not only in the establishment, but also in society. We convey to the client a message of acceptance, empathy, support, and protection, in order to facilitate these transition processes for them. Many addicts still find it difficult to trust professionals. Thus, simultaneous to their therapeutic work, they also attend NA support structures. The Twelve-Step Program work can significantly promote therapeutic processes (Teichman, 1989).

> Quite often, senior group members acquire highly advanced, sophisticated social skills; they are attentive to the process; they

have learned to effectively respond to others; they have developed conflict resolution methods; they tend to judge to a lesser extent, and to honestly express empathy (Yalom & Leszcz, 2006).

Hence, we also greatly encourage integrating the NA component into a client's detoxification stage.

I have addressed the general principles of working with SUD, I will now outline the basic stages of their treatment:

Stage One: A Client, A Clean Addict, Must Make the Choice to Accept Professional Help

I tell my clients:

Imagine a situation where you are struggling for your life drowning in a terrible sea storm. From the lifeboat, someone extends their hand. The instinctual response is always there, namely, the human desire to live. Yet the choice is in your hands. If you are overcome by shame or anger, if you fight with one another for your place as survivors, you will all drown. The savior, your friend, or staff members are offering you help to survive. You can do it. Extend your hand for help, extend your hand to your savior.

Stage Two: Acknowledging the Difficult Experience and Including It In Treatment

A client's awareness of the stress and trauma episode that they experienced is of great importance. It is important to integrate their awareness of the past sense of adversity with present therapeutic work.

The traumatic experience has many effects. It is advisable to explore and consider these effects. The traumatic experience can affect a client's emotions, thoughts, interpersonal relations, behavior, views, and even their hope for the future (Williams & Poijula, 2002). Client awareness and knowledge of the past is a first, highly essential step in treating stress and trauma memories.

Many clients repress traumatic experiences from their lives. Some even dissociate themselves from recalling the experience (Lindy, 1989; Zomer & Bleich, 2005). Acknowledging traumatic experiences is not enough. There is great importance, as early as in the treatment's initial stage, to assist the patient in paving a new path in their life, find new meaning, set and new goals. We allow patients to develop in this way in the therapeutic setting offered at Rothschild 2. Many initiatives taken by clients at Rothschild 2 have flourished, such as the petting zoo we built. These are only part of the therapeutic process that relies on the therapeutic setting and Animal Assisted Therapy (see also Chapter Eight).

Stage Three: Client Security in Therapy and Identifying Personal Tragedy

A client begins to identify their own tragedy by hearing the life stories of their fellow group members. They may receive the impression that all of their peers have tremendously suffered psychologically at some time point or another in their lives. Working on stressful and traumatic memories among the new group members often occurs by listening to the senior members and their distress.

A life of psychological suffering, life under threat, pursuit of every red cent, humiliation, assault, violence, and substance abuse remain out of the therapeutic setting. We ask the client to enhance their appearance and tidy themselves up, in order to prevent the return of delinquent behavioral patterns. In return, we convey a therapeutic message of acceptance and warmth. "Instilling and preserving hope are a key component of any psychotherapy," (Yalom & Leszcz, 2006). They also fulfill an important role at Rothschild 2. Our therapeutic setting is a beautiful natural spot, that is rich with greenery. The sound of birds singing and guinea pigs chatting floats in through the windows. "Sit down and connect to the tranquility and peace," we offer clients. "Leave your daily life and struggle for survival outside."

While registering at the treatment center, a client is questioned about why they have abused substances for such a long time, to see whether they can identify the point they experienced the distress that initially led them to choose drugs. We do not obligate a client to respond to these questions. Rather, we merely expect them to thoroughly explore and reflect their own insight regarding themselves. I feel that deep down, all of them know the answers.

By filling out the assessment forms, we introduce ourselves to a client's family history; their personal background and history; what kind of coping skills they possess; whether they have ever studied or worked; how the substances come into to their life, what kind of personal suffering they have been through, and when and where it occurred. Clients manage this stage together with one of the staff members through initial individual sessions. The assessment process is a long process, conducted by a social worker who serves clients from the beginning of treatment as their case manager and throughout the entire therapeutic process.

By establishing this therapeutic stage for a client at the center, we ask them to choose an animal from the petting zoo for which they would like to care. Once a client has assumed responsibility for treating animals, their inner empowerment process begins as well. From that moment on, even if a client still struggles to survive without drugs, they are now responsible for another living creature, an animal that needs their strength, attention, giving, containment, food, water, supervision, and care. This is one of the most fascinating moments of our work at Rothschild 2. From this point on, we are establishing a new therapeutic situation. Although the client is still under the initial assessment of their psychological, physical, and personal condition, from this moment on, they are restoring some control in their life, which develops through their care of another living creature (broadly discussed in Chapter Nine).

In this week's group therapy, suicidal voices emerge. The harsh conversations to which clients are exposed in the various groups arouse their own rough memories of the past regarding stress, trauma, and mourning. I am particularly concerned on Thursdays. The treatment center is closed on Fridays and Saturdays and these 72 hours are crucial. A patient who copes with suicidal thoughts on weekdays needs support during off hours as well.

Judy, a 24-year-old woman suffering compounded grief, recalls the profound tragedy of losing her husband and young child in a car accident.

Michael, a 23-year-old single man, recalls the fatal car accident in which his older brother, also addicted to drugs, was killed.

Sassi, a married man and father to a five-year-old son, has been at the treatment center for only two weeks. He identifies with the harsh dialogue expressed in the group. I can tell by his body language (Yalom & Leszcz, 2006), as he nods his head while hearing Judy's and Michael's stories. I call on Sassi to speak up. "You greatly identified with the conversation's subject matter," I tell him.

> *I very much empathize with the talk here. Only a month ago, I attempted to OD again. I have already experienced clinical death several times. I have always wanted to die, but I can't understand why. That's the answer that I'm searching for at Rothschild. I want to understand my behavior and change it.*

This is the first time Sassi has spoken in the group. Since his first days with us, he has demonstrated curbed rage. I guided the staff to avoid any close therapeutic contact with Sassi, since I saw he was still not mentally ready for it. "He might be very impulsive and violent," I said.

I still do not know his life story, but based on theoretical models I have established (see Chapter Ten - The Cycle of Suffering), I assume the impulsive fits of rage he mentioned are an outcome of post-traumatic issues resulting from a stress episode or harsh abuse he experienced in the past. I am exposed to such conditions, as well as others, at work with my patients on a daily basis. These are often trauma symptoms.

Judy has not eaten in several days. She speaks of an intense desire to use drugs again. "I can't live. I don't want to. I know my child is big now. He is four. They are waiting for me up there. There is life after death. I miss my husband and son."

Michael barely speaks. He is drawn into himself, indifferent. I see him shed tears when he hears his fellow group members. The initial difficulty in treating him stems from his thundering silence, which threatens to flood everything violently, like a tsunami.

The following session is expected to begin at 11 a.m. This is an Animal Assisted Therapy group, the last group session prior to Week's Closure. I consult the staff on how we can recruit Judy, Michael, and Sassi into the therapeutic process, through which we can grant them confidence and personal empowerment as alternatives to their despondency, depression, and despair.

During the break, I see that Judy is taking an interest in a pair of new pink parrots who arrived recently at Rothschild 2. In the past two weeks, all the mice she was taking care of had died. She associated their death with the own loss of her family. The mice's death served as a kind of a trigger, a hint that aroused her painful memories. I ask her if she can muster some strength to care for the new parrots. She thinks for a while before saying yes. This is the first time this week I have seen her smile.

Sassi still does not have an animal of his own to care for. I ask him to clean and repair the mice cage. He becomes alarmed and excited: *"No way! Are you punishing me? I won't do it. All I can think of is death."*

In response, I explain to him that sometimes life brings crises like death.

> *You know this, and I suppose you have met with it several times in your life. The main thing, though, is that you are able to hold on to life. You can restore control over your life if you build the cage from scratch, and then see a new family of mice move in. Try to hold on to life, rather than sticking to memories of death alone, even if they constantly arise.*

While working on the cages, I see Sassi scrub the cage floor clean. In the day's final session, he speaks of his wish to see new animals in his cage. Undoubtedly, he leaves for the weekend feeling stronger.

Michael, too, still has no animal to care for. I attribute that fact to his condition. He hasn't found his footing within the therapeutic group. I suggest he take the empty terrariums, which had been donated to the center, and clean them: *You don't have an animal of your own to care for yet, but you will when the aquariums are clean and ready, and when you feel you are able to care for an animal.*

Michael scrubs the terrariums, and seeks help from his fellow group members. During the session, I pass by them at the petting zoo, and hear him fantasizing about a lizard he wants to put in the terrarium. He looks different.

Stage Four: Go Easy on Yourself When You Recall the Trauma, Cope Without Avoidance or Denial

Many years of avoidance, trauma experiences, and memory repression are what sustain drug abuse. A sexually assaulted individual, beaten daily by their parents, or harshly abused psychologically or physically, is usually incapable of bearing his mental suffering without using drugs. The feelings of helplessness, humiliation, rage, revenge, fear, and psychological pain channel through the substance.

Many clients marry and start their own families at an older age. Many women avoid the company of men, not wanting a reminder of the cause of their trauma. Men avoid intimacy for similar reasons and with similar concerns.

> *Members who are sexual abuse victims greatly benefit from the experience of universality. An integral part of these groups is the intimate sharing, often for the first time in a member's life, of the hows and whats of the sexual abuse they underwent, and the psychological damage they suffered because of it (Yalom & Leszcz, 2006).*

Denying the event, self-blaming, or employing an all-encompassing statement such as, "All women/men are the same," often occur. Avoiding social interaction reminiscent of the trauma's setting such as sounds, smells, music, the smell of alcohol and cigarettes is common. Refusing to walk in the dark, staying home alone, and avoiding parties, getting into a car or riding a particular bus line are only a few of the constrictive actions taken by clients to avoid recalling the traumatizing, stressful experience (see also Chapter Nine).

We offer clients various ways to cope: On the one hand, we encourage them to avoid events associated with the tough memories in their life. On the other hand, we convey the following message:

> *You can allow yourself at your own time and pace to begin sharing your stressful experiences with others. Share only what you can and are willing to bring at this point. In due course, you will realize how relieved you feel. The tough events you experienced are past events. They are not taking place now. You are now in a different setting, a sheltered one. We are by your side, your fellow group members are here for you. We all attempt to assist you as much as we can.*

PORTRAYING THE EMOTIONAL EXPERIENCES ASSOCIATED WITH TRAUMA

- Complete a questionnaire outlining a client's trauma
- Record distress units caused by the trauma
- Relate the trauma in order to reminisce but not to overwhelm
- Practice calm breathing, realistic introspection - me

Figure 7: Portraying the Emotional Experiences Associated with Trauma

This week, I witness the following interaction:

Akhmed is 35 years old, born in Acre, married and a father of three. He has been treated at Rothschild 2 for approximately four months. Akhmed served a 15-year prison sentence. He ridicules women, saying he enjoys to see them lose control and cry in anger.

Michal, a 25-year-old single woman, born in Jerusalem, has been at the center for three months. She mocks Akhmed because he is primitive misogynist, a cruel, and chauvinistic brute. In many of the group sessions they engage in aggressive arguments.

When I notice two group members in conflict, I believe they are very likely to be significant for each another in therapy (Yalom & Leszcz, 2006). Current incidents within the therapeutic structure, threaten the group's secure, supportive environment, so I'm obligated to intervene immediately in such cases. Another prospect raised by Yalom & Leszcz is the presence of dispute and conflict within the group, constituting "resistance to a more intimate connection, manifesting as the members' attempts to maintain negative relations rather than connecting." Currently, the group's course is complex and sensitive, because this group has many stress and trauma victims. Therefore, I must intervene in the conflict to moderate the group climate.

In the past few days of group sessions, even when the professional staff has intervened and made an effort to avoid a conflict in relation to gender, ethnicity, religion, gang-relations, sex, or any other issue, a clash between Akhmed and Michal has been inevitable. For Akhmed, Michal is merely a trigger, reminding him of his mother, whose screams were "like a siren going off," who struck him with a belt, and gave his younger brother burns with white-hot skewers. His mother passed away when he was eight years old. Her image will always be one of punishment, devoid of nurture.

For Michal, Akhmed is the Arab guy who abused and humiliated her while she was using drugs; a dealer in Lod, who watched her suffer withdrawal symptoms. Akhmed was the one who had forced Michal to give him oral sex while all his friends witnessed her humiliation, and then joined the act themselves. Michal views Akhmed as a cruel, abusive figure. She needs to be released from the influence of Akhmed and his tastes, while Akhmed needs to be released from the influence of Michal and her peers.

Stage Five: Physiological Elements of Trauma and Detoxification from Drugs

We identify typical physiological reactions among individuals suffering post-trauma and complex post-trauma symptoms. Among most who seek treatment at Rothschild 2, we witness common physical reactions as well (see Chapter Four). Symptoms include, for example, breathing difficulties and heart problems, chronic pain and digestion problems (Herman, 1992; Teichman, 1989; Foa, 2004, 2006; Najavits, 2002; Williams & Poijula, 2002). Among addicts in the initial stages of detoxification, on breaking a long-term drug addiction, we identify additional symptoms: joint pains, nausea, diarrhea, nasal drip, weakness, and body tremors (Teichman, 1989; Green, 1995; Nadler, 2002).

As the physical detoxification progresses, after being clean of drugs for several days, new physical symptoms often appear. Sometimes, a client feels a toothache, left unattended under heroin's influence, and their body becomes prone to seasonal illnesses of which they were not aware during their years of addiction (flu, backache, leg pain, headaches, and joint ache).

The physical symptoms mix, often confusing the trauma-victim, and sometimes even confuse the caregiver. How, therefore, can we know if an individual who feels chest pains is suffering post-trauma or complex post-trauma symptoms, one of the many detoxification symptoms, or real angina? How are we to know whether the headaches, digestion problems and other phenomena are an outcome of medical problems, rather than post-trauma symptoms in situations of prolonged physical pain? We first eliminate any medical findings, and then turn to addressing the mental symptoms.

Gil, a 45-year-old single man, lives with his elderly parents in a two-bedroom apartment in Tel Aviv. On completing the first stage of drug detox, which lasted several days, he complained of varied somatic pains. He was convinced of his physical symptoms, and no physical or medical examination could have ever proved to him that he was perfectly well. When Gil progressed through the treatment stages, simultaneously detoxing, his therapist was introduced to his traumatic past. He related the sexual assault he experienced as a child, criminal abuse, witnessing severe acts of violence towards his friends, as well as many years of drug abuse, attempting to repress any difficult memories.

When Gil shared the sufferings of his life with us, his face broke out in a sweat. His hand clutched the left side of his chest, apparently in pain. Every few weeks, on a regular basis, he sees his family physician, asking for further physical examinations. So far, the results have shown normative health for a man of his age.

Gil was suffering varied physical symptoms: Physical problems typical of an individual his age, a physical condition compatible with many years of substance addiction, and the physical symptoms typical to trauma survivors.

STAGE 6: THE IMPORTANCE OF CONFIDENCE IN THE THERAPEUTIC PROCESS

> # IT IS NOT OUR FAULT

Image 2. IT IS NOT OUR FAULT

Throughout therapeutic work addressing stress, abuse, and trauma, I encounter hard feelings of guilt and shame. I often notice a new group member having trouble getting involved in the more advanced treatment stages, as long as he keeps to himself his secrets associated with shame and guilt.

In therapy, clients are introduced to other individuals who also experienced abuse and psychological suffering as children. The group members empathize with the suffering of others, understanding that they were merely victims of circumstance, absorbing the notion that they are to learn how to set themselves free of profound shame, guilt, rage, and feeling internally dirty (Yalom & Leszcz, 2006).

Guilt

Williams and Poijula (2002) propose to treat trauma victims through recording their feelings of guilt. We explore how a client was or was not accountable for the events. Are they really the one to blame for their assault? Are they accountable for it?

The question this raises relates to the responsibility of a trauma victim in these situations, and what can facilitate the process of learning to forgive themselves. I suggest asking clients to bring a childhood photograph to therapy. The picture allows them to see how small or weak they were back in those days. While exploring the photograph, most of them realize that they are not to blame for the trauma they experienced. Clients may also facilitate by process of assimilation, in which they accept the explanation that it makes no sense that as a child they could have been accountable for a situation in which they themselves were the victim.

A trauma victim's feeling of guilt often stems from false beliefs that their actions are what brought on the assault, or that because they did not react to the event, they could have prevented death, injury, or rape. We often notice these reactions among soldiers who feel guilt when a friend who had replaced them on the mission was injured or killed (Seligman & Solomon, 2004).

Healing does not guarantee freedom from guilt. However, clients should learn to adopt more realistic thinking in attempting to investigate whether or not they were accountable for their experience.

Yasha—born in Poland, 28 years old, married and a father of a three-year-old son—has been clean from drugs for two months. In therapy, he relates the trauma he experienced:

> I was eight years old when we went out for a walk on the frozen river bank on that cold Christmas morning. We ran and horsed around, when I suddenly saw Maria fall into the frozen river. She had been running away from me. I saw her eyes gazing at me through the half-transparent layer of ice. I'm certain she was calling for help, extending her hand for me to pull her out. Bubbles came out of her mouth. The current carried her away, and we couldn't see her anymore. I am the one to blame. I have felt this every day. I was the one who had offered the other children to play with me. I had chased her. Even the other children's parents blamed me.

The therapeutic process that a trauma victim undergoes is a long one. There is no short-term formula to relieve feelings from trauma. I do not believe any professional who raises false hope in this regard.

There are various ways to facilitate healing of guilt for a survivor of stress and trauma:

1. Allow the client to discuss the loss and grieve for it

2. Offer the client a healing program or experience to ease their feelings, possibly by assisting another individual

3. Tell the client that it is important to remember what happened; such a traumatic experience cannot be forgotten

4. Suggest the client distinguish the guilt from the sense of accountability

5. Offer the client a realistic, different outlook on their feelings of guilt

6. Teach the client a way to respond to their inner feelings of self-accusation and unrealistic guilt through new assumptions they establish regarding themselves

7. Tell the client they must learn how to come to terms with past events

Yasha could not have prevented the tragedy related to Maria. He was a weak, helpless child himself. "Allow yourself to grieve for her, but don't assume responsibility," we told him. "Now that we see how devoted you are to your wife, to your son, to your friends, and the way you care for your dog, we see how much love for others you have in you. We know the tragedy will remain a part of you for the rest of your life, but you should not feel guilty."

Shame

A client may feel shame when they are in a situation where they are unable to respond. The shame arouses a terrible feeling toward themselves, which does not go away through expressions of anger or crying.

A client who feels guilt is questioned about their involvement in a stress or trauma event: Do they realize they are not perfect and cannot control events in which they are involved, including their traumatic event? The fellow group members' empathy toward their feelings often facilitates them to overcome their feelings of shame.

Loss

During trauma, experiencing loss leading to sorrow is quite frequent. The first goal of therapeutic work on loss with a new client is to discuss the sorrow of the loss with them. We experience loss when loved ones or friends die, or during rough moments of bidding farewell to those dear to us. I must assist a client in accepting the reality of the death of a loved one. I have found that the most approproate way of coping is when I ask a client to list all the things they lost with that person's death. I tell clients: *Your loved one died, and with them many things died, and we can discuss them. Your loved one died, and left you happy memories as well.*

At Rothschild 2, we have established a memorial area for clients who were not able to create one. I was inspired by Herman's (1992) book to establish the memorial. She mentions the change in feelings of Vietnam War survivors throughout the United States after they constructed monuments in memory of their friends who had died. Remembering the dead fulfills an important role in stress and trauma survivors. I expect that within a therapeutic process addressing loss, through a process of assimilation and learning, a client can come to terms with the death of another. Coming to terms involves accepting a new life status, since life will never again be what it used to be.

Yasha experiences tremendous shame, since he did not meet the expectations of Maria's mother, who had relied on him to save her daughter's life. The feelings of shame arise and flood him constantly. Months and years after that episode, he was still waking from nightmares until he found that he could escape through heroin.

In the treatment offered at Rothschild 2, Yasha released for the first time in his life, the profound sorrow he felt about Maria's death. Thanks to the support of his fellow members in group, he allowed himself to grieve the loss of Maria and to realize that she would never return. Yasha shared this rough feeling of loss that he had experienced as a child, endless suffering because of his friend's tragic death. I believe we assisted him in processing that loss. We also assisted him in acquiring new tools for coping with the loss and the memory, and eliminating the need to return to drugs.

Stage Seven: Difficulties in Emotion Regulation (anger management, self-harming, taking risks)

Najavits (2002), one of the leading figures of emotional regulation therapy with trauma victims and drug addicts, states that the first thing an addict suffering PTSD seeks is safety. This is common among people with SUD. Professional therapists realize that it is only natural for a client to seek safety and peace of mind after their personal safety has been destroyed because of a traumatic experience. Restoring emotional balance following months and years of emotional chaos is merely a natural need for balancing psychological feelings.

At this stage of treatment, maintains Najavits, we encourage a client to access community resources, raise their awareness of their own body, as well as focus on personal nurturing and modifying of their former behavioral patterns.

At Rothschild 2, these stages are built into a patient's integrative therapeutic structure. Implementing emotional regulation and seeking safety as treatment consists of three stages:

- Stage One: **Safety**
- Stage Two: **Mourning**
- Stage Three: **Reconnection**

The treatment approach consists of the following instructions:

- Remain in a safe place - it is important to feel secure in the place where treatment is administered

- Respect yourself - we respect you too. You are an equal among equals

- Cope with your life difficulties and challenges and with your desire to avoid feeling pain - all without turning to drugs

- Make the present and the future better than the past - it can be done without using drugs

- Learn to have faith and trust others - we assist you by maintaining confidentiality

- Take care of your body and your health - go for periodical, routine check-ups which you haven't undergone in a while

- Seek the help of those you can trust - your partners in the journey, therapists, relatives, sponsors

- Detox from drugs is necessary in order to facilitate recovery from PTSD. Recovering from PTSD, in turn, allows solving your addiction issue

- If one therapeutic approach is ineffective, try another approach. We do not promote a method at the expense of your recovery

- Never give up. You can always approach us when you face difficulties, feel sad, or any time you consider using again

The purpose of treatment integration as an interactive model for PTSD and SUD related intervention does yield outcomes where approaches that address those issues separately have failed (Najavits, 2002). Integrating post-trauma treatment with treatment addressing the addiction issue, constituting the core of this book, is merely designated to teach the client of the relationship of both disorders and their implications. I keep telling my patients:

The change in your ability to regulate your emotions is a change that has resulted from prolonged trauma experiences suffered throughout your lives. Your limited ability to express emotions may prompt self-abuse. Identifying your emotions is a vital stage within the process of learning to regulate them.

I offer patients to check the Emotions List (Image 5.) to express which emotion illustrates a difficult feeling or moment of pain and disappointment, or a moment of happiness, joy, and accomplishment. Present emotions can manifest a past event (trauma, for instance). It is important to know how to distinguish emotions related to present events from emotions relating to the past.

I ask patients to focus for a while on certain emotions, not under circumstances of losing control or dissociation:

Try to identify the source of the emotion you are experiencing. If necessary, go far, even back to the traumatizing event. What do you feel when you recall that stressful episode? Try to face the emotion within you, in a different way, through action. Strive to solve the distressing situation by identifying it. Don't go with the difficult feeling alone. Don't try escape from it through sleep but talk about it instead. Search for another way to express the emotion; write a letter or do something else, exercise, attend a group therapy session, work on the NA Twelve Steps. It is also important that you express your pain and longings. Draw back from that emotion. Do not focus on it. Instead, restore daily life activities.

Expressing Emotions
We offer our patients additional ways to express emotions:
1. Learn how to identify clues or triggers arousing different emotions within you, and record the differences between your feelings and various emotions

2. Practice modes of responding to emotions, which you may encounter even before you have identified them

3. Practice role-playing with others, such as your therapist, in situations that express your emotions

4. Discuss your feelings with others

5. Practice emotions with which you feel more secure, and then seek feedback

6. Practice relaxation in order to cope with highly intense emotions

7. Write down the emotions (see Image No. 5) that give you pleasure and those that do not, but accept them all. Which emotions do you not want to experience; which emotions embarrass you, and how do you cope with them?

8. Describe the emotions you avoid expressing because you fear rejection, neglect, punishment, or criticism

The patient learns to identify antecedents that trigger negative emotions (in association with the risk of relapsing into substance abuse):

1. Catastrophic interpretations of events and episodes

2. Demanding, compulsive speech, employing words such as "must," "should," etc.

3. Excessive use of generalized words such as "never" or "always"

4. Negative labeling – "I'm dumb," "It's impossible," etc.

5. Categorical thinking – "I am an idiot," "I'm stupid," etc.

6. Black and white thinking – a situation is either good or bad with no intermediate status

This week I spent one of the most difficult hours ever within my work as a SUD therapist. Shosh, 25 years old, clean of drugs for three months, joined us approximately a month ago. She related a gang rape she underwent eight years ago. Our therapy groups are co-ed. Shosh had yet to express her emotions within the group. Before she arrived at oiur center, she had coped with the feelings of rage, shame, guilt, and anger through drugs.

One evening, after telling her story, Shosh felt weak and lonely, because she thought everybody would be talking about her biggest life secret. She expected her fellow group members to call her and support her, even in the evening hours, when clients are at home. But most group members did not call her. The women of the group didn't want to trouble her with their concern while the men didn't want to embarrass her, because in group, she had said she hated all men in the world.

Shosh was intensely agitated and risked relapse. As group facilitators, we were aware of Shosh's emotional condition and very concerned for her. We called her in the evening, taking interest in her and strengthening her. We said: *Your emotional condition will improve the further you go into the therapeutic process. Hang in there. The whole group loves you and is thinking of you.*

The next day, Shosh arrived at the group session. She had survived one of her most challenging days; a day when she had revealed the sexual abuse and rape she had experienced. She managed to stay clean.

Identify Your Emotions

Neglected	Welcomed	Shocked	Insufferable	Beautiful
Accepted	Neglected	Guilty	Tense	Attractive
Pained	Dependent	Calm	In love	Admired
Affectionate	Happy	Drowned	Desperate	A role model
Lonely	Sad	Secure	Happy	Father
Unfriendly	Defeated	Revengeful	Disappointed	Mother
Amused	Curious	Responsible	Stingy	Son
Angry	Devastated	Tormented	Generous	Daughter
Preoccupied	Nervous	Rejected	Sensitive	Grandson

Anxious	Odd	Pained	Indifferent	Granddaughter
Apologetic	Unstable	Vain	Dark	Great grandson
At peace granddaughter	Happy	Preoccupied	Satisfied	Great
Nervous	Precious	Guided		
Irate	Grateful	Useless	Hard working	
Embarrassed	Satisfied	Disappointed	Squanderer	
Cheerful	Giving	Unsatisfied	Extroverted	
Enthusiastic	Raging	Unsociable	Narcissist	
Lazy	Full	Understood	Depressed	
Yearning	Fulfilling	Unaware	Smiling	
Doomed	Friendly	Unappreciated	Crying	
Controlling	Sympathetic	Ugly	Imaginative	
Distressed	Sweet	Confident	Appreciating	
Desperate	Dumb	Problematic	Assessing	
Disappointed	Amazed	Trapped	Knowledgeable	
Special	Stimulated	Tortured	Masked	
Devastated	Regretting	Adaptive	Hypocrite	
Desperate	Ashamed	Tired	Obnoxious	
Conscious	Envious	Weak	Scared	Uncle
Traitor	Isolated	Pleased	Apprehensive	Aunt
Bitter	Irritated	Peace loving	Startled	Cousin
Bored	Preoccupied	Sick	Refreshed	
Courageous	Angry	Poor	Exhausted	
Serene	Interested	Sad	Hungry	
Talented	Unstable	Crazy	Thirsty	
Courteous	Innocent	Fortunate	Cold	
Cautious	Untalented	Loyal	Warm	
Joyous	Deficient	Worthwhile	Well-liked	
Collected	Humiliated	Wonderful	Friend	
Secure	Hurt	Retreating	Friend	
Contradicting	Faithful	Wiped out	Reliable	
Connected	Hopeless	Defeated	Liar	
Satisfied	Helpless	Tired	Manipulating	

Insane	Glad	Warm	Phony
Stupid	Guilty	Vulnerable	Supportive
Exposed	Irate	Victim	Supporter

Figure 8. Various Words Expressing Emotions (Williams & Poijula, 2002)

Stage Eight: Changes in Attention and Levels of Cognition: Addressing Dissociation and Sudden Forgetfulness Among SUD Patients

Dissociation and depersonalization are phenomena often emerging in response to highly stressful episodes. Among addicts who seek my treatment, I encounter many who suffer these responses. Dissociation is a situation where events and experiences, usually connected and integrated into one's mind, are separated and split (Zomer, 2004).

We understand that for a trauma victim, this phenomenon fulfills a defensive role. Depersonalization allows an individual, a victim of physical or sexual assault, to dissociate themselves from the terror of trauma and the psychological pain associated with that wound. Dissociation allows the victim to function, as with drugs or highly effective medication, and relieves their psychological pain.

Addicts who seek our treatment after long-term use of substances such as heroin, cannabis, or ecstasy, report similar phenomena. These clients dissociate from their emotions and from their very existence through drug abuse. I have concern for patients who exhibit dissociation from the psychological pain caused by trauma.

In treating SUD, we notice that on the one hand, dissociation allows the trauma victim to shift their harsh experiences and intrusive memories (see Chapter Three), yet prolonged dissociation, which lasts even after the danger is gone, is maladaptive (as I demonstrate in Chapter Nine), and sometimes even activates a delayed recovery function. Dissociation distracts the processes of traumatic experience and recovery from it. Moreover, it could damage social, emotional, and cognitive functioning.

Throughout the defensive process involved in dissociation, a shift occurs, allowing the victim to distinguish between thinking processes and emotions. In other words, the memory of the trauma does not become conscious and therefore remains emotionally unprocessed. Such a dissociated traumatic memory may remain within one's soul like burning lava threatening to erupt at a time of anger.

I witnessed such a process in Vladi:

Vladi, a 35-year-old married man, owns a modern, well-equipped electronics workhouse for repairing musical instruments. He's been clean for four years. He is very pragmatic, rational, and unable to express emotion. As a child in Russia, he was a highly gifted student. His parents paid attention only to his grades, but the fact that a boy in the neighborhood sexually abused their son for approximately a year, went unnoticed. In order to survive and withstand the stress associated with the abuse, Vladi disconnected his emotional world from his cognitive world. He succeeded in channeling his high abilities toward mathematics and electronics studies, but he never allowed himself to even approach a state of emotional expression. He tried several times to emotionally respond to the goings on in group, but he never succeeded in doing so. The group knew well that Vladi was the rational type.

When he relapsed into drug abuse, following his second divorce, we assisted him in understanding that a he needed a change of course. "Without careful, dedicated work on your dissociation, we cannot assist you in rebuilding your emotional life," we told him. "Without an emotional world of your own, you will face great difficulties in fulfilling your social, interpersonal, and spousal roles. It's possible you realize this based on your experiences in the past few years." We were also aware of the risks. We knew Vladi's encounter with his emotions might prompt a severe functional regression on his part.

I believe that, thanks to the support of his therapist and his fellow group members, his functional regression would be only temporary.

Stage Nine: Somatization, Physical Response, Chronic Pain, Digestive Difficulty, and Breathing Trouble Symptoms among SUD

As therapists for clients who experienced stress, abuse, and trauma, we must be familiar with their common and typical somatic responses. Our psychotherapeutic training does not allow us to chalk up symptoms we notice as somatic phenomea, and requires us to refer them for examination by a physician or a psychiatrist. However, identifying key somatic symptoms among trauma survivors may facilitate us in understanding their distress and even grant us therapists some peace of mind in a professional context.

Stage Ten: Prospects of Medical Treatment for SUD

Selective serotonin reuptake inhibitors (SSRIs) affect the serotonergic system (the system releasing serotonin to the nerve receptors) in the brain. Following the development of the first generation medications in the 1980s, we can see constant, intensive development of these medications and other medications for anxiety and depression.

Now, in the early years of the 21st century, psychiatrists skillfully adjust medical treatment to correspond to each individual's problem. Doctors assemble medications in various combinations based on the symptoms people suffer. A client feeling a lack of sexual desire due to one medication may receive a different prescription. An individual who feels lethargic may receive a different medicinal combination that will better assist them.

More working instruments are available to professionals today, thus they are able to assist stress and trauma victims by means of both therapeutic and medicinal tools. Currently, SSRIs present as the most effective antidepressants in the treatment of post-traumatic stress disorder because of their effectiveness in decreasing all types of symptoms typical of this disorder (Seligman & Solomon, 2004). Through SSRIs, it is possible to treat the intrusive symptoms, as well as avoidance, hyperarousal, depression and prolonged restlessness, panic attacks and impulsiveness, alcohol and drug addiction, and any symptoms associated with stress and post-trauma episodes. SSRIs combined with psychotherapy create significant improvement.

Throughout my 20 years of working with trauma and addiction victims, I, too, have adapted to the vast pharmacological developments in these treatment fields. As opposed to the early 1990s, when most professionals treating addicts had little knowledge of how to combine medical treatment and psychotherapy, in recent years, we are noticing a growing number of professionals implementing combination treatments, namely, psychotherapy and medication.

Furthermore, in the early 1990s I had rarely heard of SUD and NA support members willing to acknowledge the effects of medicinal treatment recommended by psychiatrists. Their fears of the addictive effect of the medication (even if approved by a physician) made them wary. In recent years, I have encountered a growing number of SUD patients willing to be referred to what is known as "medical consultation" and take the recommended medication on a regular, ongoing basis.

So too is the case with the approach of NA's voluntary organizations. The members of these organizations have grown to acknowledge that SSRIs are not addictive, certainly not if they are taken according to a physician's instructions. The medications serve as a necessary, supportive crutch for a client at the beginning of their long therapeutic journey. Hundreds of trauma victims, including drug addicts, can now witness the significant improvement in the lives of their peers who agreed to take medication combined with psychotherapy.

Dina, a 35-year-old, single mother to an eight-year-old girl, presents the view of the SUD patients who refuse to take medication. She has been clean of drugs for approximately twelve years. She continues, however, to suffer panic attacks, prolonged bouts of depression, and difficult mental distress. Even in the toughest moments of crisis, she refuses referral to a medical consultation:

> *I don't want to hear your suggestions. I won't replace one addiction with another. If I take medication on a daily basis, I become an addict again. I can't think of having to take medicine every day for the rest of my life... I've heard other members in the group say that the meds damage sexual desire. It's out of the question.*

Ami, a 40-year-old single man, has been clean from all drugs for two years. Ami presents the view of clients who have agreed to a medical consultation:

> *I am very grateful now, every second of my life, for agreeing to go for a medical consultation with a psychiatrist. I was concerned with the possible stigma, and how my friends, who said that medication was for lunatics, would react... I had also heard they decrease the libido, and that did happen in the beginning of treatment. However, my therapist supported and encouraged me to try a different medication. I knew I wouldn't relapse, not even for a day, into the panic and depression I had had since childhood. I am not willing to relapse into drugs, delinquency, arrests, fights, and prison. I don't have any strength left to handle the depression anymore. Thanks to the medication, I manage to lead a structured, relatively normal life. I sleep at night. My psychological condition is more balanced, without the mood swings I suffered before and after I was an addict. Everybody notices the significant change in me. I even danced drug-free at my nephew's wedding for the first time.*

My sweet dog, Choco, suffers from epilepsy. She had an epileptic fit during one of the group therapy sessions, with convulsions, an unfocused gaze, fully body spasms. I treated Choco with an injection of valium prescribed by the veterinarian. We waited for her to recover and I asked the group to continue working. The conditions weren't easy for Choco, the group members, or me, because Choco usually welcomes each group member joyously, with an excited bark, and she is the sweetest when she naps, paws crossed. Naturally, it's difficult to see her convulsing helplessly on the floor.

For one of the women in the group, Choco's fit triggered the memory of a difficult childhood experience when she had witnessed her friend passing out after a fight with her parents. Another group member offered his help to care for Choco. The dog's convulsions reminded him of how he had nursed wounded soldiers during the First Lebanon War. "Blood, so much was blood spilled there," he recalled. Another client burst into tears, recalling her father's fatal heart attack when she was eight years old.

I further discuss life events, trauma, animals, therapy, attention to events and situations, and compassion, in the following chapter.

CHAPTER EIGHT

Animal Assisted Therapy for SUD

◾──◾

Giving birth to a litter of rabbits has always brought excitement to the Rothschild 2 petting zoo. When one of the pink, bald bunnies falls out of the shelter, Kamma the dog collects it in her mouth, and brings it to the group therapy room, safe and unharmed.

In this chapter, I cite several excerpts from my published articles (Pirani, 2005, 2007). In the context of SUD treatment, integration of the therapy and techniques in the following two disciplines is an important component:

1. Working with adversity and trauma victims
2. Working with substance abuse victims

In Israel, training to integrate both disciplines is almost non-existent.

I return to addressing the treatment principles of adversity and trauma victims, which I addressed in the previous chapter.

Many clients who come to the Rothschild 2 treatment center suffer from severe mental and physical conditions. They come bearing a life of stress, trauma, delinquency, and addiction. Society and their families have rejected them, so they go physically and emotionally neglected for months and even years. We are required to integrate rules necessary for the addicts' rehabilitation, including the empathy, warmth, understanding, and support required in treating prolonged trauma and drug addiction victims (See also Foa et al., 2004; Zomer & Bleich, 2005; Seligman & Solomon, 2004; Brothers, 2004; Williams & Poijula, 2002; Najavits, 2002; Ouimette & Brown, 2003; Foa et al., 1995, 1997, 2007).

We are strict in treating our clients with the treatment plan we developed at our establishment and strict about caring for the animals based on the following principles:

1. **Honoring physical needs**: The staff needs to secure a place to sleep and food for a client and a place where they can shower. First, a therapist wishes to provide a client with shelter and privacy while honoring their most basic needs. On detox, clients feels intense pain, that appears as toothache, chills, joint pain, etc.; they need assistance in initial medical treatment. Every client caring for an animal is required to keep its habitat clean, as well as to provide it with food and water, notice if it is wounded or suffering, or keep it away from the other animals, if attacked.

2. **Confirming a client's condition**: We provide clients with an explanation of the emotional phenomena they are experiencing, and guidance in terms of how to cope with it. The professional staff praises clients on their decision to seek help and engage in treatment, introducing to them the group to which they will belong, namely, a group of clients who have suffered, but will not keep on suffering. Clients observe the way of life typical of the animal they care for. Although their communication is not verbal, they are able to convey messages through other channels of communication, by which a client will be able to tell if the animal is happy, scared, hungry, thirsty, sick, wounded, etc.

3. **Orientation**: The staff assists clients to settle into the therapeutic setting. A client's adjustment to the treatment center is simultaneous with assimilating the framework of disciplinary rules. A "shadow," namely a senior rehabilitation program participant, guides a client through their first steps. The staff is attentive to a client, letting them share their life story, but only as much as they feel capable of addressing at that point. If the professional staff feels psychological intervention should be combined with medical intervention, we suggest a client be referred to a medical consultation with our psychiatrist. Before leaving the center, a senior client hands over the animal for which they were caring to a new client who is beginning their treatment process, as though passing on the baton in a relay race; passing on their experience, acquaintance with the animal, and knowledge accumulated throughout the six months of caring for the animal.

4. **Establishing Limits**: A client needs to accept the disciplinary and structural rules of the center. Sometimes, the staff's ability to assist is limited because of budget or professional personnel limitations. At Rothschild 2, a public, ambulatory rehabilitation structure, rules are strictly enforced, as are activity schedules. Teamwork with clients and their attitudes toward themselves and toward their fellow clients, and the treatment with which they provide the animals is closely watched. So, the petting zoo also follows the same rules and its own schedule. A new client learns that they must provide the animal under their care with food and water on a daily basis. We expect a client to care for their animal's needs before having their morning coffee. "The animal has been waiting for you all night. It couldn't ask for anyone's help. Take a look, take care of it, help it."

5. **Establishing an empathy-based relationship**: Clients are encouraged to emotionally share their past grief and losses.

The professional staff at Rothschild 2 is sensitive to a client's adjustment difficulties with the transition from delinquency and the criminal world, where they had their trust in the establishment and society, to their integration into the therapeutic process.

Under these circumstances, an interesting comparison emerges: The professional staff is required to accept, empathize, support, and protect a new client while the client is expected to express empathy, support, protection and attention toward the animal in their care.

As stated, within the framework of treating an SUD, we are required to outline integrated intervention paths as follows:

1. **Empathy toward suffering and trauma**: The professional staff and the therapeutic program alumni explain to a client that rehabilitation and withdrawal from many years of substance addiction is a difficult therapeutic process, both physically and mentally. Everybody makes an effort to support a new client throughout this process. Our experience shows us that at this stage, many clients will experience emotions that have been repressed for many years - memories related to stress, trauma, sexual assault, loss, physical violence, and even the memory of the damage and hurt they've caused others.

2. **Psychoeducational guidance**: Guidance and encouragement are given toward taking rehabilitative action. The professional staff assists clients in identifying the relationship between harsh emotional conditions and an intense desire to use drugs. Clients are accustomed to escaping their stress and trauma-related memories, the psychological suffering, anxiety, rage, and depression, by using drugs. While engaging in the therapeutic process, a client realizes there are many more individuals within the group who are experiencing the same harsh feelings. Based on the experience of those who have undergone the therapeutic process, and the

professional opinion and feedback they receive, they learn to feel better as the therapeutic process progresses.

3. **Assistance in inducing cognitive balance**: A client receives the explanation that the many feelings they are experiencing at that moment are extreme emotional reactions. Their body needs to resume its production of cerebral neurobiological chemicals, which it probably ceased doing through the many years of substance abuse. The body needs to resume regulating their responses to various emotional reactions. Observation, as well as adopting a new mode of thinking, is highly important at this stage.

4. **Guided imagery**: The professional staff often starts group therapy sessions with breathing and body relaxation exercises to relieve tension. Through guided imagery, a client learns how to relax their body muscles, to inhale air into their lungs, and slowly exhale. The body of an addict is usually tense because of its consistent "emergency state,"; we retrain the body to restore its natural, relaxed and calm state. At this stage, it is important that the professional employees instill a sense of confidence within a client. A client is to feel assured that their fellow group members will not harm them either physically or verbally, and that they will not be ridiculed for their weaknesses. We emphasize to clients that sharing secrets with fellow group members is not mandatory, but only if it feels right.

5. **Further treatment and progress**: A client gradually integrates into the therapeutic structure. They witness the empowered graduate patients, and how they have evolved and experienced great relief over time. A client learns that this is a long therapeutic process. Later they receive psychological support and personal therapy. Additionally, we offer them to be involved in other therapy groups, including support groups that run in their neighborhood on a daily basis.

Clients realize that the treatment center's discipline and rules are intended to protect, rather than harm them. The therapeutic technique implemented in SUD intervention relies on commonly known principles of psychological rehabilitation in adversity and trauma:

- A client's reaction is a normal reaction to a lasting, extreme condition (many people in the same condition act the same)

- Many clients, who are substance addicts, approach us seeking assistance in terms of a referral to National Insurance, or legal assistance. Based on our deductive experience, we assume they are carrying the burden of a traumatizing past full of suffering, even if they did not openly state it when they first approached us

- Frequent reactions: The professional staff is to be acquainted with SUD's common behavioral characteristics, including defense mechanisms, denial, repression, rage and anger outbursts, and the intense desire to return to substance abuse

- Failed treatment: A percentage of clients seeking treatment at Rothschild 2 have previously sought treatment through numerous frameworks. Presumably, treatment in some of these frameworks constituted an experience of disappointment or failure. Thus, we convey the following message, both explicitly and implicitly: The professional staff is at your assistance, and will do its utmost to prevent any further harm to you.

Animal Assisted Therapy (AAT)

Animal Assisted Therapy is one of the instruments I have adapted with the professional staff at Rothschild 2 to suit SUD treatment (Pirani & Teichman, 1999; Pirani, Fishelson, & Zacks, 2001; Pirani & Shani, 2003; Pirani, 2004). This therapeutic instrument allows a client to reveal their repressed memories. Additionally, it allows the professional staff to identify psychological pain and note transformations of traumatizing events, through a client's care and attitude toward the pet. Treating SUD through animals is merely an instrument through which a client's condition may be inferred (Pirani & Shani, 2003). Furthermore, this type of therapy allows the formation of a "therapeutic setting," where a client acts just as a child would play within the "potential setting," a term coined by Winnicott in 1970.

In this chapter, I illustrate how animal assisted therapy facilitates treating Dalit and her peers Yaron, Efrat, Benny, and Judah. As mentioned previously, a traumatizing experience is causally related to future psychological damage: The effects of childhood abuse on adult psychopathology are reviewed in the many articles I cite in Chapter Two. The traumatizing episodes usually involve severe feelings of threat, to both life and physical wholeness. Some of these episodes reappear as intrusive memories, a sense of paralysis, emotional dullness, dissociation from others, lack of reactivity to one's surroundings, and nightmares. Other episodes in that category manifest as hyperarousal, which involves disruption related to behavior control and compulsive fears, as stated in Chapters Two, Three, and Four.

As mentioned above, traumatic episodes often damage relationships. They challenge basic interpersonal relations, as we witness through Dalit's relationship with her fellow group members. Many clients have reported losing basic trust in others because of physical or sexual abuse, verbal violence, and even witnessing terrorist attacks. In such extreme situations, an SUD addict will feel emptiness, tremendous vulnerability, a feeling of worthlessness and lack of meaning, as well as the feeling that "they are part of the world of the dead, rather than the world of the living," (Herman, 1992). SUD clients often experience emotional detachment, apathy, inability to experience human emotions, restlessness and discomfort. It is important to mention that some therapists assume that a traumatic dissociation's action is morphine-like, causing disconnection of the pain from the emotion (Atkinson, 1996; Herman, 1992; Munitz, 1994). Other approaches, however, refer to the drug as symbolizing a container, filling up with and absorbing intensely inexhaustible emotions (Amali, 1995). This assumption appears in various therapeutic contexts, manifested within the gradual process of change a patient undergoes throughout the course of therapy.

Dalit and other clients who come to Rothschild 2 treatment center are adults. It is evident that for years, they have suffered issues related to basic trust, as well as a blow to their ability to develop initiative, as portrayed by Herman (1992) and the normal course of their personality's development, as portrayed by Amali (1995). Indeed, even when clients are adults other issues such as delinquency and substance addiction, somatic manifestations and nightmares—known as the symptoms of post-traumatic stress disorder syndrome—(Munitz, 1994; Teichman, 1989) mask their past trauma.

SUD clients treated at the Rothschild 2 treatment center often report that for many years they felt detached from their emotions and thoughts, unable to control them. In the chapters addressing therapeutic intervention, I demonstrate that these feelings disappear for the most part when integrated into more advanced therapeutic processes.

The core of psychological trauma involves banishment of one's strength and disconnection from others (Herman, 1992). Hence, there are many therapists who assume that recovery should be based on re-empowering a patient and enhancing their confidence, through reconstructing their traumatic story, as well as by forming new social connections in their new social surroundings. The new social connections formed among group members assist them in acquiring new psychological skills, replacing those damaged by the traumatic experience, which manifested itself as many years of psychological suffering, emotion repression, and drug abuse.

Animal Assisted Therapy is a therapeutic technique that has been implemented at Rothschild 2 treatment center for approximately eight years and is enacted in two main therapeutic settings: The clinic and the therapeutic setting. I facilitate the group along with Liat Shani, a certified Animal Assisted Therapist.

In the day center group, approximately fifteen patients come for a rehabilitative treatment lasting six months, Sunday through Thursday, 8 a.m.-2 p.m. The group absorbs new clients on a waiting list basis. When a client completes six months of treatment, a new patient takes their place. The Animal Assisted Therapy group takes place twice a week, Mondays and Thursdays at 10 a.m.-11.30 a.m. At the beginning of the session, the group's senior members and the facilitators welcome new patients recently admitted to the treatment center. We explain the unique style of the AAT group to the new patients. Then, the clients gather into teams by their preferences for the animals. Within the framework of the AAT group, the clients care for hamsters, rabbits, a dog, hens, ducks, pigeons, mice, and parrots.

Following a short introduction of the new clients to the group, and explanations of the petting zoo work procedure, they engage in the work and care related to the cages and animals under their care for a 20-minute time stretch. During that time, Liat and I walk among the clients, engaging in work related to the cages, and consider the therapeutic contents rising from the clients' encounters with the animals. Meanwhile, we formulate a therapeutic theme for the group discussion, to be held when the work with the animals is completed. During the discussion, the group and facilitators sit in a circle, allowing everyone to see one another.

Here I outline some of the AAT group sessions from my years of work:

Dalit and the Rabbits, Mamush and Nanus

Dalit, a young woman about thirty years old, came to group about a month ago. She had also married a drug addict. Foster care services had taken her one-year-old son into custody, because he had been diagnosed at birth as suffering from withdrawal syndrome. The birth of a baby diagnosed with withdrawal syndrome involves, as part of the procedures at maternity wards in hospitals, social workers and welfare services. If the professionals receive the impression that the mother is incapable of caring for the baby, the baby is put into temporary foster care, where it will be cared for until the court's ruling, to either be returned to its mother's custody or given up for adoption.

When Dalit came to the treatment center, she was unkempt: Her clothes were old and torn and her hair was uncombed. Scars cover ed her very thin arms and face, and she limped on her left leg, a matter I'll address later. Dalit's brown eyes mirrored her plea *Help me save myself. Help me return my only son to my arms.*

Initially, the group members have trouble accepting Dalit. Her appearance is far from appealing, her behavior is rigid and unfriendly. This behavior is typical of a woman who has learned to survive with users and abusers, losing her interpersonal relations in the process.

Dalit was born into an immigrant family of ten, who lived in poverty and underwent a great deal of trouble while trying to integrate into Israeli society. As a child, one of her older brothers raped her many times over a long period. The rape would always take place in the afternoon or at night. We have not been able to receive clarification from her as to whether or not any of the other family members knew about the rape, or heard her cries. At ten, her behavior at school severely worsened, and she was sent to a boarding school in a nearby town. She remembers the intense longing for her family, but none of her family members made the effort to visit her. Her brother continued to sexually assault her, even when she would come home for school holidays.

In her adolescence, she adopted provocative behavior, which in retrospect can be interpreted as a cry for help. She slept with many older boys to get attention; sexual assaults and acts of rape would go on while at boarding school as well.

At 16 years old, she dropped out of boarding school but would not return to her bitter home. She associated with boys and girls her age who were wandering the streets, started smoking pot and soon became addicted to hallucinatory drugs, ecstasy, and heroin. As part of her survival efforts, she learned she could receive drugs for free if she slept with the person providing her the dose; boys her age, from boarding school or the street, adult men, or even her dealer, who later offered her the option of prostitution.

She developed a dependency on the drugs, which provided her with an illusionary peace of mind, temporarily numbing her emotional pains. At 25, she got into a fight with one of the drug dealers who had seduced her into prostitution and served as her pimp. Afterwards, he had tried to run her over with his car. In hospital she spent many months in rehabilitation and treatment. Her limp is a consequence of that episode. Approximately a year later, she had an unplanned pregnancy that she wasn't aware of until her final months of pregnancy. When her son was born, it was apparent he was suffering withdrawal symptoms.

Dalit was referred to the Rothschild 2 Treatment Center by a social worker from the welfare services. With a strong motherly instinct, she wanted her child back in her custody. In her early days of treatment, soon after her son was taken from her, she sank into depression and despair. In group, Liat asked her to choose the animal she would like to care for. Dalit chose a pair of scruffy rabbits from the nearby kindergarten, who had not been cared for during the summer vacation.

Assuming Parental Responsibility through the Animal Assisted Therapeutic Process

Following a substance detoxification process, Dalit was admitted into the day center therapy group. In the group, she underwent an initial process of acquiring basic behavioral skills, which facilitated her in integrating into the treatment and adjusting to her new life without drugs. Throughout the therapeutic process, Dalit related the prolonged physical and sexual abuse she underwent as a child, and the continuous depression into which she had sunk in those years. "The solution I adopted," says Dalit, "was to use heroin, so I didn't feel pain."

After six months of treatment, Dalit graduated to the second stage. We established the following therapeutic goals for Dalit:

1. Assume daily responsibility of the petting zoo in the therapeutic setting from 8-10 a.m. The staff believes that daily performance at the mini zoo keeps up Dalit's personal strength and her self-confidence. The staff appreciates Dalit for her personal effort and willingness to care for an animal within the therapeutic setting.

2. Maintain a well-arranged, consistent daily schedule, even after the first six months of treatment and sobriety. It is important to show up at the treatment center on the days and times scheduled, and that you are present at the treatment. We hope that during this course of time you learn additional modes of arranging and controlling your life.

    The staff expected to see Dalit's self-confidence improve, and it did. Gradually, she stripped herself of her former identity, "the bad one", "the hurt one", "the contaminated one," and adopted a new identity. She began forming new relationships within the group and her therapeutic environment (see the process outlined in Figure 1A).

3. Rent an apartment and move into it permanently, to allow yourself to develop a life of your own. Indeed, Dalit found an apartment, bought basic appliances, and resumed cleaning her own home, cooking, and having friends over, and progressed into her new life, one day at a time.

4. Emphasis is on your continued learning, allowing you to further enhance your verbal communication with the therapists and your peers, simultaneous to developing your initial parenting skills.

We notice Dalit becoming more attentive to others and more self-aware. Encouraging outcomes soon emerge. I report to the court on the initial outcomes of Dalit's evolved behavior, and in another court hearing, at which her new maternal abilities were discussed, the judge accepts our recommendations. The judge allows Dalit, guided by the Rothschild 2 professional staff, to prepare for a future session with her son, who is still in foster care.

Identifying, Connecting to and Employing Emotions, in a Developmental Process Through AAT

Yaron, a 40-year-old, twice divorced father of three from both marriages, came to the treatment center for another rehabilitation attempt, having dropped out in 2002, since he had been unable to cope with the intense emotions he had developed toward one of the center's female patients.

He reports a condition I interpret as emotional dissociation toward his children. He claims that his inability to feel anything toward his children, along with his incapability to express joy or sadness, cause him intense frustration, resulting in his regressive behavior.

Here are biographical details about Yaron's life that I have recorded: He was raised in an unpredictable, mentally and physically abusive setting, where, as he stated, he always feared the unexpected. While treating Yaron, I identify robot-like behavior, to some extent, a strength with which he learned to survive in his latest years as a neglected, hungry, and beaten homeless man. Yaron related to me how, through those years, he had learned that any emotion would be, eventually, "a waste of mental energy needed to survive," (see process in Figure 1A).

I assign several therapeutic tasks to Yaron, aided by Rothschild 2's therapeutic setting:

1. Choose an animal at the petting zoo, care for it, and look after it. Feed the animal, change its bedding, and observe its daily behavior.

    I assume this activity might enhance Yaron's initial feelings, developing his sense of control over his surroundings, and thereby, his responsibility for his own life.

2. Hold the animal you have chosen (a Siberian hamster) for 30 minutes daily.

    I assume that the contact between Yaron's palms and the hamster, would encourage emotions from Yaron of compassion, love, anger, rejection, and even care toward the animal. We discuss these emotions throughout the therapeutic process.

3. Illustrate your emotions to the group. It is important we hear repeatedly the feelings that arise from your encounter with the hamster which you are caring for. Through these feelings, we can attempt to understand other emotional states that you have trouble expressing to the group.

4. I ask Yaron to take note of his own inner voice, to connect to his inner feelings, and to pay less attention to how others respond to him.

Up to that point, most of Yaron's responses, mirroring, and attitudes had been directed at his therapeutic group members. I notice that he begins to develop an initial emotional ability for intimacy with others, simultaneously to his renewed ability to form new social relations. This ability has improved within the therapeutic group, allowing him to feel that he is not alone in his human surroundings. A few weeks later, we saw Yaron speaking to the animal he cares for, being more attentive to it than just its basic needs. In addition, his responses to other group members seemed calmer, allowing him to reintegrate into the group, and receive feedback and reinforcement. It seems that Yaron is successfully connecting to his emotions.

Nursing – Empowering Feminine and Maternal Strengths

Efrat, a 39-year-old single woman, speaks at the therapeutic group about her mistrust of men and her firm decision not to marry or have children. She relates a harsh relationship as a child with her mother, which involved continuous verbal violence from a terrified mother. At a young age, her mother unexpectedly died of a heart attack, forcing Efrat to serve as a mother to her four younger siblings. "I felt as though I was losing the most glorious years of my life. In those years, I became addicted to hardcore drugs, because only they eased the feeling of loss."

When I notice she takes a special interest in an orphaned rabbit kit, I propose several therapeutic goals to her:

1. Feed the kits with a pipette to facilitate their survival. The process that simulates nursing is an experience that will arouse maternal emotions.

2. Create nursing schedules – I suggest Efrat establish prearranged nursing hours for the kits. These instructions are important because they allow Efrat to control her surroundings and the time she has on her hands. We assume that through this established activity, Efrat will acquire other tools to function in her new life without drug abuse.

3. Attempt to seek help from any of the group members in times of need. In this way, we strive to assist her in developing her abilities to trust and believe others.

The nursing process brings up intense emotion in Efrat, and is overwhelming for her. The same thing happens to the other group members. Nursing becomes a sacred time, when any activity within it receives their full attention.

The serene therapeutic setting of rabbit care allows Efrat to gradually establish a sense of confidence and control, inducing initiative. Efrat gets to know the kits – the active one, the curious one, the confident one, and the calm one. I notice that while she cares for the kits, she projects her own nature on them. For example, when she expresses fear of accidentally hurting a rabbit kit during the care and nursing process, the staff encourage her to keep it up. I further praise Efrat for her devoted care of the kits. "Their growth and development is evidence of that," I tell her. I feel I am successful in empowering her strengths (see Figure 1A).

Efrat chose names for the kits, and even asked to take them home for the weekend, so she could continue caring for them.

Nursing allowed Efrat to open up emotionally, and even led her into a new intimate relationship. She shares her childhood trauma with the group, and even dares speaking of the notion of having children in the near future.

Functional Empowerment Through Assuming Responsibility as an "On Duty" Member

Benny, 25 years old, comes to the treatment center absorbed in his feelings, egocentric, lacking any initiative or confidence in his social relations, and indifferent to the feelings expressed by his fellow members. His appearance is unkempt, and, based on the professional staff's initial impression, he appears to lack any giving abilities, both toward his fellow group members and by his attitude toward the animals.

In the professional literature, Benny's responses are known as "robot-like." Emotional responses are perceived as a waste of vital mental energy. Benny has lived this way throughout his own struggle to survive in the past few months. During the assessment process, I also realize that Benny is suffering from depression that is disrupting his sleep, damaging his appetite, and overwhelming him with harsh feelings of despair and hopelessness.

As a child, Benny's parents had continuously abused him, physically and mentally. His mother would scream at him and hit him, regardless of his behavior at a given moment. She would berate and emasculate him, which deeply wounded him. His father, on the other hand, was detached and emotionally distant from him, and completely ignored his emotional needs. As a child, Benny saw his father as a helpless figure who just stood by, uninvolved in his life.

Furthermore, Benny reveals a high level of personal and social functioning abilities, of which we had not been aware. He completed a combat military course with honors in a military training program. For many years, he expressed his harsh rage toward his parents through self-harming and blame. Later, all that was channeled through delinquency and drug abuse (see process outlined in Figure 1A). Over the years, Benny developed a distorted estimation of his abilities and self-confidence. His self-confidence remained dependent on the evaluation and appreciation of others.

I am interested in re-empowering Benny's mental strength, enhancing his self-confidence, and re-establishing his ability to achieve. It's important that Benny connect to his fellow group members.

Throughout treatment, he relates how he feels about his excellence in military service, how it was unnatural, and just covered up for his lack of self-confidence. Several weeks later, I assign Benny to the on-duty cadet job, where he must establish the animal caring schedule, assign work tasks to others, inform the staff when to replenish the food supply, and report on safety measures.

The new position demands Benny's leadership and verbal skills, as well as the ability to be attentive to his peers by force of his position as the group's liaison to the staff.

Over time, thanks to gaining the staff's trust and the help he receives from his fellow group members, his self-esteem returns. Benny learns to employ his personal and mental strength. This is evidenced in the positive feedback he receives from his peers.

Empowering a Patient Who Was a Victim of Physical Abuse by Integrating the Professional Staff as a Parental Model

Judah is a 30-year-old single man, an immigrant from Russia, who is very thin and pale, and who appears pathetic in his outlandish attire, with his gel-smeared hair and the odd hats he wears. He comes to the treatment center apprehensive and afraid. He seems to lack self-confidence, is embarrassed and passive. Apparently, he isn't motivated to check where he stands on the waiting list for the day center. When he doesn't show for registration day, the professional staff does not give up, and asks him to register, time and again.

Approximately a month after his admittance to therapy, he shares with the group his story of the physical and mental abuse he experienced as a child. His father would beat him and lock him for days in the backyard shed, like "a caged animal," as he put it. Judah relates how his father ignored the emotional damage it caused him.

One morning, he arrived agitated and weeping. He told the staff about addict friends he previously knew who had caught him on the street. They had violently searched his body to see if he was carrying. This humiliating episode had hurt him deeply, bringing to the surface the feelings associated with the trauma he experienced as a child. We try to encourage him and let him share the episode with us.

Being attentive to Judah's mental condition, we try to convey a parental model different from the one he knows (see Figure 1 A). I seek to assist him through continued therapy, in spite of his emotional difficulty.

One day, he approaches me rather shaken. He shows me the parrot he had been looking after: it has an injured leg, which had caught in an iron wire. With great sorrow, we are forced to cut off the wounded leg, for the sake of the bird's survival. I praise Judah for his sensitive and professional treatment of the bird, and I witness the compassion and care he expresses towards it. The staff supports Judah as well, in the presence of all group members, for his quick, efficient action toward saving the parrot's life, and we ask him to continue caring for it. The group is very touched by the story, reinforcing his efficient performance. For him, it is another powerful emotional experience; from being an abuse victim in the past, he is now serving as a savior of another, caring for a victim.

I feel that Judah is testing my behavior, just as I test his. I assume that by observing me, he is learning about my constant care and concern for the animals, which constitutes a different parental model to the one he has known, one in which parents express sensitivity toward their family members, and care for them.

A few days later, I notice the significant change in Judah's appearance. He has removed his hat and has stopped applying gel to his hair. He smiles more, is more confident in his conduct, and is more involved in group. I assume he is undergoing a powerful, corrective therapeutic experience.

In this book, I often mention that substance use is one way of coping with PTSD. I demonstrate that some clients respond to traumatic memories by avoiding them and their compulsive thoughts, which costs them their day-to-day functioning due to anxiety. In Chapter Two, we mentioned the relationship between addiction to psychoactive drugs and a client's past stress and trauma experiences. The study indicating that 85 percent of people suffering post-traumatic stress disorder develop issues related to drug addiction, accounts for the large number of addicts who are post-trauma victims and who we encounter at the Rothschild 2 Treatment Center. It is for good reason that Briere (1988) reports that childhood abuse victims tend to use substances and alcohol more than other patients do. For those victims, the substance often serves as an escape from their anxiety, depression, and mental stress.

In our work with SUD, we are further identifying increasing evidence of how drugs block emotions. On the one hand, the drug serves as some emotional response to an addict's search for feelings of warmth and love. On the other hand, it blocks their ability to feel emotions and mental pain.

I demonstrate the approaches that assume that use of drugs brings on some intermediate state at the point where the physical and mental aspects meet. In other words, a drug can either bridge these aspects, or even disconnect them, and, at any rate, serves as a mental mechanism for survival (Amali, 1995). According to Amali, this state manifests when an "illusionary intermediate domain is formed due to the use of substances," which provides an imaginary sense of confidence and a false sense of protection. In relation to this approach, I state that without the drug, for a long time the SUD patient is unable to gain strength from their own personality or ego to cope with the stress they face.

If we know SUD relies on an illusionary "transition object" (Amali, 1995; Winnicott, 1971) throughout the therapeutic process, we assist the client to search for another "transition object." It is important to state this assumption along with our understanding of the relationship between an addict's life and the way the substances affect them. Drugs have qualities that affect one's ability to feel emotions, thereby serving the need to dull past trauma. Often, addicts use substances as a "transitional act," unconsciously perceiving the drug as a regressive defense mechanism to fulfill their need and protect them from their feelings. Those supporting similar approaches assume that drug use illustrates a circular process of desperately clinging on to the illusion it induces, and the trouble letting go of this illusion.

We notice that substance abuse serves as a kind of "storage tool," or "container" allowing emotional flooding on the client's part on the one hand, and on the other hand, a "filter" or "processor" of harsh or insufferable feelings.

Paradoxically, Amali (1995) mentions that substance use as a behavior is designed to maintain life while searching for meaning, yet its outcome proceeds onward to sometimes result in risks related to self-harm, abuse of others, and sometimes death.

Self-abuse and loss encountered by many clients simultaneously to their prolonged addiction raises another comment mentioned in previous chapters of this book, within the framework of discussing post-trauma. Some unfair correspondence is formed in this case, or, alternately, some conceptual comparison that society has not yet been able to assimilate.

There's a difference in the suffering experienced by trauma victims who receive a certain extent of public acknowledgement, as in terror, war, and captivity victims (Herman, 1992), to the suffering experienced by other trauma victims, who have not yet been sufficiently acknowledged by society, and whose damage is an outcome of physical, mental, or sexual abuse (see Figure 1A).

Indeed, retrospectively working with SUD patients at the Rothschild 2 Treatment Center, has often yielded a voice of disappointment in the society within which they were abused. This disappointment stems from the fact that society offered them no aid, which they in fact found in substance abuse. "The drug provided us with a temporary cure for our harsh feelings – anxiety and depression, pain and mental stress – and also granted us feelings of self-confidence, happiness; relief from inhibitions, and even increased self-esteem," they state.

Substance abuse may deceive SUD clients for many years. On the one hand, it can induce a feeling of inner relief, an illusion that they control their feelings and abilities to form social connections, as well as induce feelings of being outgoing and open in intimate situations, and the power to cope with authorities. On the other hand, substance abuse can induce rigid illusions of distorted abilities, as well as the presence of imaginary strength, which poses difficulty to an addict in terms of interpreting reality correctly.

With SUD, inner anticipation (regarding anxiety, depression, pain, and lack of self-confidence) meets the corresponding drug effects (the SUD patient has the feeling it fits like a glove), then an omnipotent illusion ensues, where the drug acts as the container to their personal needs (Amali, 1995).

Throughout the drug detoxification process and continued therapeutic process, a new framework of defense mechanism can be proposed to the SUD, replacing defense mechanisms that were supposedly formed by the substances. The therapeutic structure provides addicts with a new defense mechanism, an external guarding system and an internal deterrence system. All these serve as defensive walls, stopping clients from relapsing into substance abuse. The professional staff wants the therapeutic structure to allow addicts to undergo a process of renewed mental growth and development (see Pirani & Shani, 2003; Pirani et al., 2001).

THE PROCESS

Causes of PTSD and stress ⟶ Continuous mental condition ⟶ Adaptive and non-adaptive
Intermediate functioning ⟶ Availability of mental energy (+) ⟶ Outcome

Constriction • Hyperarousal • Intrusion

- Captivity
- Verbal violence
- Physical violence
- Natural disaster
- War

Sexual assault
PTSD

client's low functioning

- ♦ Available mental energy
- ♦ (-) mental energy channeled toward repression and stress (+)

- Circularity to non-adaptation
- Anxiety
- Depression
- Substance abuse

- Reconstruction of trauma within the "therapeutic setting"
- Empowerment
- Verbal expression of emotions
- Corrective mental reconstruction
- Social support

High-functioning of the client

- ♦ Available mental energy
- ♦ (+) Mental energy channeled toward stress (-)

- Enhanced quality of life
- Capability of emotional expression

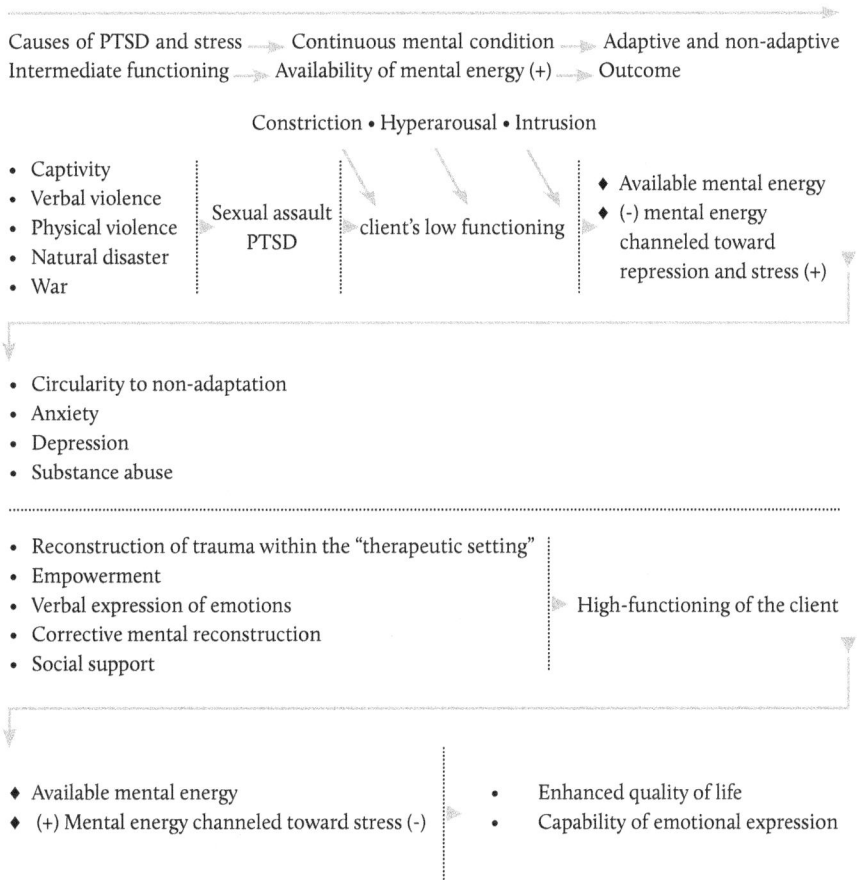

Figure 1. The new intervention technique through Animal Assisted Therapy (AAT) releases mental energy in coping with traumatic memories, thus facilitating higher personal functioning

At this point, I continue to address AAT that serves the Rothschild 2 treatment staff as a therapeutic intervention technique to treat SUD in a therapeutic setting.

Our clinical experience often implies that addicts with SUD indeed need some new container to hold their lost basic confidence, the same sort of "magical" feeling their mother was supposed to grant them as children (Amali, 1995). We aim that the therapeutic group members, the professional staff, and other people in an addict's new social field are capable of moderating the impression left by a tragedy, and influence, in some degree, the recovery processes.

Therefore, there is no doubt that clients are granted the opportunity for renewed mental growth through the therapeutic group at the sheltered setting offered by Rothschild 2, the mutual human concern that develops among its members, and therapeutic techniques such as Animal Assisted Therapy.

It is clear to the treatment staff, and to me, that our efforts to empower a patient's strength by re-establishing their sense of responsibility in life and the lives of others, and by improving their functioning, as well as encouraging new initiatives, allow them to practice for their future life through carefully monitored therapeutic processes within the therapeutic setting.

Moreover, through the empowerment processes within treatment, we aim for coherence between the mutual support among the group members and a client's own self-confidence. We strive to induce a sense of autonomy unique to each client. This is an ongoing, long-term therapeutic process. The Rothschild 2 treatment staff witnesses processes in which the SUD client no longer fears being with another person, or being on their own, and can integrate into society.

We assume the therapeutic setting portrayed in this therapeutic technique is one of the instruments facilitating this change.

One of the tasks of the staff treating SUD at Rothschild 2 is the reconstruction of a clients' basic trust, in both their therapeutic setting and their new social setting.

For that person, and as a broader conceptual view, the professional staff views the whole therapeutic setting as a broader complex, which, aside from its therapeutic functions, serves as a place of rest and social gathering. This therapeutic complex provides a client with initial feelings of acceptance, security, care, protection, and understanding.

The therapeutic setting fulfills a highly important role in an addict's recovery, because it allows them to share their memories of the harsh trauma they experienced. This sharing allows them, throughout their time in treatment, to learn from the professional staff how to restore feelings of security and peace. Indeed, we notice the changes clients undergo as early as in the initial step of caring for an animal at the Rothschild 2 complex (Pirani et al., 2001). Thus, even if we have witnessed the psychological trauma as being the helpless individual's own tragedy, the intervention by the Rothschild 2 professional staff is sufficient for offering abundant help at an early stage of treatment.

Understanding the significance of the Rothschild 2 therapeutic structure is the key to understanding the unique models we have developed and the therapeutic technique I portray in this chapter. In other words, on the one hand the behavioral platform instructing a client how to behave in their new life, without substances, and on the other hand, a sheltered therapeutic structure that allows them to grow and develop.

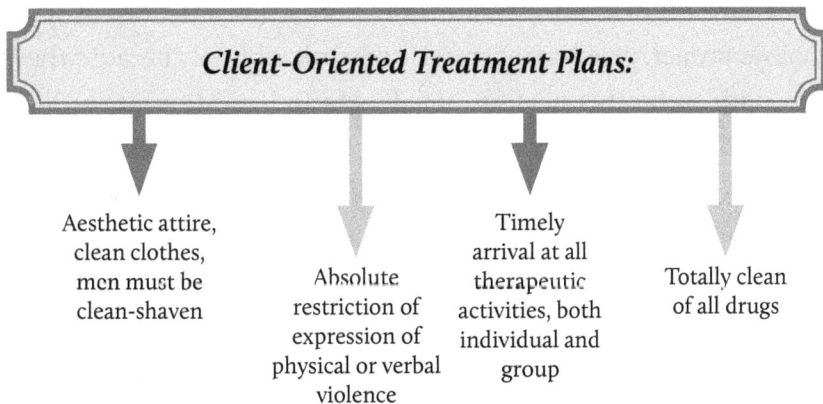

Client-Oriented Treatment Plans:

Aesthetic attire, clean clothes, men must be clean-shaven

Absolute restriction of expression of physical or verbal violence

Timely arrival at all therapeutic activities, both individual and group

Totally clean of all drugs

Figure 2. The behavior platform on which the personal treatment plan for each client is established

The continuous therapeutic work within this setting allows clients in rehabilitation to feel as though they are contained by some magic, omnipotent vessel. Based on the assumption made by the psychoanalytical approaches, a child expects to experience such an instrument in their early life through their mother's magical figure (Amali, 1995). Hence, it is clear that the treatment staff will better employ their professional ability if they succeed in inducing a secure, consistent, constant, containing, protective, and tolerant climate for clients within the therapeutic setting. In order to attain these goals, the treatment staff must work and function us one unit, as parents would act as one secure and protective family unit, which enables normal development in its children.

Issues such as interpersonal relations among group members, ethics, an individual's protection and dignity, adherence to proper attire and hygiene, and the staff's concern and interest in the SUD's emotional experiences, are conveyed as a clear and uniform, therapeutic line, which is containing and common among all the treatment staff members.

This chapter demonstrates how the Rothschild 2 treatment staff employs proper, professional modes of work, not only because they share with each other professional doubts and questions, as well as ethical dilemmas and decision making processes, but also because they show up for every discussion as one professional entity, united both in their demands from the patients and their decisions regarding them. As a professional team, we must maintain the behavioral platform's foundation in order to allow for a client's emotional and therapeutic change. It is important to note that damage to one of the "legs" holding the therapeutic "table" could damage the whole therapeutic outline (See Figure 2A).

Throughout the rehabilitation processes, the treatment staff emphasizes the therapeutic setting as inducing security and protection, as well as offering a new human society. We allow clients to recall the personal trauma they experienced and grieve over it (often while relating their life story), and strive to integrate the two so as to guide them toward other vital daily functions.

Additionally, the Rothschild 2 treatment staff functions as a "behavioral model" that holds its clients, protects them and cares for them, and for the animals at the petting zoo and within the therapeutic setting. With every step taken within the therapeutic setting, the staff members must bear in mind that they are being tested by the clients, simultaneous to the staff's testing of them. They are observing their care for the animals, whether they are feeding them, cleaning their cages, and assisting them in distress. "Therapeutic setting" interactions are constantly being tested through mutual processes; on the one hand, clients observe the staff's behavior within the therapeutic setting and on the other hand, the staff observes clients' behavior within this same setting. The feedback is certainly mutual, enriching and inspiring for both parties.

The clients' therapeutic process revolves around several circles: reestablishing self-confidence, beginning with their control over their bodies; appearance (maintaining clean attire, daily shaving for men); immediate, external control (responsibility for animals); and finally, broader control of their close environment through work and involvement in their family life (see Figure 1A).

Various writers, such as Amali (1995), Herman (1992), and Prince (1995), maintain that the recovery process is meant to occur within group relations, rather than in isolation. This is the foundation for another important principle of the Rothschild 2 Treatment Center's activity. Most of the center's activities take place in dynamic therapeutic groups, emphasizing many aspects of the behavioral complex within the therapeutic setting. We keep in mind that although drug abuse may serve as a "positive" adaptive factor at a time of total helplessness in stress and trauma, it becomes a dysfunctional adaptive factor once danger is gone.

Later, we witness a recovering addict's renewed ability to be compassionate with animals, channel emotions towards them, and provide the animal in their care with quality of life. This marks the beginning of a new rehabilitation path in a client's life. AAT has been reviewed in many articles, as is indicated in the references list. In two of my published articles, I portray the development of therapeutic instruments allowed by AAT (Pirani & Shani, 2003; Pirani et al., 2001). These articles emphasize that through caring for animals, we can learn about a client's personal content, which has been repressed and denied for many years.

In the following pages, I present several more cases to shed light on this complex, unique, and innovative therapeutic approach toward SUD, developed at the Rothschild 2 Treatment Center.

The therapeutic situations presented in the book's final chapters are single cases within a diversity of cases we encounter as professionals in an effort to assist patients suffering from PTSD. The therapeutic technique portrayed in this chapter has allowed me to demonstrate clients' experiences within some "intermediate domain" which serves as a container for another, future emotional encounter, a framework for experiencing "transition actions," (Pirani & Shani, 2003), and to present us therapists as assisting SUD in a different therapeutic mode.

The therapeutic processes I indicate in this chapter, involve an attempt to replace the negative, regressive "transition object," which was sometimes the substance abuse, with a more adaptive, permissible, and progress-inducing behavior (see Figure 1A). We feel that rendering mental energies available, rather than channeling them toward repressing emotional pain and denying traumatic emotions, facilitates a client's progress throughout the rehabilitation processes.

While writing this chapter, I must address Israel's harsh reality in recent years, which is becoming increasingly tense, stressful, and traumatic. Israeli society is experiencing a harsh reality of suicide bombings, violent terrorist actions, and a climate of anxiety and fear. Many individuals in Israel are coping with trauma and loss through their encounters with murdered or injured persons and even by their random exposure as rescuers. Many are undergoing sudden, extreme traumatic experiences in their lives. One can hear in the media how so many are raising harsh feelings regarding their faith in human society, their peers, and even in their attitude toward those in their circles, near and far. In a country replete with suicide bombings, terrorist attacks, pain, personal tragedy, and bereavement, we are likely to witness an increasingly large number of individuals who will experience phenomena of PTSD and behave accordingly.

This chapter of the book presents a different therapeutic technique, allowing empowerment, acceptance, restoration of patients' strengths and skills, and their encouragement to form new social connections. This technique can facilitate the rehabilitative, therapeutic process not only with SUD, but also with victims of other traumatic syndromes. Past factors yielding the traumatizing experience are not essential for employing this therapeutic technique. Therefore, I assume that its implementation would be beneficial for any client suffering PTSD, and there is room to think how to construct models relying on the theoretical and rehabilitative principles I portray in this chapter, to assist post-trauma stress disorder in other public structures.

At Week's Closure Group, some clients express discomfort due to the expected loneliness, and flooding of compulsive thoughts they experience over the weekend when they will be alone. Assuring that the contact sheet with the group members' telephone numbers is available to everybody, is highly important to us. It may be of assistance in moments of crisis and distress, allowing for any member to seek out a fellow member. I ask Zehava and Maya to pay special attention to Vivian, who shared her life story this week, and whose personal pain shocked us all. Zehava reminds the group members that the staff may be contacted during the weekend as well, during times of stress or crisis. Maya informs one of the group members, Miro, that Sunday will be his turn to relate his life story.

Another therapeutic instrument I discuss in the following chapter is dealing with prolonged exposure to traumatizing memories.

Chapter Nine

Prolonged Exposure Treatment for SUD

———————————————————

After one of their brothers had been snatched by the cat, the rabbit kits would flee for their lives whenever they heard sounds or sensed any unusual movement. Slowly, having safely and continuously observed their mother, the kits dared resume their play within their designated space.

Professor Edna Foa developed prolonged exposure (PE) as another therapeutic instrument for treating trauma victims. This therapeutic instrument has been experimented with and practiced at Rothschild 2 as an experiential intervention among SUD. "PE is a treatment method that assists a patient to directly cope with anxiety disorder by enhancing their quality of life. They cope with intrusive thoughts, flashbacks, and the attempt to avoid trauma-related memories," (Foa et al., 2004, 2007). Sometimes, SUD manifests in a victim as a reminder of their trauma, at which point we observe an increased craving for drugs. It is because of such situations that work on trauma among substance addicts becomes even more complicated. However, it is consensual among many experts that "exposure therapy is the quickest, most effective method for working on trauma memories, and is particularly recommended in the case of tough outbursts, flashbacks, trauma-induced fears, panic, and avoidance."

Some researchers (Foa et al., 2004; Ouimette & Brown, 2003) indicate several important principles:

1. Objectively, safe situations bear no risk within a therapy framework that triggers a memory of the trauma

2. The memory associated with the traumatic experience is different to the traumatic experience itself

3. Many findings indicate that prolonged exposure to stimuli that arouse fear, when there is no attempt to avoid or escape the memories, results in reduced fear or anxiety

As previously mentioned, one of the main therapeutic instruments common in working on trauma is prolonged exposure therapy. There are two key techniques comprising this exposure:

1. Exposure through imagery
2. Exposure through in vivo methods

Therapists employ one of the techniques mentioned above, based on the following factors: The nature of the patient concerned, their ability to recall the traumatizing event, and the length of time that has passed since the traumatic experience. The first technique is usually implemented when a difficulty to reconstruct the situation or to duplicate the abusive episode with no imagery is encountered. The second technique requires strict selection of patients, since exposure should avoid employing stimuli that could worsen the patient's physical or mental condition.

Although many researchers support the exposure technique, the professional literature also indicates points of criticism related to this technique, and they are to be considered, particularly in working with substance-addicted trauma victims:

1. Patients who suffer childhood trauma sometimes remember unclear flashes of memory, which renders recollection through imagination more difficult.

2. Anger is a common phenomenon in forgetting processes among PTSD victims. This response should be acknowledged, since anger throughout treatment could prompt an emotional blockage and even temporarily sabotage the process.

3. It is important that trauma-related memory treatment be implemented among former addicts, along with participation in an NA program. It is known to therapists who work with addicts that a negative mood intensifies cravings for a substance, especially among people coping with traumatic memories. Participating in an NA group may serve as another aid in coping with the therapeutic processes.

4. There are PE therapy groups which do not reproach a patient for relapsing into substance abuse while participating in the exposure group, and do not withdraw them from the program, but rather, discuss it within the group's forum (Ouimette & Brown, 2003). To the best of my knowledge, such a structure may not exist in most treatment establishments supervised by the Ministry of Welfare and the local authorities. It is advisable to explore this discussion's ramifications on addicts' recovery rates, throughout future exposure processes.

5. It is important to identify causes for substance relapse prior to a client's participation in the PE group. For instance, if they relapse due to negative emotions, we must assist them in developing other coping mechanisms to prevent them from using.

6. Triffleman, Carroll, and Kellogg (1999) suggest that addicts clean from drugs for a long time supervise and support new patients

within the treatment program, because they will be more skillful in identifying which patient has not yet developed mechanisms to cope with their negative emotions, thereby preventing them from participating in the PE therapy. In Israel, former addicts train in a one-year course, and serve as regular staff members, and work in the various treatment units to give this support (Hovav, 2002).

Today, I received a letter from one of my clients. She related to me how, this week, two years after having completed a therapeutic intervention involving the PE technique, she met on the bus one of the men who had sexually assaulted her. At that moment of anxiety, paralysis, and rage, she recalled me and the PE therapeutic group. Just as we guided her at group, she took deep breaths, regained her composure, and called her therapist at the first stop, so as not to deal with it all alone. The aggressor saw her make a call, and got off the bus at the first stop. In her letter, she writes:

> Amir, only you were on my mind... I felt relieved only in the evening, having showered and cleansed myself thoroughly... I am telling you this because it is because of you and Zehava that I was able to pull through the PE therapy group.

In this chapter, I portray intervention processes within the therapeutic group that engage in gradual exposure to traumatic memories. I portray the processes bound with painful exposure to the traumatizing memories, and identify the associated guilt, as well as establish a safe place for clients. I also portray the process of change which allows clients to successfully cope with the repressed psychological pain, and muster renewed strength. This is the point to express my gratitude for the privilege I have been granted as a therapist to witness the outcome of treatment and see that clients restored to their former selves, but with one key difference; with renewed strength. The female client who wrote me the letter had participated in one of those therapy groups.

Studies in the trauma fields indicate that approximately 70 percent of the adult population in the United States has experienced trauma in their lives. Studies argue that eight to 15 percent of people who have experienced trauma will develop symptoms of post-trauma, defined as an anxiety disorder both in the medical catalogue ICD-10 (2002) and in the work of Tiano (1989). In Chapter Three, I indicated that there is an extremely high rate of drug addicts who suffered trauma and developed post-trauma prior to lapsing to substance abuse. This demonstrates how many professionals assume that drug addiction is merely one of the non-adaptive ways of coping chosen by a trauma victim who has not received professional assistance (Ouimette & Brown, 2003). Again, drug addiction functions as supposed self-medication, a path chosen by the trauma victim in order to blunt their inner pain. Substance addiction functions as immediate relief for that pain, because of its ability to affect feelings and emotions. However, as for coping with anxiety issues resulting from the trauma, substance addiction is non-adaptive in the long term.

Foa's approach assumes that avoiding anxiety-arousing situations serves to preserve post-trauma symptoms. The prolonged exposure technique she developed is based on the assumption that recurrent, live exposure to situations or elements a client avoids due to anxiety or stress related to their trauma, will moderate their feelings and behavioral patterns.

This chapter portrays an initial experience among trauma victim-addicts, within the prolonged exposure technique. This chapter also presents several interventions in small groups of former addicts, who suffered post-traumatic symptoms due to traumas they experienced in their lives. The advantages of the professional technique of PE for these clients are outlined in this chapter. Furthermore, this chapter portrays the feelings of frustration and helplessness encountered by the treating staff, in an attempt to facilitate trauma victim–addicts.

Prolonged Exposure (PE): The Therapeutic Group

In 2004-2005, we implemented the PE therapeutic technique in three therapeutic groups. This therapeutic technique allowed us to integrate the treatment for substance addiction issues and trauma issues. Prolonged exposure has been a key approach in the past 20 years of trauma-related work. This approach calls therapists to lead interested clients to expose their traumatic experiences gradually and continuously.

Assisted by the professional staff of the Rothschild 2 treatment center, I established small groups, consisting of three to four clients. Addressing trauma is a rough, challenging therapeutic process. We realized that trauma victims often report that thoughts related to the traumatizing experiences arouse their feeling that the trauma is occurring at that given moment. While recalling the trauma, past events overshadow the present, obstructing the individual's ability to plan and think ahead. It is important to clarify to patients that they are not experiencing trauma at that moment, and that trauma-related thoughts are not dangerous (Foa et al., 2007, p. 15). Addressing trauma requires a high degree of self-exposure, trust in the facilitators and group members, and coping with extremely harsh feelings of rage, humiliation, guilt, anger, shame, and more (Herman, 1992; Foa et al., 2007).

The PE program is a plan consisting of two parts. The first part, "Exposure Through Imagery," is where an individual brings the traumatic experience back to life through imagination. The second part, "Exposure Through In Vivo Methods," is where a client must face particularly dangerous situations they have avoided since the trauma due to fear or because it reminded them of the trauma (Foa et al., 2004, p. 45; Foa et al., 2007, p. 2).

My choice to work with patients to the depth of their traumatic pain is based on my professional outlook. I assume that repressed traumatic memories affect the way the repressing individual behaves and moves along. I usually visualize memory repression as a situation where one is trying to sink a ball underwater. The force of buoyancy, like the power of memories, pushes the ball up to float on the water's surface. I view an individual who represses their memories as investing energy in submerging the ball under the water, while the ball's tendency is to float to the surface. Human psychological energy is naturally limited, as is any other energy type. According to this image, if I invest energy toward submerging the ball, I will have less energy to swim. If I repress traumatic memories, I will possess less mental energy to channel towards coping skills and psychological growth.

In practical terms, the work involved in Prolonged Exposure is well-organized therapeutic work, integrating a protocol written by experts of worldwide reputation in the trauma field (Foa et al., 2004, 2007).

At Rothschild 2 treatment center, we characterize this therapeutic intervention by the following elements:

- Working with addicts in the initial stages of substance detoxification. This work requires knowledge and unique professional practice (Green, 1995; Teichman, 1989)

- Intervention in cases of trauma resulting from abuse and violence among substance addicts (similar to psychological components of trauma induced by terrorist attacks, war, or rape), as stated by Foa et al. (2004), Zomer and Bleich (2005), Herman (1992), NATAL (2003), Foa et al. (2007)

- Two facilitators for every three to four clients within a small therapeutic group, rather than individual work with a sole client, as suggested by the protocol, due to scarcity of treatment resources (Zomer & Bleich, 2005), and reliance on the power in a group

- Treating prolonged abuse victims is an interventional process that usually takes place many years after the abuse occurred. This interventional process sometimes serves as late treatment of complex post-trauma symptoms (Herman, 1992; Shalev et al., 2001; Pirani & Shani, 2003; Pirani, 2004)

In the following section, I portray an episode from one of our sessions, and the dilemma deriving from it:

In a therapeutic group, one of the clients brought up a vague feeling of threat. She felt that in the treatment center, within the broader framework of activity, an individual who had sexually assaulted her was present. The feeling of this female client aroused emotional turmoil among the group members and facilitators. On the one hand, rage, revenge, and repulsion toward the aggressor arose. On the other hand, emerged concern for the victim, fear that she might take revenge on the aggressor, and concern for the uncertainty and vagueness yielded by the situation. The client indicated the likelihood of her identifying the aggressor to be approximately 20 percent. As facilitators, we allow abundant support, to facilitate coping with anger, rage, shame, and guilt. As part of my professional view regarding the issues yielded by repressing the traumatic memory, as aforementioned, I asked the client to recall further details regarding the aggressor. She indeed succeeded in recalling the address of the house where she experienced the assaults. Her level of recollection immediately rose to 80 percent. The greater the client's recollection level became, the greater my tension level rose. What would be revealed with their identification? After all, the aggressor must be a member of a therapy group equivalent to the client's PE group. As the scope of recollection expanded, the assaulted client indicated a desire to hurt the aggressor. Her humiliation, hurt, and helplessness had aroused her rage, revenge, and desire for violence, and I feared a physical outburst and potential harm to the aggressor. Perhaps I should not have asked the client to recall?

While writing these lines, I recall the emotions that flooded me in that session. On the one hand, I empathized with the victim's feelings; helplessness, anger, revenge, shame. How can an individual hurt another so harshly? On the other hand, there were my feelings as a therapist, including pity, compassion, concern, and a great deal of anger and rage.

Then, I began questioning myself; how do I protect, assist, and support the victim? How do we, as facilitators protect the aggressor? (Information regarding prospective third party physical harm can be found in the Social Workers Law.) Zehava, the counselor with whom I co-facilitate the group, possessed a clearer view of the issue: "I am on our female patient's side, and I will convey the message: 'I am here for you.'"

I conducted professional consultations with the relevant parties: manager, supervisor, and professional colleagues.

As a therapist, will I be able to assist the client in maintaining confidentiality while the third party could be assaulted? How am I going to face the client who asked for full anonymity, when I am obligated to prevent third party harm, in an establishment I manage? How can I keep treating a male client who has assaulted a patient of mine? To whom am I to be loyal? How would the professional ethical code, the supervisors, the superintendents, address the issue? These are dilemmas and questions not addressed in this chapter of the book.

Now I portray a few of the PE group sessions, namely, the intervention method and its contents.

Groups Implementing the Prolonged Exposure (PE) Technique: Group Session Description

The group forms a circle, sitting in the therapy room. Zehava and I are the facilitators. We select a quiet room, where no external stimuli reach us. We disconnect the phone and hang a sign on the door: "90-minute Group Therapy in Session." The professional staff is instructed not to enter or distract the session.

The group will meet for 10-15 weekly sessions, of approximately 90 minutes each.

We light candles in the room, dimming the lights. The group consists of four sober clients, and two facilitators. The circle formed is small and intimate. The first part begins with a few minutes of silence. Everybody sits with her or his eyes closed, connecting to themselves. Some sessions begin with relaxing music such as the sounds of whales or the waves, the sound of the rain falling in the forest, or birds twittering. The climate is peaceful, and I feel as though we are successfully establishing a safe work setting for the patients. The second part of the therapeutic intervention includes breathing exercises, practiced by both the group and the facilitators, inhaling air into the lungs, slowly exhaling, and vice versa (later, I demonstrate how this exercise serves to calm the autonomous nervous system. This exercise fulfills an important role for many anxiety and post-trauma victims (Foa et al., 2004). The group consists of two male patients, two female patients, a male facilitator, and a female facilitator. We believe it is important that each patient be able to identify with one of the facilitators based on gender. We strive to induce a climate of intimacy and a sense of security within the group. The session is representative of a human encounter of smaller scope. We assume that a small group will instill in patients a feeling of trust in their peers and facilitators, so that, eventually, they will feel safe to open up to us.

Clients must be sober in order for them to experience emotions without the substance's influence. This is one of the most vital conditions for receiving treatment at Rothschild 2. The clients have undergone an initial professional interview by social workers, confirming their capability of coping with the trauma exposure processes. In the months preceding their group work, we determined our impression regarding each client's capability to discuss a past traumatic experience and rely on their therapists and peers within the group. All clients have freely chosen to participate in the group. We have notified them and explained the mental difficulty involved in any therapeutic work exposing trauma, as well as of the likelihood of feeling discomfort for a short stretch of time, resulting from the traumatic memories. "You may feel worse before you feel better," (Foa et al., 2007, p. 17). Simultaneously, the clients receive an offer to maintain phone contact with the facilitators throughout the group activity period.

As a group facilitator, it means a lot to me that I can rely on my co-workers, colleagues, managers, and the psychiatrist we hire. On the one hand, I am excited and tense. On the other hand, I feel protected and safe with my professional standing.

I begin:

> Today is our first session. Following the explanations and breathing exercises, each patient will fill out a questionnaire (an In Vivo Exposure Task List, Foa et al., 2004). This questionnaire aims at measuring the distress units experienced by a client. Distress Units (DU) are a numerical ranking describing your feelings on a scale from zero to a hundred. You describe any feeling that arouse distress or anxiety, which usually leads you to avoid thoughts or action. Zero is the calm end of the continuum. Describe a certain episode in your life, and if you feel calm rather than anxious or threatened, mark zero or any number near it that represents your feeling. One hundred is the turbulent end of the continuum. The greater your degree of distress or anxiety, the higher the number you must record, namely, the closer it will be to one hundred. Furthermore, each client in the group will fill out another written questionnaire, a Post-Trauma Interview (Foa, Zinbarg, & Rothbaum, 1992), which questions socio-demographic information and trauma episodes you wish to relate.

I outline several numerical DU examples described by clients in the three different groups (names have been changed to protect our clients' identities). In June 2005, Y. writes, "I give 45 to my feeling when I see parents of others; 100 for meeting people I do not know."

In June 2005, A. writes, "100 is the mark I give to the smell of Noblesse cigarettes; 100 to male body odor; 50 to situations where I am yelled at; 10 when I hear someone relate a rape he or she underwent." (See chart at the end of this chapter).

In August 2004, L. writes, " I give 90 to the thought of speaking to my friends about all I have been through; 70 is the mark for my feeling when I visit my mother at the psychiatric hospital; 30 is the mark for visiting friends with a mate."

In January 2005, V. writes, "100 reflects my feeling when I am home, alone, and suddenly I hear a terrible scream; 100 reflects how I would feel if people ridicule things I say; 50 is for the feeling I have if I meet an individual who looks like my abuser; 30 is for feelings that come up while speaking to my aunt of the abuse." (See Chart 2 at the end of this chapter.)

In January 2005, R. writes, "90 for how I feel when I meet one of my rapists on the street; 60 when I see the uncle who raped me; 15 for the anxiety I feel while I shower." (See Chart No. 3 at the end of this chapter.)

R's Exposure: Intervention Outline

R is the client who wrote me the letter I cited earlier in this chapter. I choose her case to begin portraying the therapeutic proceedings within the PE group.

R. takes deep breaths; the dam holding back her tears collapses... She is a 28-year-old woman, pretty, thin, and blonde. She is accepted and well liked in the group. The group is sitting in a circle, which allows each patient to form eye contact with their peers. Moreover, sitting in a circle allows physical support of a client, for example, at a time of need, a group member may give a comforting pat on the shoulder to one of their peers who is sitting next them.

> *I remember living as the partner of a drug dealer who provided me with drugs. One day, I took a huge dose. In fact, I used up everything he had brought. It's hard to understand how I didn't OD. He came home and was furious. Maybe he was experiencing withdrawal symptoms or owed some to others. He asked me to go with him to the deal, where several men suddenly attacked me... I remember some were Jews and others were Arabs. They hit me, undressed me and raped me, one after another. I remember, it was so twisted how some of them pissed on me to humiliate me even more. Then they tied me to a tree and left. I cried, and then I went silent. I was in shock. For a while, I felt as though it hadn't happened to me. I can't understand how the dealer didn't protect me. I thought he was my partner.*

R. sobs. Her fellow group member, A., pats her shoulder. Zehava, the female facilitator who is sitting opposite her, asks to exchange seats with Y., who is also next to R. Zehava, too, pats R.'s shoulder. Through the gentle caress, Zehava conveys to the patient a message of care and physical support, letting her know she is not alone. It seems that R. is reliving the trauma. I ask R. if she wants to keep on relating. "You don't have to continue. Breathe deeply." R. takes a few deep breaths, and continues:

> I remember how disgusting they smelled. I remember a grove of trees, darkness, fear... I was afraid they would kill me.

Every few moments, R. pushes away the hands of A. and Zehava, who are trying to pat her. It seems that at that moment she is unable to be touched. Zehava, being an experienced staff member, knows how to accept this rejection, which a new therapist or counselor might misinterpret as rejection on the client's part and even be insulted.

Zehava: "R., we are here for you. You are in a therapeutic group who loves you. You are in a structure that wishes to protect you. You are not there now."

R.:

> *I feel fear. Sometimes, while walking down the street, I meet the people who assaulted me. Some live on my street. Sometimes when I feel this terror, I feel physically paralyzed. I feel as though they might attack me again. What can I do in a moment like that? What can I get out of being in a group at the treatment center? What can I get out of you loving me?*

She bursts iton tears and now yearns for a hug. A. responds to her and hugs her warmly.

Several group sessions later, we reconstruct the episode. This is the prolonged exposure. Each session is devoted to reconstructing, repeatedly, the traumatic episode, in detail. The reconstruction allows the memory coded as fear and terror to convert into words. To recall the ball imagery, the ball submerged under the water is not a threatening monster. One can allow it to jump out, without feeling terror.

In one session, I offer R. a verbal justification of her feelings up to that point.

Me:

> "You went through a very harsh episode that you have shared with the group. We are very proud of you for that, for your courage and your willingness to honestly share such a troublesome episode in your life. You are here now. That episode is in the past. Those were times when you were addicted and helpless. You were not aware of your condition and the prospect of receiving help. You did not even dare scream. Now you are here, clean of drugs. You can see other people on the street, and you can assume that if

you scream, they will come to your assistance. You can imagine us by your side, call us in a moment of distress and speak to us. You can breathe deeply, as we have practiced, whenever anxiety and fear arise.

Now I feel it is important to demonstrate to R. that, thanks to the breathing exercises, she can relax the hyperactive autonomous system, which manifests in rapid heartbeat, sweating, and a feeling that adrenalin is flooding the body (Foa et al., 2007).

R. nods.

"We ask you to call us in a tough moment. We'll speak to you, and be there for you."

On January 26, 2005, while filling out a DU follow up questionnaire, we review the issues we ranked three weeks before, according to the feelings experienced. This procedure occurs for purposes of comparison and tracking. The equivalent questionnaire presents only those DU situations the patient had recorded the previous month (four PE sessions before), without the mark they recorded the first time when they filled out the questionnaire. Patients reassesses the DUs and records them again (See Chart 3 at the end of this chapter).

It is important to note that, aside from the PE therapy group, R. participated in three other groups on a daily basis, and met the social worker for individual sessions at Rothschild 2 day center.

In the second questionnaire, R. marks a future encounter with her attackers at 30 (a 60-point decline in her anxiety level); she marks the prospective encounter with her uncle 50 (a ten-point decline), and her anxiety while showering receives 30-40 points (15-25 points up).

We notice R.'s anxieties have significantly evolved. Some of them have been greatly relieved, while others demonstrate an increased anxiety level. This is a stage in working on trauma where she "may feel worse before she feels better."

V's Exposure: Intervention Outline

V. is the guy who wrote: "100 is the mark reflecting how I would feel if people laugh at things that I relate." Revealing a traumatic story is a moment experienced as difficult by any client. Sometimes, it is at that moment that the client feels as though they have been stripped of all of their defenses, and they are vulnerable to harm. These are the moments when it is particularly important to convey to a client the feeling of a protective professional setting (also see Reel, 1997, 2002).

V. comes with an intense desire to speak up. I assume that in a small group setting he feels more secure than in a larger group. He relates: "My mother met a man after her divorce. A man who had been a friend of my father's before he died. I know they were violent criminals and drug addicts. My father had been murdered, and my mother let that man into our lives. That man wanted to discipline me, but he was not my father and I would not accept him... One day, he was approached by people who told him that they suspected me of stealing money from them... He wanted to show them how strong he was, so he forced me to admit to stealing. I was aggressively beaten by him, which is something I was used to...But that time, it was not enough. He forced me to give him oral sex. It was awful. I feared him to death so could not refuse. I was terribly disgusted and humiliated. That episode recurred, time and time again. I wanted to tell my aunt. I kneeled and kissed her feet. I begged her to listen to me, but she wouldn't. She did not want to believe. I continued experiencing sexual assault until I ran away from home and joined a group of boys who used drugs."

Y. pats V.'s shoulders, as if telling him: "I am here for you." V. continues: "How can I trust the group, how can I believe a stranger would want to help me if my own aunt wouldn't? I have no trust in people out there."

I sit by V. He is a tall, thin, blue-eyed man. His face is full of pimples. I am sitting next to a patient who was sexually assaulted. Will he be able to accept my empathy, my willingness to strengthen him? I try to pat him lightly on his shoulder. V. flinches. He is not willing to accept my pat. I understand him. It is a common, recurrent response, to recoil from any human touch, typical of sexual trauma victims.

Me: "V., you shared a rather harsh episode of your life. You receive tremendous support from your fellow group members. In the group, we heard you and nobody made fun of you. Rather, we feel the opposite: I think we all appreciate your courage and honesty. In other groups, I have heard many stories of guys who underwent assault as adolescents or children, but not many have managed to relate their stories with such openness. You are brave! We realize you were helpless, scared, threatened. Even the strongest, bravest soldiers can break down in conditions of fear and threat, in combat, in captivity.. You are not there now. You do not use substances, you are "a knight," as you yourself described yourself... Look how close to the group you became while you spoke."

I can see the tension in V.'s face dissipate. It is evident that the apprehension from the response he feared has somewhat declined. Neither did V.'s story draw away others nor did it cause others to disrespect him.

Similar to what I described in relation to R.'s treatment, n the second questionnaire, which was distributed to the participants on January 26, 2005, four additional sessions after he had recalled the traumatizing episode, and simultaneous to other therapeutic activities in which he was involved within the treatment center, V. recorded the mark 80 for the fear of sitting home alone while hearing a terrifying scream (a 20 point decline); 30 points for the fear lest people ridicule him if he would relate his story (a 70 point decline, compared to the first questionnaire), and zero (namely, 30 points less) for the feeling he experienced while relating his story to his aunt (see Chart No. 2 at the end of this chapter).

We assume that repeating the tale of the traumatic episodes facilitated him in somewhat reducing the helplessness he was feeling.

A's Exposure: Intervention Outline

A. is an immigrant from the Soviet Union. Her hair is tied back, and her brown eyes brim over with tears. A. is more connected than the rest of the group to emotional content. "I wish to relate a gang rape I underwent as a teenager. I went to a club with friends from school, where I was awaited by ten boys who had been drinking alcohol. Before I knew it, they raped me one after the other." She grows silent, allowing W. to hug her. They both cry in each other's arms. Zehava employs one of Prolonged Exposure's guidelines, namely, the in vivo reconstruction; not allowing the harsh memories to draw away our mental strengths; not to invest our limited mental strengths in favor of submerging the ball under the water.

Zehava: "What can you remember from that terrible episode? Try to connect us to the harsh experience you went through."

A.. takes a breath, "I remember them smelling of Russian cigarettes... the odor of sweat... I am shocked, ashamed; with the first, I still tried to resist. I was more humiliated than physically hurt by his slap."

Zehava: "A., you are here, with us. You are not the same age. You are in another country. Nobody knows you from those days. You are beautiful, you are loved, we are very touched to see W. hug you and cry with you. We are proud of you for relating your story today. You went on for several moments, relating a very troublesome episode in your life. In our next session, we will try to hear you again, and at length. It is important you let go of harsh feelings you're holding on to in the recesses of your memory. It is important you express fear with words."

On November 9, 2005, five months following that session, A. reports the following: I mark the cigarette smell at 50 (a 50 point decline compared to the mark given five months before); masculine sweat odor – 50 (a 50 point decline compared to the mark given five months before); I mark 25 for what I feel when I hear somebody relating a rape they underwent (a 15 point increase) (see Chart No. 1 at the end of this chapter).

With A., too, we notice a change. On the one hand, tension and anxiety conditions have declined. On the other hand, there is an increase in the DU mark in relation to the feeling, resulting in increased tension and anxiety.

There are measurement conditions where, after a while, we notice increased anxiety or distress. We assume this increase could be associated with several factors, which are to be further explored:

1. Greater degree of clients' openness and sensitivity to emotional states; openness which takes place within therapeutic processes in the "Prolonged Exposure" group. For the most part, an increased DU mark at this point reflects more intense feelings toward those DU reported earlier in the process (a prospective interpretation of this change has been aforementioned – "you may feel worse before you feel better")

2. Continuing or quitting the therapeutic process. V. did not continue his individual and group therapy at Rothschild 2, since he lives in another town. R. did not continue her therapeutic process, for she went on maternity leave. Hence, the higher rankings of anxiety and distress reflect a declined feeling of confidence and emotional stability provided by the integrative therapeutic structure.

Apparently, the feeling of confidence and calmness induced by the very process of trauma exposure requires a certain time period of therapeutic maintenance; a process which, under the circumstances, was impossible for V., R., and A. at some stages.

A., November 2005: "Now I can say that I do not blame myself for what I went through. What happened was not my fault. I know how to distinguish my reality from my past. I feel part of the normal population."

In May 2006, nearly a year after her participation in the "Prolonged Exposure" group, having given birth and resumed individual treatment, A. describes the following: "cigarette smell; mark zero (another 50 point decline); masculine sweat odor, mark 10 (a 40 point decline); when somebody relates a rape episode, mark 25 (identical to previous assessment's mark)."

I now portray the qualitative data analysis I conducted. Additionally, I attempt to clarify and provide further justification for the data, as in the form of insights and implications I have come across.

There are various approaches to trauma treatment, based on a diversity of theoretical models. Some therapists, in their treatment methods, rely on the assumption that engaging in past memories and traumas within treatment is dangerous to the client's inner, psychological life. In their opinion, engaging in trauma may be compared to scrtaching off a scab that again begins to bleed. According to this approach, an individual will recover from the trauma memories through their own, natural recovery power, and any further attempt to address those memories might prompt their regression to a state where the trauma wound is open, infected, and dangerous. Other therapists rely on a theoretical viewpoint which I possess as well. They assume that traumatizing memories are to be addressed differently in therapy. Trauma treatment can initially be compared to treating a scab without thoroughly cleaning the infection. The wound must be opened and the infection must be cleaned, allowing for a fuller recovery.

This comparison implies that traumatizing memories bear daily ramifications which are manifested by present anxiety and avoidance processes. The harder we try to escape the traumatizing memories, the more they continue to haunt our lives and be a part of them, just as an infected wound will keep on causing us pain (Foa et al., 2003; Ouimette & Brown, 2007). Prolonged Exposure is one of the therapeutic techniques derived from this approach, which calls for past traumatizing memory exposure so as to facilitate life in the present.

At this point, I turn to discuss the clients themselves. The significant change A. underwent from June 2005 through May 2006 can be clearly noticed.

A., whose feelings were marked as 100, which expresses the highest DU intensity, as of June 22, 2005, marked 0-10 DU as for her feelings regarding the same elements by May 18, 2006 (see Chart No. 1 at the end of this chapter). In other words, A. could not bear to smell cigarettes and masculine sweat, nor could she hear her partner speak to her during intercourse. Within less than one year, she is again able to experience sexual intimacy, smells, and sounds without feeling distressed and anxious.

For R., the change trends were different. On the one hand, an improvement was noticed. One the other hand, there was a regression in terms of DU within the time periods explored. R. reported 90 DU on January 5, 2005 in association with a prospective encounter on the street with those who raped her. A year later, on January 26, 2005, her feelings significantly declined, reaching 30 DU. Why is it, therefore, that the DU climbed again to 60 on July 5, 2006? Is this a recovery process characterized by ups and downs? Is it a consequence of R.'s withdrawal from treatment and support?

The facilitators and professional staff assume that R.'s recurrent increase in DU feelings could be accounted for by her seeking treatment in another town, as well as her long maternity leave and withdrawal from the therapeutic structure. At any rate, the facilitators presume that this matter is to be re-investigated with future therapeutic cases.

For V., too, the change following the Prolonged Exposure processes indicated a significant improvement on the one hand, and regression on the other hand. On January 5, 2005, V. gave the mark of 100 DU to his feeling of hearing a terrifying scream while at home. On January 26, 2005, his feeling declined to 80 DU, and in November 2006 further declined to 70 DU. On January 5, 2005, however, V. marked 100 DU fo his concern that people would ridicule him when he related the trauma he had experienced. Later, on January 26, 2005, while still in therapy, he marked his feelings as 30 DU, which is a significant decline, while on June 11, his DU mark drastically climbed to 90. In interpreting V.'s feelings, the professional staff assumed that his withdrawal from the therapeutic structure and move to another town were the cause for the resumed intensification of distress. In this case, too, I suggest this matter be further explored in future therapeutic cases.

To sum up, I assume that treatment through "Prolonged Exposure" bears advantages in working with addicts who are trauma victims. However, because of the depth and sensitivity characterizing the therapeutic work, this treatment method should comprise professional teamwork, involving social workers, a psychiatrist, and a counselor. Further studies regarding the advantages and disadvantages of the treatment method may facilitate in drawing clearer conclusions.

The small "Prolonged Exposure" therapy groups ended after approximately twelve sessions. In the three experimental groups I gave we attained rather interesting outcomes. For the most part, the outcomes portray significantly declined anxiety, terror, and shame among the patients who participated. A graphic chart illustrating these feelings is presented in Charts 1, 2, and 3 at the end of this chapter.

As a group facilitator, I felt great professional satisfaction. I noticed that the participants of the Prolonged Exposure groups experienced direct outcomes, which positively affected their quality of life.

The discussion portraying this intervention group, as well as many years of work with substance addicts led me to construct a theoretical model, which I explore in the following chapter, namely, Chapter Ten.

The theoretical model indicates a consistently circular relationship of the following variables:

1. The preceding event – the trauma

2. The response to trauma unaddressed – post-trauma

3. Substance use as self-medication to ease the psychological pain – the addiction

4. The action taken to obtain money in order to use the substance resulting in further psychological pain – the delinquency and suffering

In order to cease this circular relationship, interventional therapeutic techniques which address trauma are to be implemented, such as Prolonged Exposure.

This theoretical model is titled The Cycle of Suffering.

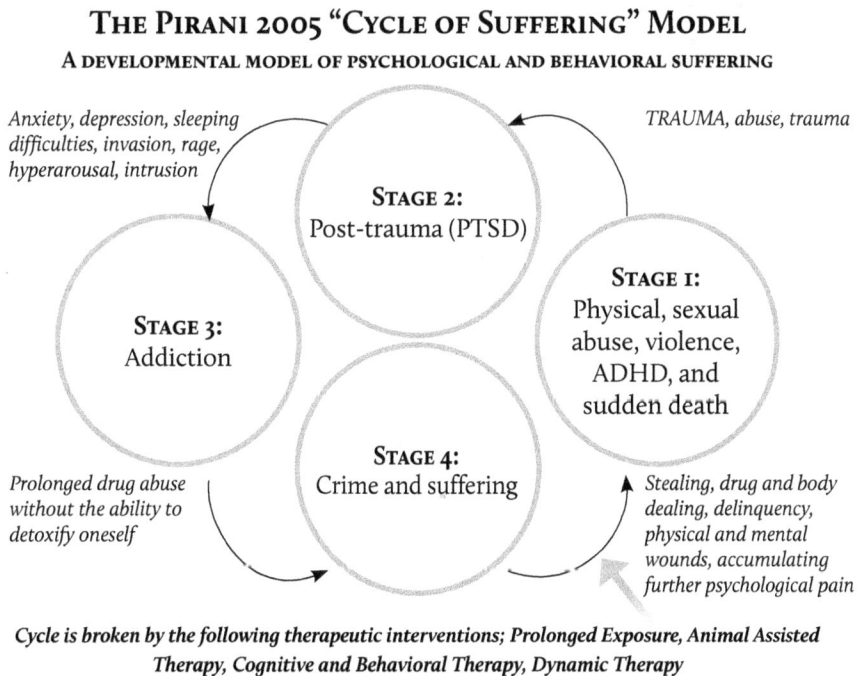

THE PIRANI 2005 "CYCLE OF SUFFERING" MODEL
A DEVELOPMENTAL MODEL OF PSYCHOLOGICAL AND BEHAVIORAL SUFFERING

Anxiety, depression, sleeping difficulties, invasion, rage, hyperarousal, intrusion

TRAUMA, abuse, trauma

STAGE 2:
Post-trauma (PTSD)

STAGE 1:
Physical, sexual abuse, violence, ADHD, and sudden death

STAGE 3:
Addiction

STAGE 4:
Crime and suffering

Prolonged drug abuse without the ability to detoxify oneself

Stealing, drug and body dealing, delinquency, physical and mental wounds, accumulating further psychological pain

Cycle is broken by the following therapeutic interventions; Prolonged Exposure, Animal Assisted Therapy, Cognitive and Behavioral Therapy, Dynamic Therapy

Figure No. 9: Illustration of the different stages in the Cycle of Suffering

Table 1: A.'s Follow-Up

Date/Subject Measured	22/6/05	9/11/05	18/5/06
DU index Recoiling from the smell of Noblesse cigarettes	100	50	0
DU index The smell of masculine sweat	100	50	10
Speaking during intercourse	100	10	0

Table 2: V.'s Follow Up

Date/Subject Measured	5/1/05	26/1/05	11/06
DU index Hearing a terrifying scream while at home alone	100	80	70
DU index People who ridicule the trauma	100	30	90
Speaking to my aunt of the trauma at home	30	0	80

Table 3: R.'s Follow Up

Date/Subject Measured	22/6/05	9/11/05	18/5/06
DU Index Encountering the people who raped me	90	30	70
DU Index Encountering the uncle who raped me	60	50	60
DU index Anxiety while showering	15	35	100

Chapter Ten portrays the cycle of suffering theoretical model. The chapter analyzes the circular flow of events prompting SUD to recur through experiences of trauma, psychological suffering, and hurting others. The Rothschild 2 professional staff has established its goal of stopping this Sisyphean circularity in a drug addict's life, by means of various therapeutic interventions.

CHAPTER TEN

The Cycle of Suffering

Once upon a time there was a rat that despised its nose, just like that
She learned her lesson through a costly operation
Nose is inner nature, the heart's external manifestation
While the external change will cause only aggravation
An honest, fun-loving rat
Needs no arrogance or all that strife
But a rat ugly from within
Never would it be able to hide it for life

This chapter portrays the cycle of suffering theoretical model that I have developed, and broadly addresses the four components that I briefly cited in the preface.

My mobile phone rings. On the screen, an unidentified number appears. I am home by now, but some inner voice instructs me to take the call.

"Amir, this is Loria, Tanya's mother. Do you remember we agreed I would call you when I found her? She is here with me, but she won't look at me."

Loria sounds distraught and confused; her voice is broken, "Dirty men come to take away my only daughter. I am standing right next to her. You promised to come."

Loria is a mature woman in her early 50s with an impressive presence. One evening, about ten days ago, she showed up at my office. In a tonally off-key Hebrew with a heavy Russian accent, she desperately begs for help:

> *My daughter is killing herself. She is using drugs. She works the streets every evening, prostituting by the Tel-Aviv old central bus station. She does not know what she is doing. I have tried locking her in at home, but she jumped from the second floor and ran away. Nobody helps me. You have many patients. I have only one daughter.*

Her sentences are short and confused. Her voice echoes tremendous panic. She does not cry and seems peaceful, but deep inside, she is torn. Every evening, she stands helplessly at the Tel-Aviv old central bus station beside her daughter who is dazed by the drug's influence, gazing in terror and restrained rage at the men coming to pay her for a quickie in a dark alley.

Through the years, various psychological theories have attempted to account for the motives and causes of prolonged substance addiction. Those theories have yielded various therapeutic techniques, some of which were discussed in previous chapters of this book. It may be noticed that while professional intervention with combat and terror victims is employed swiftly and relatively near the time of occurrence

(Zomer & Bleich, 2005; Seligman & Salomon, 2004), stress, trauma, and childhood sexual assault victims are treated only after many years of psychological suffering. The same also applies to many SUD patients, namely trauma victims who are also addicted to substances.

The cycle of suffering is a new theoretical model I have constructed, illustrating the prolonged substance addiction process through a scheme. The model accounts for the proceeding through which a branch from the "substance addiction tree" forms; a branch feeding on stress and emotional trauma. The PTSD branch, which stems from substance addiction, expands to be manifested by the symptoms indicated in Chapters Three and Four. I encounter this addiction domain among most clients who come to me for treatment at the public services. I am convinced the public feels and knows that the percentage of people experimenting with substances has grown in the past decade. Some researchers indicate this constitutes approximately thirty percent of the population. Only a few will develop an addiction issue, and only a certain percentage of those will seek professional help from the public services (Pirani, 2005; 2004). Drug abuse is a lengthy addiction, from which one may not recover without external professional help.

Throughout the book I have indicated that deductively, our treatment of approximately three thousand substance-addicted clients since 1992, implies a strong relationship between prolonged substance abuse and a clients' past, most of whom have experienced stress, trauma, and abuse. This is a shocking statistic, both in terms of its associated findings and implications. In Chapters Two, Three, and Four of this book, I demonstrated how stress experiences relating to physical and sexual violence and abuse which induce a feeling of existential or physical threat to the assaulted individual, leave the victim with harsh post-traumatic symptoms if not treated professionally as soon as possible after the event has occurred.

In Chapter Two, which cites the epidemiological data, I indicate that many studies imply a relationship between severe stress, physical and sexual abuse, and future substance addiction. I cite the following few studies again:

- Females who were sexually stalked as children are at a four times higher risk to develop major depression, compared to those without such a history. These females are significantly likely to develop bulimia and chronic PTSD.

- Children who underwent stress and abuse will demonstrate experiences of guilt, flashbacks, nightmares, various phobias, depression, and substance and alcohol abuse in adulthood (Herman, 1992).

- More than two thirds of the males and females treated for addiction rehabilitation reported childhood abuse or neglect (Ford, 2003; 2006).

- 71-90% of female adolescents and 23-42% of male adolescents treated at "Maina" addiction treatment center reported a history of childhood sexual abuse (Rohsenow et al., 1988).

- Adolescents who were sexually abused as children are doubly at risk to develop substance abuse issues, compared to those who were not abused as children (Ford, 2003, 2006).

I referred to the phenomenon of using various drugs by an addict sometimes, in an attempt to apply self-medication to their suffering soul. This self-medication is administered by some percentage of clients who are victims of a traumatizing experience. Perhaps these clients unconsciously chose to facilitate their psychological pain in that mode. This matter, as mentioned previously, has been known to therapy-related professionals for many years (Tiano, 1991; Teichman, 2001; Pirani, 2005; Shoham et al., 1987; Reel, 1997, 2002; Green, 1995; Foa et al., 2004; and others). There is no doubt in my mind that the meaning found in abusing substances is a non-adaptive act, nor is it effective in curing the individual psychologically in the long term. However, the phenomenon's prevalence demands a different professional attitude to the one that is currently common.

Drug abuse often yields further burden to substance addicts, in physical and mental suffering (Najavits, 2002). Arrest and imprisonment; physical beatings; prostitution, drug dealing, theft, and burglary in order to fund substance abuse; physical neglect; disease; family breakdown; and even death are the fate of many substance addicts, which I portray in the Cycle of Suffering. Based on this theoretical model, I offer an account concerning circular, endless processes, witnessed in association with prolonged substance addiction. Stress, trauma, post-trauma, and psychological and physical suffering, often trigger processes that, when not properly treated, prompt the client into prolonged substance addiction.

Breaking the cycle of suffering both theoretically and practically is essential, in order to facilitate an effective treatment to guarantee effective substance rehabilitation, including treating the traumatizing memory, trauma symptoms, and a client's traumatic, psychological suffering. This therapeutic intervention is required in order to allow a client to resume daily functioning without substances, as well as restore their family relations.

At Rothschild 2, breaking the cycle of suffering is employed by means of unique therapeutic techniques, a few of which I have outlined in this book. Through these interventional processes, therapists convey to their clients an attitude of acceptance and empathy, while establishing behavioral boundaries, thereby allowing clients a more thorough involvement while re-establishing their personal boundaries.

A clients' trust of their therapist allows them to integrate into the therapeutic setting offered by Rothschild 2, which, in turn, facilitates working on the memory they carry as a consequence of the severe trauma they experienced. Without establishing a firm, secure therapeutic foundation where a client feels protected and contained, their exposure to the trauma experiences repressed for many years through substance abuse, will not be facilitated (Pirani, 2005).

I maintain contact with various units that treat addicts. Most of them perform decent, important therapeutic and rehabilitative work, which does not always entail delving into recollection and past trauma exposure. The therapeutic need to address past stress, trauma, and abuse-related memories arouses when the therapist notices that a client's treatment is not progressing at all, and they relapse into substance abuse whenever they encounter feelings of rage, shame, guilt, anxiety, depression, nightmares, or terrifying dreams.

Other situations from which I have learned about a lack of progress in prolonged addiction processes (stemming from trauma) are manifested by intrusion, avoidance, and constriction symptoms, which were addressed in Chapters Three and Four. In relation to addicts treated by the public services, it is clear to me that therapeutic processes addressing behavioral, cognitive, functional, system, and/ or rehabilitative aspects are not sufficient. Furthermore, in prolonged addiction conditions, it is essential to therapeutically address the sources of psychological trauma experienced by most addicts.

I assume that even touching on the therapeutic addressing of an addicts' traumatizing memories would yield high success rates in treatment and rehabilitation. In coping with prolonged drug addiction among SUD, a different kind of intervention is required.

This chapter broadly portrays this notion while addressing the Cycle of Suffering and summarizes the theoretical concept presented in this book.

The Cycle of Suffering

I indicate that, in medical terms, I compare psychological symptoms caused by extreme stress and psychological trauma to an open wound on the body. On the surface, the wound seems to be characterized by distinct signs (an open, bleeding wound forms a crust, a sign of healing). On the inside, the wound's state of healing is not always as clear.

The same applies to post-traumatic psychological symptoms: The external symptoms seem to be psychological and behavioral manifestations known to professionals. They must be thoroughly investigated and assessed. I portray many of these in the chapters addressing trauma and the chapter addressing post-trauma (Chapters Two and Three).

However, just as bandaging a wound and applying various creams will not always prompt the anticipated healing, so too in terms of treating a psychological wound. We call for for a different type of treatment when the SUD's previous psychological wound is known to us; a wound which, in many cases, preceded the patient's substance addiction. Just as in the state of a prolonged physical wound, in which healing is never fully complete, so too in ceasing the abuse of a substance. If we do not succeed in completing psychological treatment in depth, and particularly, if we do not consider the prospect of past traumatic, psychological wounds and do not know how to maintain the therapeutic process, then the former addict will not restore full functioning. Furthermore, they are very likely to resort to substances in times of crisis and stress.

Just as thorough, complex, and professional treatment is required in healing various types of inflammatory diseases, the same is required in psychologically treating SUD. As professionals, we are to induce psychological healing which will be effective, significant, thorough, and balanced. Yet it will not be achieved without therapeutic work among those SUD who have been wounded by stress and psychological trauma. Treating memories of past trauma, stress, and abuse experiences is required in order to form a sound foundation for the SUD's physical and psychological detoxification, as well as to prevent the recurrence of behaviors aimed at coping with psychological distress processes by means of substances (see Figure 9: Portraying the various stages within the Cycle of Suffering, p. 245).

The Cycle of Suffering Theoretical Model

Stage One: The Trauma

In Chapter Two, I demonstrate that various psychologically and physically stressful experiences induce an existential threat, which causes psychological trauma to many people. I have reviewed many studies indicating epidemiological findings that estimate that 40-80 percent of the world population will experience at least one potentially traumatizing episode in their lifetime. I have also indicated that among those exposed to traumatizing experiences, too, symptoms diagnosed a month later as PTSD tend to remain.

The following are events perceived as an existential or physical threat:

- **Severe domestic physical violence** a child experiences from one of their parents, siblings, or another family member is one of

336

the causes of trauma deduced from the diagnosis questionnaire analyses given to any client coming for treatment at the Rothschild 2 Treatment Center

- **Sexual assault** by a father, mother, or any other relative is another highly prevalent cause in our epidemiological findings, as outlined in Chapter Two

- Daily **verbal violence**, and extreme, consistent emotional deprivation, both damage a child's self-confidence, inducing the development of a future post-traumatic syndrome

- **A drunken parent** who hits their children regardless of their actions, creating an intense feeling of helplessness in them

- Children who suffer **Attention Deficit Disorder** encounter consistently impatient responses in their home, at school, and in their social encounters in various structures, often marginalized among their peers. These children can be drawn into involvement in acts of violence, as well as into feelings of a consistent lack of self-confidence and other severe psychological experiences (Manor & Tiano, 2005)

- **Sexual, physical, or verbal abuse** with peers or a one-time violent encounter also characterize substance addicts who approach us for treatment

- Children and adolescents who witness the tragic outcome of **disaster** following the loss of a relative in a car accident, a sudden death, terrorist attack, or fatal natural disaster, have had exposure to severely traumatic experiences (NATAL, 2002)

All these experiences are to be accounted for in the context of a client's traumatizing experience as well as in relation to their innate neurophysiological and personality composition (also see Zomer & Bleich, 2005; Seligman & Solomon, 2004; Teichman, 1989, 2001; Reel,

1997, 2002; Tiano, 1991; Foa et al., 2004). These episodes may integrate to form a rigid, post-traumatic response structure characterized by post-traumatic symptoms, to be portrayed in detail in Stage Two of the Cycle of Suffering.

Stage Two: Post-Traumatic Symptoms

In Chapter Three I mention many PTSD symptoms known in the professional literature and evident among SUD sufferers. We must emphasize these symptoms at the diagnosis stage and as an integral part of understanding the circular process of Stage Two in the cycle of suffering. (See appendix, lecture December 17, 2007, at the "Addictions" conference in Haifa.) Symptoms include prolonged anxiety; nightmares and flashbacks of the trauma; feelings of guilt and shame associated with the abusive experience; recurring severe depression; disproportionate rage; and avoiding experiences and even food associated with the trauma. We must consider these symptoms, including sleeping difficulties and concentration difficulties, continuous damage to interpersonal relations, and over irritability while filling in the SUD diagnosis form for those who approach us to seek treatment through the public services. Clear dissociation distinguishing thought from feeling, past memories coloring the present and varied responses to human company are also significant post-traumatic characteristics.

Symptoms that remain ignored professionally for many years heavily influence an individual's behavior and feelings, making them a different individual to who they were prior to the trauma.

Traumatic secrets carried by a client from childhood, continuous biting of nails, and a decline in social integration and schooling could constitute a red light, signaling danger. These are often the traces of damage left in a client's soul by the disaster and trauma. If no proper professional solution is provided at the stress and trauma damage stages, a victim will be more likely to experience future PTSD symptoms.

At a more advanced stage, with no other professional solution available, a victim might experiment with substances, as a temporary solution to cope with their harsh feelings and post-traumatic responses, which, however, will only escalate their future psychological condition. Experimenting with drugs, as outlined in Stage Three of the Cycle of Suffering, is a temporary, non-adaptive cure. An SUD client supposedly succeeds in easing their post-traumatic mental syndromes, yet the very act causes them to bury their memories and experience them deep down in the depths of the unconscious, burying them and the severe trauma they experienced (Zomer & Bleich, 2005; Pirani, 2005, 2007).

Stage Three: Substance Use and its Impact on PTSD Symptoms

We categorize drugs into different groups of effect. Among therapy professionals, some categorize substance types by their psychological effect on humans (Teichman, 1989; Green, 1995; Michael, 2007). Within academia, research, and the medical profession, some assign the action as the chemical effect on our brain's neurophysiological and biochemical structure (Tiano, 1991; Khantzian, 1985, etc.). Still other professionals portray the social and sociological effects of drug abuse (Denzin, 1984; Teichman, 2002).

In the Cycle of Suffering theoretical model, I divide drugs into two categories, based on their functional effect on an SUD client:
- Substances inhibiting emotions, psychological pain, and memories among SUD

- Substances enhancing SUD's self-confidence, self-image, and social outgoingness

The range of effects of these substances on users is not a dichotomous one. Some inhibiting substances affect one addict differently than they would affect another addict. Some addicts consume a mix of substances, yielding contradictory feelings and effects. There is a transition between consuming one substance category to another substance category (cross addiction: Michael, 2007). Addicts, depending on an individual's fiscal abilities and their lifestyle, consume some substances during different use periods. These substance categories can be outlined as follows:

- Substances inhibiting a user's emotions: alcohol, marijuana, benzodiazepines, and others
- Substances intensifying a user's emotions: cocaine, ecstasy, alcohol, LSD, and others

Acquaintance with this categorization as early as in the initial SUD diagnosis and treatment stages is important, since it facilitates identifying an addict's motives for drug abuse. Does an addict abuse the substance in order to overcome anxiety and depression or to avoid an emotional encounter with their memories associated with stress and trauma they have experienced? Perhaps they abuse a certain drug in order to enhance their self-confidence, uplift their downs, and for interpersonal and social relations.

Stage Four: Crime, Delinquency, and Further Psychological Suffering

Drug use requires large sums of money. Even a wealthy individual will soon lose most of their property if they become addicted to drugs. At the public treatment center, we are familiar with situations where

SUDs swallow tens of thousands of dollars a day for substance use. Much of the money is earned through drug dealing and prostitution.

Delinquency also results in a user experiencing further stress, involving psychological and physical suffering. Delinquents get arrested at some point, serve prolonged imprisonments, are harmed by their delinquent human surroundings, harm their relatives, and suffer harm from their responses. In addition, they could suffer various inflammatory diseases, other disasters or even death (see Chapter Six).

An addict experiences these conditions as severe stress episodes and further trauma experiences. The Cycle of Suffering comes full circle, only to restart. It begins moving in the same circle again: traumatizing experiences, trauma symptoms, more intense substance abuse, delinquent activity, and further suffering.

Prolonged Exposure (PE)

Chapter Nine presented a therapeutic approach which was the subject of an experiment at Rothschild 2, whereby the PE treatment method facilitated individuals directly coping with an anxiety disorder. I mention the method's professional goal as assisting patients in enhancing their quality of life "by coping with the intrusive thoughts, flashbacks, and attempts to avoid memories associated with trauma," (Foa, 2004, p. 13).

We first experimented with this therapeutic model at Rothschild 2 as a new SUD treatment technique (the model received the blessing of the technique developer, Professor Foa, who was updated of the model's achievements and challenges while implementing it with this population).

I again portray some of the investigation and implementation points specific of this therapeutic intervention, as conducted at Rothschild 2:

A. In PE, the therapist dictates and prompts a client's daily agenda, while other intervention techniques (mostly dynamic ones) allow the patient to set the daily agenda's tone and even the pace of progress.

B. PE is mostly implemented as an individual therapeutic intervention. Due to difficulties relating to budget and resources, at Rothschild 2 it is implemented within a small therapeutic group (three to four clients and two therapists).

C. PE has been implemented within several experimental therapeutic groups at Rothschild 2, as one component of a broader therapeutic setting provided to the patients, including individual treatment, psychiatric consultation, urinalyses, group therapy, and an established rules and behaviors framework.

D. PE has proven to be a technique suitable for treating psychological trauma victims. Those who intend to employ it can undergo a relatively short training, and it yields decent therapeutic outcomes relatively quickly (Foa, 2004, p. 12). Unfortunately, while writing this book, due to a different prioritization and limited professional resources in the welfare field in Israel, the treatment staff does not undergo this important professional training.

Prolonged Exposure's Therapeutic Process – Case Studies in Other Aspects of the Cycle of Suffering

Alex is a 26-year-old single man living with his mother, stepfather, and younger brother. He has been clean of all drug types for approximately half a year, following 11 years of addiction. He participates in various therapeutic groups, is an NA member, and wishes to join the PE group to cope with the anxiety attacks and rage he has experienced for a long time. In the group session, Alex relates the merciless rape he experienced as a child by his sister's boyfriend. Back then, when he sought his sister's help, she rejected him and his complaints. Shortly following the rape, he developed post-traumatic symptoms, including fear to walk or hang out alone, sleeping difficulties, inappropriate rage toward his peers, emotional dissociation, trouble forming new social relations, depression, anxiety, and substance abuse. Using heroin helped Alex dull the feelings of humiliation and rage that would rise in him whenever he recalled the rape. Using cocaine allowed Alex to engage in crime with no fear, to obtain money to fund his substance abuse.

Throughout the brief therapeutic process, we witnessed a decline in the intensity of his distress and anxiety, which was apparent in the relief he felt by the end of the PE group. Alex's intensity of feeling was measured through questionnaires distributed to him and the other group members on the second and tenth sessions. The outline of Alex's therapeutic process integrates well into the Cycle of Suffering theoretical model:

Stage One (the trauma): Alex experienced a severe sexual trauma, which was not addressed through professional treatment.

Stage Two (post-trauma): Alex developed post-traumatic stress disorder symptoms.

Stage Three (substance abuse): Alex sought psychological relief, an outlet he found through substance abuse.

Stage Four (delinquency and further suffering): Alex engaged in crime in order to fund his substance abuse. He got into further trouble, legally, resulting in further psychological suffering. All this induced additional traumatic experiences for him, which continued moving in the Cycle of Suffering.

As mentioned previously, the PE method is one of the treatment techniques implemented at Rothschild 2. I notice that treatment by the PE method assisted in breaking the circular process of suffering and addiction, enabling the interruption of the Cycle of Suffering. Because of the relief in symptoms associated with the post-traumatic experience, a treatment that interrupts the cycle of suffering is sufficient to increase recovery rates among SUD, an issue which should be further explored.

Anat is a 25-year-old woman living with her boyfriend in his home. Anat has two sisters, and she maintains daily contact with her family. Anat has been clean of all drugs for nine months. In the group session, she relates a harsh rape she underwent approximately two years before by two young men. The therapists are aware that Anat has a history of prolonged sexual abuse that took place at the boarding school she attended from age 12-14. In the group session, she shares the numerous difficulties she experiences during intercourse with her boyfriend. Moreover, she is not willing to be alone, even in her own home, and she fears an encounter with her aggressors on the street. She experiences difficulty falling asleep at night, and anxiety attacks on rising in the morning.

She abused heroin for ten years, since she realized that substances blunted her harsh emotions. In her last years of addiction, she engaged in prostitution.

Facilitator: "Anat, you have described being raped by those two guys as the most distressful traumatic experience of your life. You indicate the distress units as 100." Anat confirms by nodding her head, relating the traumatic experience to the group as best she can. Based on the instructions she received from the group facilitators, she tries recalling every detail related to the terrifying moments she experienced. She describes the alley where the assault took place, the aggressors' appearance, the sounds and the smells, all her memories from the rape.

Facilitator: *Close your eyes and try to recall your most difficult experience, where you were lonely and terrified. Now you are here, with us. You are not alone or helpless. If you feel anxious or stressed, take ten deep breaths, as we practice in every session.*

Anat: *I am on my way home, from the movies. The street is dark. I know I shouldn't have turned there. I always make dumb decisions.*

Facilitator: *This is not your fault. You are criticizing the steps you took. Try to recall your feelings and thoughts while walking home after the movie ended.*

Anat: *I feel like someone is following me. I am startled and paralyzed with fear. The taller one asks me to borrow my lighter to light a cigarette, and then slaps me hard* (when Anat mentions this, she trembles and cries; a female group member who sits beside her hugs her for a brief moment). *I remember begging them to leave me alone. They hit me like crazy, undressing me. I was so shocked. I watched the whole episode as a side observer... I remember the thick smell of alcohol and sweat. That's it...I can't go on.*

Facilitator: *Anat, we are here with you. We love you. Keep up the deep breathing. It helps a great deal to relax the* body (Anat's female fellow member gently pats her, hugging her. Anat seems to have returned to reality from her travel in time). *Anat, that's enough for today. We appreciate your courage. We feel that today, you are coming out as a winner.*

Rape Exposure Processes - Eight Sessions Later:

Anat: *I recall the taller aggressor. I feel anger and contempt toward him. I cannot understand how he dared hurt me like that in an alley. Although now I do not walk alone, if I would ever meet him, I would look him in the eye, and cry for help. The street is full of people. I feel strong now. I will not let the aggressor witness my humiliation.*

Facilitator: *Anat, how would you rank your feelings today on a prospective encounter on the street with your past aggressors?* (Note: The clients usually do not remember the grade they recorded at the second session).

Anat: *Of course I pray it won't happen again, but I feel less terrified and more in control of the feelings associated with these memories. 50 represents my current feelings.*

Anat reports a decline from 100 to 50 on the numerical scale measuring her feelings of anxiety while she recalls the traumatic episodes.

We account an outline of the PE process that Anat underwent over ten harsh therapeutic sessions in the Cycle of Suffering theoretical model:

1. The trauma consisted of rape episodes in Anat's past, the latter not being addressed through professional treatment.
2. The PTSD symptoms were sleeping difficulties; Anat's fear of being alone; and her fear of encountering her aggressors. Anat also faced difficulties related to interpersonal relations with her boyfriend.

3. Substance abuse supposedly eased Anat's harsh emotions associated with recollection, anxiety, and emotional overload, yet prompted her to further suffering and crime.

4. Further suffering and crime followed in the form of engaging in prostitution in order to fund substances.

Anat's PE treatment, simultaneous to additional individual and group therapy, facilitated Anat's ability to experience the harsh memories of her past, without allowing them to guide her actions. At the time of writing this chapter, Anat has been clean of all substance types for three years and two months.

Akhmed, 35, divorced and a father of three lives in a mixed town in the northern part of Israel. Akhmed has attempted detoxification several times, though unsuccessfully. Additionally, he has tried to commit suicide several times by taking tranquilizers and cutting his wrists. Akhmed seems quiet and introverted. He looks embarrassed. He used heroin for 23 years and was in state of clinical death a few times. His life was saved thanks to medical treatment adiministered at the hospital. The northern district's treatment staff doubts Akhmed's psychological strength: he is suicidal, with an extensive psychiatric background.

The PE group facilitators request to review Akhmed's past psychiatric assessments:

On patient examination as per your request, we witness anxiety attacks and simultaneous tension, sometimes immediately on waking, rapid heartbeat, choking, and shortness of breath. Usually, in order to relieve these feelings, he uses heroin... Additionally we witness dissociative episodes requiring psychological treatment.

Another psychiatrist wrote:

> I examined Akhmed following a suicide attempt involving an overdose... his stomach was pumped at the hospital... the examination indicated no signs of major depression or active psychotic signs... has been known to the system for many years... I recommend further treatment at a substance abuse treatment center.

These reports imply that Akhmed was a substance addict for many years. He had attempted suicide before; he suffers anxiety attacks, sleeping and waking difficulties, as well as mental confusion. Akhmed didn't receive a diagnosis of major depression or psychotic symptoms. An individual like him could dwell in cycles of psychological and physical suffering, since the treatment system addressing substance abuse victims has focused on the outcome of his psychological trauma for many years, namely, the substance abuse, rather than its cause, namely, the psychological trauma itself.

At this point, the discussion focuses on the new theoretical model of treating addiction, namely, the Cycle of Suffering.

I expect a professional who works with SUD to employ a professional, focused outlook on the characteristics implied by the various diagnoses, in order to piece the diagnostic information together. In many cases, as mentioned previously in this book, "deductively among most clients," all these characteristics manifest as PTSD, which stems from stress or trauma experiences. Using substances as a means of self-medication affect clients as a temporary, non-adaptive cure in the long term.

Substance abuse requires abundant funding sources, which an addict must provide for themselves. Therefore, they will often find themselves engaged in delinquent activities. The diverse types of delinquency prompt arrest, beatings, prostitution, and various types of humiliation that prompt further traumatic elements, as well as other episodes of psychological suffering.

The Cycle of Suffering is interrupted by means of various treatment techniques; focused treatment aimed at relieving PTSD; cognitive behavioral therapy; group therapy, where the client participates in support groups; PE, AAT, and other therapeutic approaches.

As of the writing of this book, Akhmed has been clean of drugs for two years and four months. He refuses to take medication, because he used to suffer harsh side effects due to such treatment.

Sun's story:
I used to meet Sun every Sunday at 7:30 p.m., outside the clinic. It was dark by that time, and I was tired after a long day of work. I had trouble conducting sessions with her. Sun told me of her life with the Bedouins in Sinai.

> I arrived in Sinai with no particular goal. Like all of my contemporaries, I wanted to take a break from life, find one of those huts on the Sinai beach, enjoy the beautiful landscape and the absolute freedom. I wanted to get away from my parents and their burdensome supervision. I wanted to be among young people, in nature, do drugs, and think of nothing.

> I was always a bit more daring than my friends were. I felt as though I needed to try to experiment with everything in life, otherwise, I might feel as though I had missed something. I can say this feeling is rather troublesome, often driving me to take dumb actions I regret.

Now, as a mother to a three-year-old girl, I shiver with fear when I recall the risks I took. But in my early twenties, an inner voice urged me, time and time again to try everything. Have no fear. What could really happen to me, rape? I had experienced such situations as well. No, I had no fear. I would repress those thoughts with nonsense thoughts: So what if some driver rapes me while hitchhiking. As if that's the most terrible thing that could happen... I'd be submissive with him. I wouldn't resist, so he wouldn't be violent. I could get through that. What could happen? Sex is sex. I have been with dozens of men. What would be any different?

Love, emotions... I didn't know what they were, anyway. Sex stimulated me physically. I felt an intense urge to experience sex. Maybe it was part of my obsession. During intercourse, I received some attention – caresses, kisses, breathing. I knew no other form of contact. I did not know what a mature relationship was like. I didn't understand what love was. I'll probably talk about this more later on in the treatment.

My early sessions with Sun surprised me. Her outgoingness while speaking of her past, the depth of disclosure she reached was rare among my patients, certainly at such an early stage. Apparently, Sun was quite quick to trust me. I thought perhaps that she had been through other therapies in her life.

On one of my trips to Sinai, I went out on my own, with a large, worn out backpack, and no watch, mobile phone, or calendar. I wanted to take a break from life, forget the mundane, everyday world, lacking any meaning or worth; the desperate world I had lived in during my last few months in Tel-Aviv.

I arrived at a small fishermen's village by Nuweiba in Sinai. I found a nice, small shack far from the village center. South to it, along the

*shore, many other shacks were scattered. To the north, I could see
endless sand dunes. To the east was the Red Sea. There were palm
trees and bushes, pure serenity. A huge, black Bedouin tent stood
there. I couldn't see any Israelis or tourists there, only Bedouin women
dressed in black, sitting by the tent. I could see only their eyes peering
through their veils.*

*The Bedouin men fished; some sat underneath the palms and smoked
on the nargila pipe. Every hour, one of them would come with small,
white coffee mugs, giving them with sugar cubes to the family men.
I quickly learned all the customs associated with the Egyptian hash-
smoking culture. The special high it gave me made me feel very
special. My senses sharpened. The endless sea was colored deep blue,
merging with the horizon. I felt an absolute sense of freedom. My
animism fitted into the desert scenery. I undressed and lay on the
sand. I felt no shame or embarrassment. I loved my body and drew
pleasure from the way the sand touched it. The hot desert sun burned
my body, so every half hour I ran naked into the ocean, wetting my
body and returning to my sandy tanning bed. I loved to tan, it made
me feel most sensual. Now I have trouble saying whether I indeed
felt as though the young Bedouin was eyeing me. Perhaps there was
a strong feeling of power and control to it, as though I were the
queen of the desert.*

*On the second day, I fell asleep on the beach, maybe because I was
so high. When I woke up, I saw Mussa eyeing me with lust. He was
sitting approximately ten meters away from me, in his white clothes,
muscular and handsome. This time, I felt embarrassed. He would
not take his eyes off me, and did not blink or cast his gaze down.*

*I hopped for a final dip in the ocean. When I emerged from the water,
his longing gaze at my wet body aroused my lust as well.*

While I was wearing my yellow jalabiya (robe), *I was wondering what it would be like with a Bedouin. Do the Bedouins have sex like us? Perhaps their sexual behavior is violent? What if he hurts me and my fear stops me from asking him to stop.* "What could happen," *I calmed myself down, as always.* "He will probably just come, and then leave me alone." *This was always the way things ended up when I was not prepared. I know it may sound a bit odd, but I was even aroused by that.*

The espresso we are drinking now reminds me of the coffee I drank with Mussa then. I had to muster the courage to ask him for a cup of coffee. I was not embarrassed, just had the feeling that I had control over the horny Mussa. We started talking. His Hebrew was excellent, and he told me he was attending Cairo University, and was spending his semester break in his home village. He was very polite, charming, and handsome. The dry, chapped skin on his feet repelled me, but the more I got to know him, the less I was repelled. Mussa suggested I climb the mountain with him at night, and wait for sunrise with him. "Never in your life have you seen such a gorgeous sunrise," *he said with a smile revealing his white teeth. As always, I did not hesitate. We went toward the mountain, riding a camel. We landed in a deep valley, by a hidden water pool shaded by green flora; it was a stunning oasis, appearing surprisingly among the endless sea of sand. The hash Mussa offered me was much stronger than what I had been used to, and in the light of the shining sun, I was filled with wonderful relief, which I had never felt before. I was surrounded by such a romantic climate, that I felt like running downhill, naked.*

Suddenly, Mussa stopped talking, and he did not look like himself. He became an animal and raped me by the light of the rising sun. It was more terrible than anything I had imagined. For the second time in my life, I lost trust in humans. The violent memories of the

rape would come to me every night in the form of nightmares. So I
started using heroin and became addicted to the false peace it gave me.

For me, Sun's story raised one of the most complex dilemmas to which I was exposed in the final week of December 2007; it called to light a dilemma regarding the limits of the therapeutic discourse whether to allow patients at Rothschild 2 to speak in group about their feelings of falling in love and emotional involvement. I questioned whether it was right to raise such feelings in a group discussion, while the therapeutic group members were at the beginning of their emotional, intimate, and exhausting journey toward ending their drug abuse. Wouldn't it open a Pandora's Box whose contents would harm anyone who dared open it?

We encourage our patients to do therapeutic work on memories related to trauma, family life, falling in love, and betrayal, while avoiding any such discourse in the initial treatment stages and any other situations that could arouse emotional expression and falling in love among the therapeutic group members. I am aware that many clinicians would claim that in a therapeutic group every topic needs addressing. We have had quite an argument in this regard amongst the professional staff.

Additionally, the group holds an equal count of males and females. It is clear to us that this situation could induce mutual attraction among them. As treatment staff, we know that the initial stages of therapy that follow physical detoxification could spur their feelings to become highly intense, which does not always reflect the true nature of the objective experience characterizing two individuals in love.

As mentioned before, this constitutes a highly significant point of discussion regarding SUD treatment. The group is in a rather delicate state. Most clients are still fighting for their lives without drugs, and any relapse might bring on an overdose or dangerous involvement in delinquency and crime. Hence, the treatment staff is to employ serious judgment, prioritize intervention, explore what can promote treatment and be alert to the risks factors within it.

In my opinion, when one is drowning in a stormy sea, the struggle should be for life first. It is not a time to fall in love. Regardless, I recommend postponing such therapeutic issues to more advanced stages of healing.

"Removing the Cork": A Case Study

A group case study analyzed through the Cycle of Suffering theoretical model (Pirani, 2007):

Group Status: 15 clean clients, sober for various lengths of time, ranging from two weeks to six months. The group comprises 13 men and 2 women, all absolutely clean of drugs. Their ages range from 20-50; all are residents of Tel Aviv-Jaffa, except one.

One particular week, during group sessions, I heard many detailed descriptions of delinquent acts, which are forbidden while in therapy. All patients had signed a contract clarifying the center's code of conduct starting from day one in therapy.

Client distribution by treatment in Tel-Aviv and Holon: seven patients are residents of central Tel Aviv, one is a resident of Holon; six are residents of Jaffa and three live in HaTikva and Neve Eliezer neighborhoods.

Like the other professional staff members, I begin to feel a great deal of mistrust and emotional estrangement among the group members. We feel the patients are avoiding any attempt to address their own pain directly and are speaking about shocking episodes from their pasts. The recovery process slows, and there is tension among the staff members.

According to the Cycle of Suffering theoretical model, I illustrate the situation to the group: The clients have skipped the PTSD treatment, engaging in the model's fourth stage, delinquency. Consequently, they are prompted to further psychological suffering, a risk of future substance abuse, and thus an inability to break the cycle of suffering.

The professional staff also includes professional counselors trained to work with substance addicts. At the time, two of them had been absent from the center for two and half weeks, due to holidays and sick leave. We felt their absence from the professional staff, because they are strict about rules related to discipline and behavior, had also induced an atmosphere of identification and closeness with the clients.

Additionally, a new social worker had been hired at the center, without enough experience to work with therapy groups of addicts in the day center setting. I am certain this factor also affected the therapeutic group's conduct. Even the AAT group counselor was absent that same week. There is no doubt that being a senior counselor in the organization, we felt her absence both within the professional staff and among the clients.

In order to complete the outline of our staff, we should note that in the past year another professional counselor was hired, formerly from one of the municipal addiction treatment centers in Tel-Aviv. This counselor facilitates a weekly group and is well known and liked by the clients. We regularly update him on the activity at the day center and he serves as a source of further professional power and input in terms of consulting and exchanging views.

Furthermore, two other professional counselors had joined our staff, but were not yet skilled enough in the therapeutic instruments implemented by the Cycle of Suffering theoretical model.

On ordinary days, the staff consists of experienced senior staff, whose professional presence is powerful; I possess 20 years of work experience with substance addicts, and have professionally guided each staff member. One counselor has 16 years of counseling experience and has been employed at the center for approximately six years. The staff also includes a counselor with seven years of counseling experience, and she herself is a graduate of the Rothschild 2 Treatment Center. The counselor who facilitates the weekly group has 12 years' work experience in facilitating therapy groups for drug addicts. In addition, we have a psychodrama counselor, who has been employed at the center for three years.

The staff gathers each day for established work meetings, consultations, and therapeutic case study presentations. The staff is updated throughout work hours as regards the group's therapeutic state, and of the main dilemmas rising in each group process. In adduition, we hold a professional weekly staff meeting.

Immediate staff response to the group's delinquent behavior:

- We suspended one group member for a week from the day center after he said he stole a wallet at the supermarket.
- Another member, who was in on a recent ecstasy deal, was immediately ejected from the group.

- A mentee who served as the group's deputy mentee on duty was replaced because he objected to various activities within the group and failed to open up in its framework.

- Another group member confessed to the group that he had resisted a drug-smuggling deal he had been offered. However, he told of another group member who had known about it, but had kept it a secret from the other members. The professional staff summoned that member, and other members for a conference, in order to investigate their behavioral patterns.

  The group included three patients who had come from a private treatment center. The three of them had formed some kind of a sub-group, keeping secrets from the wider group ("scratch my back and I'll scratch yours"). We could feel that the members belonging to this sub-group, contrary to other group members, avoided sharing their psychological suffering, because they feared losing the confidentiality treaty between themselves and the other patients who were not part of this sub-group.

- The 16th group member had relapsed into abusing heroin in the past few weeks. He too was ejected from the group.

- The 17th member was taken out of the group because he had been absent from the day center and group activities several times with no justified reason, and because of the concern that he was abusing substances.

- The superintendent, who himself is an alumnus of the day center, was reprimanded by the staff, for accumulating five behavior-related warnings after not following the center's disciplinary rules.

Other decisions made by the staff include re organizing the therapeutic setting at Rothschild 2. The staff reviews and clarifies the treatment center's code of conduct, reminding clients that any deviation from the behavioral norms required by the day center contract will bear consequences. The staff works toward ceasing all delinquency patterns at the center, thereby aiming to provide protection to other clients who feel threatened by the delinquency patterns:

- M. (from the Jaffa treatment unit, living in a private treatment center) is suspended for one week for verbally threatening other group members.

- A. (from the central Tel Aviv treatment unit, living in a sheltered resident flat supervised by the homeless treatment project "Someone to Run With") is removed, having failed to show up at Rothschild 2 on Sunday and without calling to notify of his absence, eventhough at the time he was serving as deputy head of the therapy group. Previously, A. had been suspended from participation in the therapy group, because his attendance had been inconsistent and he had not been cooperating in performing the tasks required by the day center.

- A.P. (from the Tel Aviv treatment center) was removed after repeatedly demonstrating delinquency patterns at the center: "I sent people to physically attack my girlfriend, so she would leave the house," and, referring to other groups members, "I used to cut to pieces somebody who spoke to me that way."

- S. (from the Jaffa treatment unit) was suspended for a week, having lied to the staff as to his absence on group therapy days, claiming he had traveled north to celebrate a religious holiday while, in fact, he had not got up on time, and asked his fellow group members to cover for him and lie to the group and staff.

- A. (from the central Tel Aviv unit) was refused his appeal to deduct two days from his detention from the day center. He received a week of detention for stealing at the supermarket.

- The treatment staff delivered an educational message to all group members: "Those unable to adhere to the rules and behavior code at the center are requested to leave voluntarily or will be requested to do so by the professional staff. The treatment staff will not allow any deviant behavior or tolerate any failure to adhere to the disciplinary rules at Rothschild 2.

As professional staff, we expect that the intensified discipline and renewed enforcement of the group rules will achieve therapeutic goals:

- The extent of direct and indirect violence among group members will decline.

  When the group members feel safer within the therapeutic setting, a more intimate atmosphere will be achieved among the group members in the various therapeutic processes.

- The staff provides extra attention to clients who seek to treat and heal themselves and who need protection.

- The staff will not overlook behavior that displays delinquency patterns, "shady business," or a threatening climate among patients.

- The organized environment allows work on the memories of trauma and "psychological suffering," thereby breaking the "Cycle of Suffering."

As previously mentioned, the Cycle of Suffering theoretical model states that clients wounded by childhood stress, abuse, and trauma, if left untreated at the time of the assault, often develop PTSD symptoms. Out of the helplessness they experience, these clients view the drug as a means to self-medicate. Drug consumption entails much money, driving clients into the delinquency necessary to obtain funds for buying drugs. Delinquency often prompts other stress episodes, traumas, and psychological pain, thereby maintaining the course of the Cycle of Suffering.

We witness immediate treatment outcomes in the therapeutic group that week

The therapeutic climate was evolving. It is evident that new intimacy was developing among the clients who remained within the therapeutic group (ten out of 15) and the professional staff. The clients reported feelings of relief following the removal of the group members who had induced a climate of threat and delinquency, as well as relief resulting from the professional staff's protection throughout that intervention.

I felt the threat floating out the window, establishing a renewed trust in the staff's professionalism, and promoting trust-inducing processes within the group. All these yielded a different therapeutic climate. The group calming process allowed the clients to share personal content with their peers, which they would not dare do before:

1. Moshe, 34 years old, addicted to hard drugs for approximately twenty years, shares with his peers the story of sexual abuse he underwent as a child by an older neighbor from a nearby block.

2. Ninette, 20, addicted five years, shares with the group the story of the prolonged sexual abuse by her father and brother, which she underwent as a child.

3. Rami, addicted 25 years, shares with the group the experience of extremely rough physical abuse by his stepbrother, with a hint at sexual abuse.

4. Yaki, addicted approximately twenty years, shares the story of the harsh violence he endured as a child, unfaithfulness between his parents, family breakup; he may also be hinting at further pain of which won't speak.

5. David, addicted to cocaine for only three years, identifies with one of the group members who has related sexual abuse, by stating: "Shame is our biggest issue." The staff feels that David is not yet

ready to share the abundant psychological suffering he endured following his parents' divorce and the breakup of his family. (His father did not allow his mother to see him, and sent him to live at his grandmother's house in Haifa.)

6. Saul, addicted approximately twenty years. His behavior is characterized by intense rage. In group, Saul relates a disaster he underwent as a child: "I asked my father to give me a ride in his car and we had a fatal car accident. My brother was killed." It is evident he is still having trouble relating further stress he has experienced throughout his life.

7. Mahmud, addicted approximately twenty years, relates to his fellow group members that he is raising a child that isn't his, after his wife cheated on him while he was imprisoned. Mahmud still seems to have further past stress experiences.

There is a new, intimate climate in the group.

• The staff applauds the group members for the personal courage each of them is demonstrating.

• The professionals assume that any member relating their survival story is progressing in treatment toward rebuilding their life. Great importance is attached to a group member's awareness of the helplessness they experienced as children and their not being accountable for the abuse they experienced.

• The staff repeatedly emphasizes the following professional view: "Your past experiences, whether you were assaulted or abused, are *not your fault*."

• The staff clarifies that no pressure will be exerted on any member to share contents if unable to do so. The very ability of the staff to absorb the rage of the clients still unable to relate their life story, sets an example for them of a different coping model.

To conclude, working on memories of stress, suffering, and trauma, intertwined with much psychological pain, is effective in breaking each client's personal Cycle of Suffering. Renewed exposure to that pain, while addressing the emotions it raises, may prevent the unconscious need to turn to drugs to self-medicate. Those who feel safe within their therapeutic setting and trust the treatment staff and the climate of confidentiality and sharing among their peers, reveal to the group members and the therapists experiences originally concealed and even repressed as personal secrets. Such retrieval can instigate a change in terms of the emotional coding a client has experienced for many years. A different response to emotions associated with stress and trauma relieve the symptoms experienced by clients, thereby enhancing their quality of life.

CHAPTER ELEVEN

Epilogue

————————————————————————————

When the wound split open all along the field of ripe grain
There was no room for recalling that pain.
Some remember each moment
Having trouble to sort it all out
Repeatedly feeling the pain, all over, all around
Failing to bridge the gap, to sort it out
Others are different
Forgetting a moment, and the moment is gone
Without a friend or two, it will not get done, more securely does it feel
Even when the wound heals;
Both will heal if they wish
Rising from the depths and out they reach.

Two days ago, Thursday, was quite a rough day for us—an intense day at work. The happenings serve as a summary of the book:

This week's final group therapy session convene in the evening. The SUD Alumni Group has been clean of drugs for at least two years now. In this group, we do not witness any relation to thoughts of using drugs, or resistance to treatment or the structure itself, but rather discussions on falling in love and intimacy, searching for permanent employment and further education. This group concludes a fascinating workweek.

At the group session, Khil discusses his feelings. He claims he has got everything he can out of treatment, sharing his thoughts with his fellow group members:

> I have been in therapy for three years. I feel strong. I have pretty much spat out all my pain by now. I want to try to cope with life without the center's therapeutic cocoon and without my friends' support.

The other group members are surprised by his words.
Silvia responds by saying, "I don't feel I know you at all."
Mary further states, "Other than bits and pieces regarding your loss, which you mentioned when you told us of your trip to Spain, I have not heard anything from you that relates to your personal life."
Arik: "I think it's too bad you won't be a group member anymore."
Gadi: "Membership in this group means more than anything to me. If I draw away from the group, I might forget where I came from."

The group addresses a variety of emotional contents and themes associated with the prospect of Khil withdrawing from the group. I, too, feel great sorrow. I have grown to love him and value his survival strength, as he faces the tremendous suffering he has experienced throughout the course of his life. I respond to him by saying, "I see your contribution to your peers in the group, the efforts you invest toward maintaining the center's surroundings. Let's try to delve into your feeling, and discuss it more thoroughly."

This week, Alex passed away, the loss of a soul I had already mentioned, and I have to conclude this week of therapeutic work in the most professional manner possible. It is of great importance that the clients do not leave for the weekend carrying open emotional baggage.

Following consultation, Effy and I decide to present the Alumni group with a question addressed to each of its members, "Try to recall an episode in your past where you were willing to do anything to be able to score."

Apparently, the group is taken aback by the question. "I do not feel like connecting," says Mary.

"Why are you bringing up our pasts again?" questions Arik. "I always had money for doing drugs."

We do not retreat:

"We find it important to connect your feeling as group members to your past feelings, which were not so long ago. See how the therapeutic process can constitute the border separating life from death."

I am pleased that a few minutes later, the group members successfully connect to past memories and emotions. The memories they present bear extremely harsh emotional content.

Silvia recalls:

When I was discharged from a three-day arrest, I experienced wicked withdrawal symptoms. I had no money; not even 50 shekels for a hit. I waited for ten hours outside a friend's parents' house. I knew that's where he was sleeping. By the time he came, my whole body was shaking, and I begged him for a small hit, which he had probably purchased for his own use. I told him: "You can ask anything you wish from me, even if it means I have to kiss your feet or lick your ass. I'll do anything." *He indeed did. Only afterwards did the bastard agree to share his score with me.*

Khil is having trouble recalling, even as he wants to embark on a new life:

I recall a ridiculous situation. I was searching for any extra shekel so I could score. I was even willing to dig in the Tel-Aviv sewage. I found a building under construction, in its final stages. I broke in and destroyed every object in sight. I remember myself in the middle of winter, walking past people like a furniture mover without a truck, carrying with a couch on my back, and asking people on the street if they would be interested in buying it; disassembling a sink or a door, and trying to sell them to passers-by on Jerusalem Street. To this day, I don't know if the cops arrested me for stolen property or because I seemed so odd and insane.

Mary recalls:

I suffered terrible withdrawal. I was willing to do anything to get my hands on some stuff. I remember going down to the apartment where I knew I would find Boris, a dirty, scruffy squatter, always doped up and holding. I found him lying naked with another addicted girl. I knew they had drugs. I could feel it in the air. That stinky guy asked me to watch them having anal sex, if I wanted to have a hit. As you can imagine, I did not say no. I puked my guts out after that. The next day, I started detox.

Gadi hints to some recalled pain. We are familiar with his hints. When he physically connects with his emotions, he rapidly wrings his hands.

I am ashamed to remember how I dragged my elderly father to the bank, and forced him to withdraw cash for me. My father was 80 years old, limping, leaning on a walking cane. I would slap him if he objected. I would hit him until he gave in. I would drag him down the city streets, in extreme heat or rain. Once I got the money from him, I would leave him standing there. I did not care how he would got home. I cared only about the drugs. There were even a few times when I pulled him with me into a cab on the way to score in Abu Saif orchard, Jaffa. Luckily, the cab drivers showed some sense. They were the ones who talked me into making a stop at home, on the way, to drop him off. I am so ashamed of my acts.

The group members continue connecting to their memories. We notice that time is up. I wrap up the meeting by expressing my thanks to those members who shared their stories. Effy reminds the group members that such painful past events can serve as an alarm to guide present behavior. We sum up the group process with "Let's never forget where we came from."

As I complete the writing of this book, I cannot help recall this group process. The days in drug rehab are undefined as a set of consecutive days when substances are not used. These days are a quality expression of time and the therapeutic process each client has undergone.

Clean days accumulate and uproot the lives of those clients who succeed, through psychological treatment, to face the past pain and suffering that they have experienced. These days are significant for clients who have succeeded in recalling the stress and trauma they experienced, which prompted them to abuse drugs, but who now are able to cope differently.

Thursday evening, 7:30 p.m. An intensive week of work has ended. I go for an espresso at the Rothschild Espresso Bar on the corner of Rothschild and Hertzl, Tel-Aviv. There, every week for the past five years, I meet Giora Shoham, a professor in criminology, law, and philosophy.

Professor Shoham voluntarily facilitates a therapeutic group at the treatment center I run. His personality, knowledge, and professionalism are the source of support and strength that helps me cope with my Rothschild work experiences and occurrences. Shoham, a brilliant, unique individual, with abundant life experience; is a precious man in his mid-70s, and always seems much younger to me. I remember having valued his therapeutic approach since our first encounter five years ago when he told me, "Do you think I come to Rothschild 2 every Thursday just to assist people, just to guide the college students through their internship with addicts? No, I do it for myself. I need this encounter just as much as they do."

I figure people out by their behavior, words, actions, and wisdom. Professor Shoham rises to hug every client who arrives at the Thursday evening therapeutic group. He always speaks to the students, the clients, and everybody else as an equal, creating a comfortable atmosphere in the conversation. I order another short espresso. The waiter is familiar with us, the odd Thursday evening couple. She returns, holding a small glass of water and a slice of lemon. "In all of my years of work, I have never met anyone like you," I tell Professor Shoham. "You are in the therapeutic arena rather than remaining distant in the ivory tower of academia. The therapeutic field needs more individuals like you."

I have met many professionals in professional discussion, contemplating theoretical thoughts and issues. I have also met many more, both during my working hours and on days when I study at the university. I have invited them all to visit Rothschild 2, to become acquainted with the rehabilitated individuals, and the models we have been implementing for the past two decades. Most have not shown up.

Saturday morning, on my kibbutz weekend duty, I rise early. My acquaintances know I cannot oversleep. I leave for Rothschild 2 to care for the animals and water the plants. This is my therapy, for which I have persevered twenty years. This Saturday, too, my path crosses observant residents rushing to the synagogue, all wearing white. This morning, I saw an adult son holding his father, physically supporting him. Together, they slowly walk to the synagogue. The father is trembling, unable to balance his body due to Parkinson's disease. Yet he carries his prayer shawl, as he has customarily done for many years. *Traditions and habits bear great power*, I tell myself. In the slowly awaking city, there are dozens of energetic, blinded-by-hormones, beautiful youths. This is the finest hour for dating and courting. Most of them still gather near the nightclub doors, which close at dawn. One of them is very near Rothschild 2 center. One couple leaves the club, slowly walking to their car. They're chatting. It's evident that passion burns between them. The man is in his 20s, wearing a T-shirt drenched in the sweat of dancing and ecstasy; his eyes are red. The woman seems to be more sober, level-headed, wearing next to nothing. The man stops by a tall, strong eucalyptus tree to urinate. They keep talking. I wonder what the old tree, our Rothschild neighbor, has heard for the hundred years it has stood there.

The streets of Tel-Aviv on a Sabbath morning; the observant are headed for their prayers; the wild youth search for another sexual experience, while I am on my way to my fortress of devotion, for another magical, peaceful morning at the Rothschild 2 zoo.

I established Rothschild 2 approximately twenty years ago. I often encounter one of the center graduates watering the garden. "You are a fixture here," I tell him. I fill with joy when I witness our graduates' contribution to the center. Thus, I believe, they continue to view Rothschild 2 as their home, thereby allowing us to keep on fostering the other kibbutz of which I have always dreamed.

One of the graduates constructed a fishpond at the center. Another graduate built a decorative rock wall, whose construction lasted many months. The water well integrates the old and the new, symbolizing suffering and recovery. A third graduate devotedly cares for the garden. It is a paradise of recovery, within a hell of cruelty and human suffering. This place is alive and breathing. Thousands receive their lives back at Rothschild 2, and many of them have significantly improved their quality of life.

I look back with satisfaction, my heart filled with anticipation as to what the future might hold. There is still so much to do.

On this Sabbath walk, our family dog is accompanying me. In the past two years, Choco, a brown and mischievous Cocker Spaniel cross-breed, has been with me every day of my work at the center and clinic. Her trimmed tail is wiggling happily, putting a smile on each person we pass. One cannot resist her human-like eyes when she begs for a pat. Kamma, the center's dog, envies Choco, grabbing every opportunity to chase us on our way home. I feel pity when I have to walk her back to Rothschild. The angry looks Kamma casts at Choco say it all.

Each year, Rothschild 2 holds an end-of-summer-vacation party on August 31, hosting some guests of honor. At this party, we receive abundant praise for our practice and work. Yet my patients, the professionals working with me, and I are not satisfied. Professor Shoham's acts prove that more can be done.

These days, I am preparing lectures, to address researchers and treatment professionals in Israel, in various conferences discussing new ways of treating addicts in the 21st century. I am excited. This year, my ideas will reach a large-scale, statewide conference, acting as a call for researchers to recruit and explore my work. I will be delighted if some of them rise to the challenge.

The reader of this book is welcome to come and observe the community life we have established within the heart of Tel-Aviv, a rehabilitated human community, clean of drugs, alive, breathing, and ever growing.

Come sit, explore, and observe. Listen to the stories of Dean, Itzik, Shlomo, the story of the recovery process of addicted clients, the victims of past stress and trauma. Some clients engage in business, supporting families and look just like you and me; sensitive individuals whose wounds were caused by others, who did not choose to become addicted to substances. Come visit and realize how, even when trauma prompts drug abuse, consequently resulting in trauma, one can recover from addiction.

References

Amali, T. (1995). *Damage to Personality as a Motive for Addiction: Poor Integration and Self-Containment.* In: D. Green (Ed.). Substances: Facts, Questions, and Issues. Tel Aviv: Ministry of Defense. Pp. 110-123 [HEB]

Aviad, J., & Roseman, M. (1988). *Drugs in Mind.* Tel Aviv: Ramot Publications [HEB]

Bar Guy, N., & Shalev, A. (2001). *The Impact of Childhood Abuse on Adult Psychopathology. Sichot,* 15, pp. 180-194 [HEB]

Bar Hamburger, R. B., & Tal, T. (Eds.)(1999). *A Decade of Substance-Related Research.* Jerusalem: Israel Anti-Drug Authority [HEB]

Bar-Sade, N. (2008). *Therapeutic Alliance and the Role of Flexibility and Creativity in Working with Adolescent and Adult Sexual Assault Victims.* Hebrew Psychology. Available at: http://hebpsy.net/classic_articles. asp?id=1675 Accessed on March 20, 2008

Berman, O. S. (2003). *Secrets and Punishment: Legally Establishing the Rights of Sexual Abuse Victims. Hevra Verevacha,* 23, pp. 185-198 [HEB]

Brothers, B. J. (2004). *Abuse of Men: Trauma Begets Trauma*. Kiriyat Bialik: Oach [HEB]

Cohen, S. (2001). *Treatment Under Pressure: The Role of Psychoanalysis in Treatment of Children at Risk for Abuse and Neglect*. Sichot, 15, pp. 196-206 [HEB]

Eshel, O. (1997). *Black Holes and Things in Between*. Sichot, 11, 3, pp. 195-205 [HEB]

Etgar, T. (1999). *Group Therapy with Adolescent Sex Offenders*. Hevra Verevacha, 19, pp. 215-234 [HEB[

Eylon, O. (1983). *Delicate Balance: Coping with Stress in the Family*. Tel Aviv: Sifriyat Hapoalim [HEB]

Foa, E., Doron, M., & Yadin, A. (2004). *Prolonged Exposure. Post-Trauma Treatment Manual*. Coping Resources Development Center

Green, D. (Ed.) (1995). *Drugs: Facts, Questions, and Issues*. Tel Aviv: Ministry of Defense [HEB]

Gur, A. (2004). *My Pimp Has Nothing to Teach Me. Dad Taught it All to Me at Home: Incest as a Key Trigger for Women and Girls Resorting to Prostitution, Substances, and Crime*. In: Seligman, Z., & Z. Solomon (Eds.). Broken Secret: Issues Related to Incest. Tel Aviv: Tel Aviv University, Adler Child Welfare Institute and HaKibbutz HaMe'uchad, pp. 457-482 [HEB]

Herman, J. L. (1992). *Trauma and Recovery*. Tel Aviv: Am Oved

Hertzano-Letty, M., & Toder, D. (2006). *Post-Traumatic Disorder as an Endless Death. Sichot*, 20, 3, pp. 314-320 [HEB]

Hovav, M. (Ed.)(2002). *Substance Abuse Victims in Israel: Treatment and Rehabilitation*. Tel Aviv: Cherickover Publication [HEB]

Israeli Psychiatric Association (2002). *ICD-10*. Tel Aviv: Dyonon

Katzenelson, E. (1998). *Between Children and Parents: The Psychology of Parents and Children*. Ramat Gan: Horim Press [HEB]

Lazar, G. P., & Zwikel, G. (1992). *Assisting Female Rape Victims: Survival or Social Change. Hevra Verevacha,* 13, pp. 67-88 [HEB]

Lindy, D. G. (1989). *Counter-Transference and Post-Traumatic Syndrome* (Trans. Arik Shalev). *Sichot*, 3, 2, pp. 94-100 [HEB]

Manor, I., & Tiano, S. (2003). *Living with ADHD*. Tel Aviv: Dyonon

Michael, A. (2007). *Addiction and Recovery: Selected Issues in Treating Addicts*. Kiriyat Bialik: Oach Publications

Munitz, H. (Ed.) (1994a). *Selected Chapters in Psychiatry*. Tel Aviv: Papyrus [HEB]

Munitz, H. (Ed.) (2003b). *Selected Chapters in Psychiatry*. Tel Aviv: Papyrus [HEB]

Nadler, B. (2002). *Lexicon of New Psychology*. Haifa: Rakefet [HEB]

NATAL (2003). *How to Identify and Prevent Post-Traumatic Response*. Tel Aviv: Independent Publication [HEB]

Nevo, R., Galvan, A., & Bar Guy, R. (2006). *Female Treatment Forum.* Jerusalem: Ministry of Labor and Welfare [HEB]

Pintzy, R., Schnit, R., & Weitzman, A. (1999). *Battered Children: Typical Profile and Assessment Instrument.* Hevra Verevacha, 19, pp. 430-460 [HEB]

Sanderovich, A. (2002). *The Relationship of Childhood and Adolescent Sexual Abuse and Adulthood Substance Abuse: Background Paper for Discussion.* Jerusalem: Research and Information Center, Knesset Yisrael [HEB]

Seligman, Z., & Solomon, Z. (Eds.) (2004). *Broken Secrets: Issues Related to Incest.* Tel Aviv: Tel Aviv University, Adler Child Welfare Institute and HaKibbutz HaMe'uchad [HEB]

Zomer, E. (2004). *To Be or Not to Be: Childhood Trauma and Dissociation Disorders.* In: Z. Seligman & Z. Solomon (Eds.). Broken Secrets: Issues Related to Incest. Tel Aviv: Tel Aviv University, Adler Child Welfare Institute and HaKibbutz HaMe'uchad, pp. 164-192 [HEB]

Zomer, E., & Bleich, A. (Eds.) (2005). *Mental Health Under Terror.* Tel Aviv: Ramot [HEB]

Zomer, E., Leventhal, E., & Tzoref, E. (2005). *Dissociative Disorders Among Substance Abuse Victims.* Jerusalem: The National Anti-Drug Authority [HEB]

Teichman, M. (1989). *Living in Another World.* Tel Aviv: Ramot [HEB]

Teichman, M. (2001). *From God's Nectar to the Poison Cup.* Tel Aviv: Ramot [HEB]

Tiano, S. (Ed.) (1991). *Substance and Alcohol Abuse*. In: H. Munitz (Ed.) Selected Chapters in Psychiatry. Tel Aviv University: Papyrus Publication

Winnicott, D. W. (1971). *Playing and Reality*. Tel Aviv: Am Oved [HEB]

Yalom, E. D., & Leszcz, M. (2006). *Group Therapy. Theory and Practice*. (Trans. Ben Tzion Herman). Or Yehuda: Kinneret [HEB]

Yalom, E. D. (2002). *The Gift of Therapy* (Trans. Carmit Guy). Or Yehuda: Kinneret [HEB]

Appendices

—————————————————————

A cat and a fox found themselves a place.
Thus, their fraud falls from grace.
The fox alone is obvious and cunning
His lies from a distance are bright and stunning.
The cat is shrewd and just as cruel.
Together they are cunning, exchanging looks,
Everyone, they will fool.
The two's deception is wretched and low
Worn on their sleeves, will forever remain and grow.

Appendix 1: Conference Lecture on Addict Assessment in the 21st Century

Lecture: Trauma and Substance Addiction
Lecturer: Amir Pirani, MSW, Director of Rothschild 2 Treatment Center and Municipal Day Center, City Center Family Department; Social Services Administration, Tel Aviv-Jaffa

Good morning, all. It is extremely exciting to address such an important issue in front of so many colleagues working in the field of addictions in Israel.

When I requested to give an address at this important conference, I saw the privilege before me, yes, the privilege to speak of the challenges professionals face in assessing substance addiction victims in the 21st century. I particularly wish to illuminate the issue of trauma.

Reviewing the professional literature in Israel reveals a very small extent of discussion and research on an issue we all face and encounter as therapy professionals, namely, the strong relationship of trauma experienced by an individual when they turn to drugs.

I am certain that many of you sitting in this conference encounter in your clinical work, on a daily basis, during sessions with your patients, the psychological trauma resulting from sexual and other types of abuse.

Why is it, therefore, that this relationship has scarcely been studied in Israel? Why does the field of addiction in Israel not offer thorough training to treat civil trauma victims, and individuals suffering from PTSD?

As a professional who has worked in the field of addiction therapy for 20 years, at the treatment center operated by the Tel Aviv-Jaffa social service administration, the encounter with addict trauma is routine.

I illustrate to you, my esteemed audience, a theoretical model I have established, and on which I rely in my attempt to account for the relationship between psychological trauma and addiction.

I would like to believe that this model, which has been of assistance to me for many years in assessing and understanding addiction issues among those who seek treatment from the public services, could be of assistance to us, as professionals, in achieving the goals we have established at this conference.

Since 1992, my professional experience with thousands of clients has taught me, through exposure to great pain, the four stages comprising the Cycle of Suffering. I established this theoretical model to account for the relationship between trauma and addiction:

1. The vast majority of addicts who seek treatment at the public service for their addiction issues experienced sexual, physical, or another type of abuse as children. This is a deductive assumption, the first stage of the theoretical model. Many are likely to question whether this deductive assumption is true. I firmly believe it is. I am certain that many of you sitting here are aware of this as well. A sheltering, client-secure professional setting can help address the root of the chronic addiction problem, namely, the psychological damage resulting from trauma. I address this issue later in the lecture.

2. The second stage of the theoretical model I established relates an even more painful story: The vast majority of people wounded by civil trauma episodes, as I refer to them, did not receive treatment in the initial stages following the abuse. There are many reasons to account for this, I am certain you will agree with me on that as well: The secret that lies within the abuse protects the aggressor and conceals the victim; a paralyzing fear prompts more and more abuse episodes; abuse victims seek dissociation and distanceing from the event; exacerbated by dysfunctional parental roles and deficient school alertness. The consequences of the neglect and failure to treat the trauma are post-traumatic stress disorder (PTSD) symptoms; expressed as explosive rage, anxiety, depression, difficulties in interpersonal relations; and nightmares. I am sure most of you are familiar with those conditions among your patients as well.

3. These children, both boys and girls, who have not received professionally treatment or assistance following the trauma they

experienced, develop PTSD, and find, at times, temporary peace of mind in drugs. Alcohol supposedly heals the pain of the soul, heroin supposedly disconnects a suffering or terrified individual from their emotions, and other drugs offer other promises. In the theoretical model's third stage, addiction serves as self-medication that the young individual, suffering an insufferable, prolonged pain of the soul, comes across. The substance allegedly tranquilizes the pain, covering an open wound. I am sure most of you acknowledge this assumption, too. What happens at this stage? By now, the addiction has become very costly, as drugs cost money, and the disrupted daily schedule also costs money, along with work, and family. The desperate need for money to purchase substances prompts the fourth stage of my theoretical model:

4. Allegedly, people who abuse drugs start to steal from their parents and other relatives, break into cars, trade their body for money, and deal in drugs. The violent pursuit of money for the purchase of substances leads to delinquency and, worse yet, to further suffering. Delinquency prompts physical violence, arrests, or imprisonment. Trading one's body prompts further psychological trauma, thus coming full circle in terms of suffering. The addict encounters further, unrelated trauma such as chronic PTSD, emotional dissociation, and substance use disorder (SUD). Therapeutic techniques addressing psychological trauma enable treatment of the substance addiction issue. Therapeutic techniques involve trauma exposure, construction of a well-organized narrative outlining a client's life and the ability to accept their suffering through Animal Assisted Therapy, and other therapeutic techniques.

Unfortunately, I am unable to address these techniques in this lecture, so, beyond the vast personal knowledge possessed by all attendants in this regard, anyone interested is welcome to browse my published articles discussing these matters.

My time is up. I have attempted to bring a professional message that diagnosis of an addict fulfills an extensive role in establishing an effective therapeutic structure! A professional, therapeutic approach to the psychological trauma carried by most drug addicts I have known requires a secure professional work setting that correctly and adequately addresses psychological trauma, thereby assisting clients.

We can assist our clients through professional intervention in psychological trauma to lift the veil that covers the past, blocking any future development or growth. Feeling better requires some suffering within therapy.

Cycle of Suffering Stages Theoretical Model (Pirani, 2007) Outline:
    The theoretical model indicates a prolonged circular relation of several variables:
1. The preceding event – **Trauma**
2. The response for the untreated trauma – **Post-Trauma**
3. Taking drugs as self-medication to ease the psychological pain – **Addiction**
4. The action(s) taken to raise funds for doing drugs, which cause further psychological suffering – **Delinquency and Suffering**

The theoretical model implies that the variables maintain a prolonged, circular relation. To interrupt the circular dynamics of this relation, we must implement interventional, therapeutic trauma treatment techniques.

Appendix 2: Standard Questionnaire

Date:_____ Interviewer's Name:_____

Referred by _____

Admission Questionnaire for Substance/Alcohol Detoxification
Personal Information

Last Name:_____ First Name:_____

ID No._____ Father's Name _____

Address:_____ Telephone:_____

Civil Status: Single/Married/Divorced/Widowed

Date of Birth _____ Place of Birth _____

Parents' Place of Birth: Father _____ Mother _____

Year of Immigration _____

Children's Names	Dates of Birth

Spouse Name _____ No. of Siblings _____

Placement among siblings (oldest, youngest, etc.)_____

If applicant has been married more than once, please specify:

_____

Education

Number of Schooling Years:_____

Type of training/trades acquired:_____

Military Service

From (date) _____ to (date) _____ Total Period:_____

Reason for exemption/partial service period:_____

Reserve Service: Serving/Exempt

Reason for exemption:_____

Employment History (beginning with most recent or current, including at the municipality):

Position	Employment Period From/To		Relationship with Employer	Reason(s) for Layoff and Other Comments

Is the applicant presently employed? Yes/No

Starting Date:_____ Salary _____

Kindly indicate other sources of income _____

What is/are the current reason(s) for detoxification/rehabilitation?

_____

_____

Is there a family history of substance and/or alcohol abuse?

_____

_____

Has the applicant been treated by social services? – Yes/No

If "yes," please specify the social services branch name _____

Caregiver's Name _____

Have there been any suicide attempts? Yes/No

If "yes," please specify _____

Have there been any suicidal thoughts? Yes/No

If "yes," please specify _____

Has the applicant been treated by a psychiatrist or a psychologist?

Yes/No

Reason for referral _____

Treatment framework _____

Caregiver's Name _____

Dates: _____

Has any family member been treated by a psychiatrist or a psychologist?

Extent of Motivation (In what way does the applicant expect to solve the problem? To what extent are they suffering from their difficult circumstances and conditions?)

_____

_____